Heritage, Culture, and Politics in the Postcolony

HERITAGE, CULTURE, and POLITICS in the POSTCOLONY

Daniel Herwitz

COLUMBIA UNIVERSITY PRESS   NEW YORK

Columbia University Press
Publishers Since 1893
New York   Chichester, West Sussex
cup.columbia.edu
Copyright © 2012 Columbia University Press
All rights reserved
Library of Congress Cataloging-in-Publication Data
Herwitz, Daniel Alan, 1955–
  Heritage, culture, and politics in the postcolony / Daniel Herwitz.
    p. cm.
  Includes bibliographical references (p.   ) and index.
  ISBN 978-0-231-16018-6 (cloth: alk. paper)
  ISBN 978-0-231-53072-9 (e-book)
  1. Social sciences and history. 2. India—Historiography—Social aspects. 3. South Africa—Historiography—Social aspects. 4. United States—Historiography—Social aspects. 5. National characteristics, East Indian. 6. National characteristics, South African. 7. National characteristics, American. 8. Postcolonialism—India. 9. Postcolonialism—South Africa. 10. Postcolonialism—United States. I. Title.

D16.166.H47 2012
  907.2—dc23
∞
Columbia University Press books are printed on permanent and durable acid-free paper.
This book is printed on paper with recycled content.
Printed in the United States of America
c 10 9 8 7 6 5 4 3 2 1

COVER IMAGE: Maqbool Fida Husain, *Maya or Tribal Girl*, painting, 1977, gift of the Chester and Davida Herwitz Collection, Peabody Essex Museum; reproduced courtesy of the M. F. Husain Estate.

References to Internet Web sites (URLs) were accurate at the time of writing. Neither the author nor Columbia University Press is responsible for URLs that may have expired or changed since the manuscript was prepared.

For Lucia and Sophia

We need history, certainly, but we need it for reasons different from those for which the idler in the garden of knowledge needs it. . . . We need it . . . for the sake of life and action. . . . We want to serve history only to the extent that history serves life.

—Friedrich Nietzsche, "On the Uses and Disadvantages of History for Life"

Contents

Preface xi

Acknowledgments xvii

One   The Heritage of Heritage   1

Two   Recovering and Inventing the Past:
M. F. Husain's Live Action Heritage   26

Three   Sustaining Heritage Off the Road to Kruger Park   58

Four   Monument, Ruin, and Redress in South African Heritage   80

Five   Renaissance and Pandemic   135

Six   Tocqueville on the Bridge to Nowhere   152

Epilogue   190

Notes   193

Index   203

Preface

My grandmother was a seamstress, come from Riga at the moment of the twentieth century. What America offered her and her clan at first was a lot of not-so-fancy footwork, as Sarah and her generation traipsed their way through the grime, the factories, the tenements, the sweat shops, the industrial sludge, the con jobs, the dirty fishmarkets, enduring unsanitary facilities, ethnic slurs, and barely treatable diseases. She sewed her fingers down to the bone, working for pennies, aching from arthritis. Every stitch was a misery, every step an agony. She and her generation eked out a living while reading the Yiddish newspapers in order to know America in a language in which they were at least fluent. But between shvitzing in the factories and freezing in the tenements she learned of another America hovering above, an America filled with enchanted histories of presidents, cowboys, Indians, Thanksgiving suppers, baseball players, adversities surmounted, untold riches obtained, and happy families living blissfully among the fruited plain. This instruction took place in the home and at the congregation, in the Yiddish newspapers and through the stories their children brought back from school. And it took place at the movies, where Rudolph Valentino hovered like an idealized mirror of the future. During the Depression this family was reduced to selling grab bags out of its garage after Harry, my grandfather, was cheated out of his little chocolate business by his brothers. It is said they were forced into selling the family dog after Harry's brothers tried to sue him out of his home (for desperate immigrant families all bets are off). My grandmother's hands grew knotted like fishing rope from the arthritis, but she taught her two boys that one day they would rise up and reap the rewards of her labor, thus making good on her travails. And they knew: knew that from the fish markets and pawn shops they would rise up to *achieve*, taking their place in the world of power, fantasy, and finesse. I like to think of her boys as most happy when, standing there in the kitchen, they are sent reeling into the future by their mother as she ladles soup, spoons gravy over brisket, serves up fish cakes hard as barnacles, catapulting them into the idealized tense of the "what will be," to the place where they will make good on all her suffering by becoming real Americans, GI Joes, success stories—their toes tapping to a Yiddishkeit inclusive of blonde chorines and jazz pianos, their bank accounts overflowing with greenbacks. In the GI tracts of these youths would be a bounteous presence upon which their forefathers, constituted in every kind of starvation and deprivation, would supp. If my grandmother's life was a deluge of traipsing and sewing, its purpose was to be a birthing process for the generations who would become doctors, lawyers, and professors, women of business and men of accountancy, dentists, podiatrists: fillers of bank accounts all. Through this great act of gestation, she—and through her, the generations of the past—would inherit America. It was not through lineages, pedigrees, through your status as a good Daughter of the American Revolution or a Son of the Civil War that you, an immigrant, were blessed with the appellation American. No, it was through your progeny and what they would become. Sarah was poor, but they would be rich; she was malnourished; they would eat Wheaties, drink orange juice, and grow six feet tall, their heads craning above sodden reality like those of the swan or the falcon. Hers was the optimism and fortitude of a people longing to be inherited by a land for over a thousand years, a people who believed they had finally found such a land in the great streets of New York, the peaks of the Catskills, and the Old Charter Houses of Salem and Portsmouth. A-M-E-R-I-K-A. Collectively disinherited when the Second Temple fell at the time of the Roman Empire, press-ganged into the Diaspora for nearly two thousand years, the Jew prayed that next year he or she would be in Jerusalem. Sarah prayed for Jerusalem, but staked her future on the forty eight states.

    My father lived his childhood in that rough and tumble landscape of anticipation. Roosevelt was there, and the Declaration of Independence and Joe Kennedy and Rita Hayworth. After the Second World War, determined to make good, he began selling handcrafted women's belts out of the trunk of his old Ford, peddling his wares to the college towns of the East Coast, determined to make good in the eyes of his demanding parents. Fear of failure sent him to the medical clinics, made him a bear of a man, impossible in anxiety. He often returned home dog tired with mere pennies in his pocket. Then a client, some shop in Amherst, New Haven, or Rochester. Soon another, then a third, and, suddenly, as if we'd already read it in the history books, it was the 1960s and he had built a designing house. His green tartan skirts, plaid dresses, leather handbags with antique finishes turned college clothing into a celebratory logo. He took farmer's satchels, mailmen's bags, job men's toolkits, electrician's belts and turned them into fashion Americana. Even the Stars and Stripes made it onto the side of one of his leather purses.

These were an immigrant's blessing on the thing he felt he never was. The genuine college guy or girl was one born into it ("Yale men" from F. Scott Fitzgerald stories about the Jazz Age, Boston girls with blonde hair who grew up baking cupcakes with bright blue icing and sailing off their own private islands into the coastal waters of Maine). When your own father never went past the fifth grade, college seems to you a magical place where you don't quite belong. What he loved was the *pedigree* of it, the kind Vassar and Smith girls carried so naturally in their strong-chinned, youthful smiles, their gleaming white teeth, their oversized varsity sweaters, their ease of breeding, their ability to ride horses. He adored their incandescent ordinariness, their lack of immigrant insecurity. To be ordinary meant freedom from a burden he felt every day: that of carrying forward the commandments of his parents, of *assimilating* and *surpassing* at the same time. It was freedom from this burden he wanted to gift to his own children—wanted and failed. But to the college girls he managed to give a logo, a mass-produced image of what they already were. His future was made by turning their daily idiom into hundred proof (bonded) heritage. A generation before him, Italian and Jewish immigrants like Frank Capra, Vicente Minnelli, and Robert Riskin had given the small towns of America (in which they'd never grown up) a similar seal of Hollywood approval, and their blessings had become part, indeed proof, of American heritage (something I will turn to when I discuss Sarah Palin and her boy-next-door husband from the oil fields in chapter 6). My father's mother, had she understood the bonding of heritage, would have been proud. But she never did understand and instead endlessly complained that my father simply catered to the goyim. She never got it that for a Jew to make good in America he or she had to enter a wider world than that of the temples and the Miami Beach hotels.

He bought a farm at the Vermont border and decorated it with Amish quilts, old American pottery, the stuff of Yankee know-how he knew only through its whiff of authenticity. That farm was his way of entering the book of sources, the script of an America he had in no way been part of, and from which he was, excepting his purchase power, largely (in the early 1960s) excluded. Yes, he'd made it into the marketplace, but until he had the past under his belt he wasn't a true blue Yankee, just a Yankees fan. And so his antique land of Vermont daffodil, apple orchard, morel, and spring blossom. His farm should have been called Green Acres, after the television show, since he bungled more or less everything. The tractor he could not drive, nor the barn door fix, the corn was grown for hungry herds of raccoons, which he failed to shoot, the pressing of apples went sour, applejack tasted of hay. Each week another episode occurred in this ongoing sitcom, which the family came to love like the TV it watched on a Sunday night while eating chicken from the bucket. It was the place to be, farm livin' is the life for me, land stretching out so far and wide, keep Manhattan but give me that countryside! The TV jingle, all *ooh la la* Eva Gabor, darling I can't fix the tractor, was in my father's hands a way of installing himself in the closed book of heritage, the one owned and operated by old Bostonians in topsiders drinking martinis at the yacht club, the club he wouldn't have joined if they had asked, and they didn't ask.

We little ones were sent to school in Brooks Brothers cotton shirts and gray flannel, as American as the apple pie we ate the Vermont way with sharp cheddar cheese. It tasted of Apple Pie the jingle, the one invented by the Madison Avenue ad men who blended into America through their wearing and branding of Brooks Brothers. Ralph Lauren came later: the man with the given name of Lifshitz who invented a way of blending into heritage by copying *up*. Ralph Lauren, my father once explained to me, changed the course of fashion design. It used to be that copycat meant cheap rip-off, the kind of shirt you bought from someone off the streets of Manhattan with a fake designer label in it which fell apart the first time tossed into the washing machine. Ralph Lauren took the wardrobes of the past, the rumpled hunting clothes of the mink and manure English country set, the pink shirt and bow tie of the yacht club supper, and remade them in finer, classier materials, turning these into set pieces for "heritage," the heritage of a hundred British and Hollywood films of "Old England" from the Ealing Studios featuring topcoated actors gulping syllables and drinking scotch neat from silver monogrammed flasks at the hunt. Old England has always sold big among the upper crust of America; Ralph Lauren simply expanded this principle. He made heritage a thing you could purchase whoever you are, democratized it so that the common man or woman could sport the clothing of princes and queens in the mall, at the movies, in their backyards, at the law office, and church picnic. You are what you wear. Identity is what you try on, available to all who have the cash or credit card to acquire it. Anyone could drape themselves in the aura of Old England (or the American West), which in Ralph Lauren designs became an advertising logo, a suit of clothes tailor-made for lawyers and stockbrokers on the rise. Before you knew it, six-year-old daughters of real estate magnates dressed in Marie Antoinette wear, clutching American Girl dolls bedecked in homespun Amish pullovers.

Those on the way up could tailor their entry through the clothing of American heritage, a heritage now largely gone, and free to arise in the form of myth. You blend into the top drawer of America by wearing its top drawers. No longer was it necessary to eat at the restricted Princeton clubs most recently known for having served Republican Supreme Court justices when they were students. All you had to do was purchase your own House of Lauren four poster bed from the Ralph Lauren palace on Madison Avenue, that kingly place of worship crammed with the bow ties and belt buckles of the past, not to mention the furniture, paintings, chintz and silk, all that Citizen Kane junk that people acquire "collecting statues." We are all royals now, trotting ourselves out on the streets of New York or waiting in line at the Upper East Side market to buy our heritage turkeys (equally pricey) so we can gather together to ask the Lord's blessing who hastens and chastens his will to make known each and every thanksgiving day.

This is heritage the marketing adventure where the aura of something from the past is bottled, turned into a branding item, and sold so that by trying it on or collecting it a person acquires status, profile, and identity. Heritage has become a branding term, conveying authenticity, excellence, the test of time for product sold as the real McCoy. And so there is the heritage guitar company in Kalamazoo, Michigan, there are heritage kayaks, heritage canoes, homes, furniture, and coins (no doubt of the realm), we have *American Heritage Magazine, The Old Farmer's Almanac, The American Heritage Dictionary*. A new breed of restaurant has arisen where the menu is all "heritage": echt cheeses from Wisconsin, old mother-in-law bourbon, meat from individually massaged cows fed on Kansas prairie grass. Everyone grows stronger and feels snappier with a bit of heritage in their mouths.

My father wore corduroy jeans, Indian vests, collarless shirts, Birkenstock sandals—always needing to stand different from the crowd. But I was blended in Brooks Brothers-wise, Lord's Prayer-wise. In this way I made my tiny entrance into America: that storybook land of recitation and ready-to-wear. Unofficial me, coming from below, a child of the child of immigrants, met heritage from above (the recitations, institutions, and tales of old) and blended.

This was the source of my interest in heritage, which has expanded since childhood. For heritage is a driver of American politics today, draping political positions in the mythology of great origins and values, dignifying them with settler spirit, immigrant achievement, and religious resolve. One cannot understand, I shall argue in the final chapter of this book, American democracy without grasping how heritage becomes political sound bite courtesy of the media. Heritage is a window into American democratic process, the place where history, myth, media, and profiling/marketing meet. Indeed, it is a central constituent of postcolonial social formations generally, of which America (settler society par excellence) is historically the first. Heritage scripts the postcolony's long arm of time, its sense of origin and newness, its will to dominion, independence, and unity. It also marks out difference, inequality (which it can sometimes seek to correct through acknowledging formerly invisible or downcast peoples). It sometimes augments internal quarrel, aims for combat, and can be brutal. Heritage is an instrument institutionalizing authority in the museum, court of law, university, stadium, TV station. It profiles and markets the past, enlarges and contracts it, all the while seeking to preserve it. Because heritage formation is central to the rise of the postcolonial nation and its practices therein, it is a marker of differences across the postcolonial world, a route to understanding those differences. My story begins and ends in America, but ranges across three continents for this reason. But I jump ahead.

Acknowledgments

This book assumed its shape courtesy of the Andrew Mellon Foundation which offered me a Visiting Fellowship in 2010 to participate in the *Archives and Public Culture Seminar* of the Department of Anthropology, University of Cape Town. Commandeered/commanded by Professor Carolyn Hamilton, that seminar is a wonderfully free-thinking exploration of new trade routes between historians, literary scholars, anthropologists, artists, curators, critics, and activists from the public sector. My manuscript in progress was everywhere aided and abetted by these co-conspirators; sometimes chapters in progress returned for repeat offense. Carolyn Hamilton, Pippa Skotnes, Njabulo Ndebele, David Cohen, Nessa Leibheimer, Nick Shepherd, Litheko Modisane, and the late Jon Berndt may stand in for others to receive my thanks.

Jean Comaroff, Ahmed Bawa, Mike Morris, Dennis Davis, Patrick Lenta, Michael Kelly, and Lucia Saks have applied their brainpower to the book at key moments of its composition, as have two cohorts of fellows from the Institute for the Humanities at the University of Michigan where I have been blessed to serve as director.

Parts of the book were presented to the Department of Anthropology, University of Stellenbosch, the Cornell University–East China Normal University Center for the Humanities, Shanghai, the University of Amsterdam Cool Passions Conference, the University of London and Open University Seminar on the Indian Ocean, the University of Michigan's Weiser Center, and the Ruins of Modernity Conference, also at the University of Michigan. This list is not exclusive, but prompts a thank you to

ACKNOWLEDGMENTS

Julia Hell, Haiping Yan, Brenda Gourley, Steve Robins, and Thomas Blom Hansen.

Certain chapters of the book have begun as published essays in *Third Text*, *Modern Painters*, *Politique Africaine*, *Hundred Schools in Arts*, and in the edited volumes *Ruins of Modernity*, *Curature*, and *Africa's World Cup: Critical Reflections on Play, Patriotism, Spectatorship, and Space* allowing me to add a thank you to Richard Dyer, Rasheed Areaeen, Peter Alegi, and Sean Jacobs.

This book was completed in Cape Town, in Ann Arbor, and on planes between. The Cape sky is a panorama in cerulean blue, the Michigan sky low hanging and gray. Either may turn tumultuous in an instant. I wrote in a state of instability. Without the company of Lucia Saks and Sophia Saks-Herwitz it would have been arduous. As a trio we turned uncertainty into delight. I offer my book to Lucia and Sophia in love and gratitude.

Heritage, Culture, and Politics in the Postcolony

Chapter One

The Heritage of Heritage

I

Heritage entered and remade in an action-packed way and right now, or in the twentieth century anyway, with all the energy and all the fault lines associated. That is the topic of this book. Heritage at the moment of agency, poised between heritage practices of the past and the desire, need, or inevitability of breaking away from them to make something new. My father remade an old farm into his own personal piece of American heritage by preserving vintage barn boards, purchasing green fields, and turning old antiques into Americana; he made old clothing into a heritage brand item for fun and profit. His entry into the book of heritage also changed it. He bought into it, collected and acquired it as if he were a Vanderbilt, Carnegie, or Rockefeller. But he also branded it with his own insignia by turning it into a *brand*. This is an immigrant's heritage, that of the newly rich who buy their ancient titles and their places on the boards of venerable institutions which one generation past would have had none of them. It is how they find their way inside: through wearing the past, collecting and marketing it. It is the case of an individual wanting in to the American dream and wanting it in a way that declares his own independence, his own access point, his own drummer. In this way the immigrant latches onto the values of America the first settler society, the first postcolonial state. He (if it is my father) acts as if he is the settler writ large, driving his car around the college towns of New England and New York as if slogging westward ho by wagon train or canoe or arriving at

Plymouth Rock by sailing ship. Thus does he magnify his own sense of self through some unique combination of history, movie, and maternal blessing, thinking of himself as Davy Crocket, Randolph Scott, some American explorer.

Across the world young nations, groups of men and women, sects, provinces, conflagrations of people of all kinds have been engaged in the project of rewriting their pasts into heritages, and in particular in that vast part of the world that can be called postcolonial or the postcolony. I lived a decade in South Africa during the moment of political transition, the 1990s. At that miraculous moment of political negotiation, Truth and Reconciliation, and the writing of perhaps the most forward-looking constitution of any nation, old heritages went into tailspins and new ones hurtled into being. Decolonization had placed its European/settler heritages in question, leaving their role in everything from museum practice to university curriculum reeling. Traditional objects (artifacts of "indigenous" culture) and the institutions with which they are associated were being pulled from the "anthropology section" of the museum, recontextualized, and given new meaning within contemporary heritage discourses. Proclaiming one's past and codifying it in museums and through tourist sites is a virtual obsession through which people aim for acknowledgment (in some social or national or transnational context) and also, as often as not, branding and marketing, profiling and cash. And yet heritage is also the object of the most profound social, national, transnational controversies. It is a headache as well as obsession. Museums, uncertain of how to stake art, retreated to the default position of one size fits all: exhibiting one of everything so as not to leave anything out, nor provide any possibly unjust emphasis on anything. The result: a smorgasbord of art, a department store of incomprehensible items. The most famous painting in the Johannesburg Art Gallery was stolen because the museum, afraid of unduly emphasizing its Eurocentric past, had stashed it in an unlocked closet with old video machines. University debated the role of classics, Romance languages, European philosophy for the new Africa, not always aware that their terms of debate were themselves a product of the philosophical heritages they were sometimes too ready to jettison. Heritage fell into question at this moment of creative inauguration. But, on the other hand, new kinds of performance and exhibition began playing roles in the preservation of community and identity values, but also the remaking of those values in the urban/contemporary vibrancies of new lives being lived, new aspirations being formulated by the young. Performance, always deep in African village and town, quickly morphed into a central vehicle for the remaking of identity, which itself, in the newly inaugurated dispensation, was caught between inherited social practice and new identities tried on in the excitement of a vast social theater called the new country. At the same time, the continuities of heritage became critical to identity and group belonging, placing a conservative angle on heritage (preservation of tradition). Between conservation and free appropriation the past was played out in—and for—the present. The past became heritage done and undone.

Political history is itself an object of heritage making. What was an apartheid struggle is now a story to be told, a set of artifacts to be put on exhibition, a collection of memoirs and history books, a legacy, the stuff of heritage making. How to rescript the story of apartheid as a heritage for the newly evolving postcolonial state: whether to tell it as a vast act of mourning and suffering or March to freedom, within the media of book or digital apartheid museum and Web site, where, when, and featuring whom, for whose jockeying to power and whose benefit and whose readership and for what national purpose? Justice becomes, in the realm of heritage making, a new kind of contest between storytelling, medium, and power. Heritage is a window into the relation of aesthetics to politics as it emerges in the postcolony. By a bizarre act of Parliament, any group that builds a new casino in the country must build an apartheid museum at the site. And so the casino just to the south of Johannesburg, at Gold Reef City, which celebrates the heritage of white mining that was the birth of Johannesburg as a major metropolis and global commercial center, fronts a highly effective apartheid museum designed by an Israeli architect (see chapter 4). No adequate history book has been written for use in the schools that would teach this difficulty and traumatic legacy of South Africa's in a way congruent with the new democratic dispensation. The country, desperately in need of a national narrative, finds itself unable to reach agreement in and on its telling. Heritage remains at the official level only partly inaugurated even twenty years into the new democracy.

South Africans of every color, creed, linguistic affiliation, and geographical location are meanwhile hard at work turning their sometimes formerly dispossessed or devalued pasts into "heritages," and this for purposes of acknowledgment, identity politics, and/or commercialization and tourism. Every nook and cranny of every city, hamlet, or rural area has some kind of heritage museum or library/archive or tourist theme park in the hope that Danish, Dutch, and British high moral tourism will stop in, look, listen, and buy. While official state heritage making and related national consciousness is highly contested, decentralized heritage, heritage from "below," local heritage making, and market-driven heritage practices prosper. In that country (and elsewhere) heritage making is a lens into the problems and prospects of national unity, state-driven narration, and nation building, the diversities of social acknowledgment and the global market forces into which the heritage game enters and sometimes wins big bucks. And also of groups, provinces, and families who seek acknowledgment, voice, power, profiling, and also, as often as not, capital gains through heritage. It is a gesture of voice, an act of empowerment and solidarity, a piece of venture capital.

II

The heritage turn was part of the logic of construction by which many late colonial societies were able to formulate their terms of identity and origin and found their national beginnings. These people at the late colonial moment are likely to see their past as a broken legacy, one that has been castigated, robbed by those in power over them. The recovery of this kind of past, a past which appears to them only in downgraded form, an otherwise lost or inaccessible past, is also a worldwide phenomenon. A past perceived to be alienated, even broken, is one that a people congregate around fixing, and the reconstruction (whether for identity and/or marketplace) is often one of fierce, implacable energy, perhaps violent nationalism.

This dynamic of break, perceived fracture, inaccessibility has been central to the postcolony, where the (precolonial) past is often perceived to have gone through what Frantz Fanon called a process of "devaluation."[1] Mortified as monstrous, primitive, incapable of modernization, colonialism turned the precolonial past into a mark of inferiority, then stuck it in the museum to be gazed at like a nude alabaster Venus missing an arm and a leg. This mortification of a people was compounded by their reeducation as colonial subjects, trained in forms of art, language, philosophy, and writing which gradually supplant the other, and which are learned from a position of subordination. They are usually seen by the colonial master as wearing this education like an ill-fitting suit of clothes, which confirms to the colonial eye their buffoonery. The motto is *You too can become a second-rate version of us, so go for it! After all, you have no choice.* And so the great game of mimicry begins, further displacing people from past.

The remaking of a dispossessed past into a "heritage" today is important in driving not only nationalism but self-respect. It is also important in the neoliberal game of profiling, branding, and marketing. How this remaking intersects with market forces is one of the most interesting questions one can ask, since it is about the relation between human aspiration, group affiliation, creative innovation, and global self-branding for the marketplace. "Heritage," John and Jean Comaroff remark in *Ethnicity INC*: "is culture named and projected into the past, and simultaneously, the past congealed into culture. . . . It is identity in tractable, alienable form, identity whose found objects and objectifications may be consumed by others and, therefore, be delivered to the market."[2]

It is a central theme of that fine book that across the postcolonies the resurgence of identity takes the form of reconstructing heritage as marketable commodity (intellectual property or corporate project). To their idea one may add that of archeologist Nick Shepherd, who points out that the very discourse of heritage is a way of globalizing the local, packaging it in a common and neutral language with immediate status and recognition value on the global stage.[3] Redescribed as "heritage," local rituals, projects, and beliefs suddenly make global sense. Heritage discourse allows local culture potential entry into the circuit of global foundations, nonprofit and humanitarian organizations, world markets by profiling and branding local culture for that globalized, neoliberal consumer system. The paradox is that, like human rights language (with which heritage-speak overlaps), global comprehensibility and recognition are purchased at the price of thinning content into a language of buzzwords.

There is a great deal of truth to Shepherd's idea, which can be confirmed by the circuitry of international conferences, foundation grants, public goods organizations from UNESCO, all using these same buzzwords, "heritage" being the most obvious, "intellectual property" a close second, with "human capital" coming in third for the bronze. The language of heritage turns local culture into a particular twist on a common tongue, just as a sweater, automobile, news program, or canned food from Peru, Malaysia, Nepal, or Italy often is. This common language makes identity a globally comprehensible, consumable item and provides local populations with relevant profile. Having (suddenly) a *heritage* makes you (potentially) an international player just as having a Web site in English does. You may even get your fifteen minutes of Andy Warhol glory, jacking up the sales of your land, property, motorbike, flora, fauna, books, or artifacts. The Comaroffs put it thus: *empowerment* is a term increasingly "connoting privileged access to markets, money, and material enrichment."[4] The very use of heritage-speak empowers by lending the speaker a sense of internationalized "profile," a belief that by talking the talk and walking the walk they are now international players. Which may well be the case, whether for the heritage ecotourism market or for the world of foundations and grants.

This happens at the expense of the thinning of content, the profiling of content through buzzwords. Heritage making finds itself under pressure to conform to global profiling stereotypes, and all heritage products begin to look alike. The world's differences thin in the global department store of heritages. But heritage making must also thicken and deepen content if the scripting of a group or nation's past and traditions, the performance of these, the ritualized presentation of them is a way of achieving depth of voice, is part of the project of self-recognition, of return from alienation. The tension between the profiling game (which thins content) and the aim of deepening the texture of the heritage voice is often very real. This is especially so because the one demands the other. Part of what constitutes recognition or acknowledgment of a group through its heritage making is the circulation of their heritage to some broad class of participants and consumers. Otherwise that heritage, however thick and complex in content, speaks only to a small number of special initiates in a tiny heritage church. Sometimes this is what is perhaps wanted (cult formation, human exclusivity and exclusion), but as often as not a group or nation scripts its past with the aim of empowerment within a wide circle of participants, within an identity politics or nation or global consumer class. And so the simultaneous need to thicken and to thin the content of one's heritage script/instruments is an ongoing condition or conundrum.

I think every act of heritage gesture today faces something of this double-edged sword: to profile for a nation and/or global consumer population while also thickening the complexity of voice for purposes of self-recognition and what the philosopher Friedrich Nietzsche would call *self-becoming* (self-creation through new self-narration). This is clearly a matter of trade-off. Sometimes it pushes heritage creation in the direction of a distributed array of products, some of which are quite complicated and deep, others thinner, more globally comprehensible. It is a double-edged sword which extends to the heritage icon, that special event, ritual, story, and/or place which encrypts so much of a group or nation's past, carries the weight of deep historical signification, but is also a global profiling instrument by which the group or nation gains immediate recognition as well as tourist value. The South African example is of course Robben Island. Robben Island is a tiny salt deposit off the coast of Cape Town where anti-apartheid political prisoners lived in tiny cells and worked digging salt during decades of isolation, connected to the wider world only through their endless gaze at the city of Cape Town and its crystal rock mountain suspended under a cerulean sky and through samizdat documents smuggled onto the island. It is an indelible site of memory, also increasingly a pit stop on the itinerary of the tourist who takes in the island along with a township between photographing the wild game at designer game parks and shopping for wire sculptures of animals, mohair shawls, and printed tablecloths—heritage items all—at the Cape Waterfront. The silence of this liminal island haunts, its aura of incarceration is too powerful to disappear into ecotourism yet, especially when the guided tour is given by a former prisoner whose recitation is a ritualized act of testimony. But the ability of this island to suspend the consumer stance and produce an experience of shock (which stops the traveler in their tracks, inviting complex reflection) may not prove indelible if/when time passes and the immediacy of the memory, its eloquent caesura, fades. As it eventually will over time. If this island is in danger of reducing to another pit stop on the moral tourist's day planner, then everything is. I will return to this in chapter 4.

A moral pit stop is not always a bad thing: Money is to be made by impoverished peoples through heritage tourism, especially if the tourist will buy the book, eat at the restaurant, purchase the heritage costume, and stay at the B and B. But a moral pit stop is inevitably the victory of thin over thick content; profiling wins out over complexity of voice. It remains within the fast-paced one-dimensional aesthetics of experience rather than in the ambit of deeper human absorption and reflection. Heritage making is therefore an *aesthetic* issue: about quality and kind of *experience* afforded in late capitalist society, not simply a moral and political issue about recognition, reparation, and social power. This is why heritage is such a prescient window onto human societies today.

But here one arrives at a prior question, perhaps the basic question. Why heritage of all things? Why should an emerging postcolonial society want entry into this particular way of framing the past, this heritage game? I mean, given how tainted the colonial practice of heritage was, how much *damage* it did to them? To answer *because that's where the money is* is not enough of an answer. More than money is at stake here: the use of a practice, of an instrument, heritage, which was a lynchpin in colonial culture and preached to the native with missionary zeal in the missionary position. Heritage practice was an act of power *over* those peoples who now want to adopt that very game. Heritage practice was a "gift" in the double-edged sense of offering and poison.[5] Why should the postcolony be so obsessed with gaining access to this particular test match? Why should the postcolony be so keen to establish national, museums and acts of modernism, bringing the texture of the past now understood as heritage into the whirl of the present? Why not be done with the heritage game once and for all and treat the past in some other way? After all, the past is infinitely rewritable, from a loose set of traditions to a distant memory to the thing that one opposes to that which one ignores on principle, etc. . . . Of all the ways in which the past has been and might be rewritten, why restage it as heritage? Why not break with the colonial construction of it altogether?

Is this the case of my father writ large: that there is no stimulus for entry into the heritage game more powerful than being an immigrant or outsider, formerly excluded from the New England Yacht Club and/or the playing fields of Eton? So you determine to create your own access points. Or you become a first-class mimic, changing your name, upgrading your accent, imitating King Charles spaniels for pure breeding?

There is no single answer to this question.

Here is one answer: Heritage has always been perceived in two ways: as the club you can't enter but also the gift you are offered from the pulpit. Colonial elites have been offered European education, Sunday roast beef, and three-piece tailored suits; they have righteously admired Dickens and company as among the best parts of themselves. Nelson Mandela often spoke this way of the importance of the literacy, literature, respect for law and morality, disciplines of thought he acquired in mission school in the Eastern Cape as a child. He is not alone. Without the positive side of heritage learned in colonial times there could be no impetus for elites to reestablish heritage as a basis of a postcolonial nation state.

And here is what the philosopher Alexander Kojève might say (following G. W. F. Hegel), were this topic to arise.[6] Apart from concepts of heritage, it would be impossible for late colonial subjects to imagine and create their own nations. The reason why the slave does not kill the master at the moment where the master/slave dialectic is resolved is that the slave needs the master around as a model. You separate from the colonizer by becoming his ways and means, which gradually become your own. To take over the languages and practices of the colonizer, to play his cricket game, is to learn to think one's own future. There is no thinking of one's own future apart from this. Benedict Anderson has made this point sociologically, about the colonial institutions through which colonial elites begin to think of themselves as geographically bounded and identified: the map, the census, and the museum. The very idea of the nation is imagined through these forms, there is no other imaginable way to think and create it.[7] And so new decolonizing nations set up museums, archives, and the like, and these do indeed empower them, instruct them; dignify their pasts with the stamp of national patrimony. But these institutions are more than models of how to become powerful. They are the very materials—the *only* materials—through which colonial subjects can conceive their futures. The process of decolonization is incoherent apart from the taking over of structure and concept from colonizer and materializing these as one's own future.

The nation is imagined through a mixture of mimicry/assimilation and oppositional thinking. Colonial elites model their own sense of national unity on heritage origins. In their thinking, writing, and political speaking a mélange of shared language, culture, experience, and history converts into a singular unity. Of particular importance for societies that have endured the repression of their pasts and the castigation of their traditions under colonialism is to rescript both as heritage and in opposition to the colonizer. Settler societies go about this differently, as I shall try to show in chapter 6 (which is why America is part of this book), relying not on a rescripted past but a self-image settler experiment through which dominion is claimed over wilderness and peoples therein and a newly ensouled identity is brought into being in the process. But, for the rest, the act of rescripting the past in a way that is heritage creating and heritage differentiating gives precedence to their putatively *precolonial* past: that part of their past which predates the colonizer's entry. The category of the precolonial is an invention by the colonizer and his museum, a way of organizing artifacts and also script cultures into historical stages that are premodern, etc. . . . There is a long history of this particular articulation of the precolonial that is central to the history of colonialism. What late colonial elites do is take over the category of the precolonial and put it to their own use. They construct their precolonial past out of a mélange of artifacts, texts, beliefs, language, old forms of life, and contemporary traditions. This precolonial construction becomes proof that they have always been a *people*—until such time as their glorious past was blasted by the colonizer and stashed in the museum. The precolonial is in their thinking a mysterious origin through which they imagine themselves as a people robbed of their old protonation (whatever that was). It unifies them in opposition to the colonizer. And it provides them with purpose, destiny: to become again the people they once were and are destined to be. The precolonial is a necessary fiction through which they write themselves as a nation.

This is why heritage making is so critical to the act of national imagination. Through heritage, colonial elites come to imagine their own national status as that which was already there in the past, that which colonialism subdued, that which national struggle must vivify. Heritage bonds a people together, legitimates their struggle, points their way to the future. Without heritage it is hard to work out how they could conceptualize themselves as a nation. And when the new nation comes into existence, heritage allows them to codify it with the stamp of origin and patrimony. The point of chapter 2 will be to show how this process informs the national museums of India and the modern art movements there.

Again, settler societies are different: their act of self-imagination sets their origin in the new experience of the land itself, the experiment in settling, the process of laying claim to dominion over place and native peoples. The values they quickly accrete into heritage, forming their origin and destiny, are a mixture of settler values (thrift, resolve, ability to endure hardship, communalism, etc.) and a mélange of moral, aesthetic, and religious values from the (European) home country. Over time the act of experiment, the aspiration to settle (to take dominion) over land and peoples becomes the script of heritage they follow. This script of a social experiment in self-creation through the imagination of settling and the ingenuity to do it wants to be endlessly reenacted for purposes of reaffirming origin, reestablishing destiny, reaffirming character: for heritage purposes. Again I shall say more about that in chapter 6.

Now, for those societies instead actively scripting a unified heritage of the "precolonial," this unity is in actual practice a symbolic and institutional construction imposed upon diverse peoples, beliefs, traditions, languages, which picks out certain versions of the past to the exclusion of others, favors certain groups as more authentic than others. Heritage is always political and all too often imposed with terror, provoking a response in the same currency. The imposition of heritage onto diverse peoples is like forcing all people to wear the same size suit of clothes—and in the same color and design. This is exactly how colonialism offered heritage to the colonized: one-size-fits-all humanity and it's of our making, not yours. And so, up to a point, the politics of postcolonial heritage simply repeat the tactics of colonial conquest with equally violent results. In India the religious/Hindu orientation of heritage led to the violence of partition, to the world of Salman Rushdie's *Midnight's Children*. Contemporary heritage practice is always a riff on past heritage practice. The logic of heritage is that of difference within repetition.

And this is at the core of my book: that heritage games repeat past heritage games, but with a difference. The key in reading a particular case is to limn the texture of difference. Often heritage games are caught between the old exultations of accreted values, the old themes of origin and destiny, and new times that require intervention in the old games. What links the chapters that follow together is this "logic" of difference within repetition. This "logic" or grammar I call *live action heritage*. Live action heritage games veer between the power and authority vested in heritage with its capital *H*, its power to exalt and sublime tradition, create destiny, generate authority, and a break from this nineteenth-century mold, an intervention in the full-scale monty of the capital *H*. The postcolony, as Achille Mbembe puts it, represents "a specific system of signs, a particular way of fabricating simulacra or re-forming stereotypes. It is not" he goes on, "just an economy of signs in which power is mirrored and *imagined* self-reflectively. The postcolony is characterized by a distinctive style of political improvisation."[8] This perspective may be extended to heritage making in the postcolony, which is central to the politics of improvisation.

Live action heritage, as often as not, preserves something of the old goal posts, aura, authority, and power associated, while also changing the rules, goal posts, power, and authority of the game. It is the simultaneous acceptance of and intervention in the terms of the *game* that is the marker of the type. The paradox that by using a practice you change it while also retaining something of its (colonial) magic is the source of much postcolonial uncertainty. Even if you are the most ardent postcolonial mimic of European heritage, even if all you want to do is replay the Anglophone past on *Masterpiece Theatre,* you still change the format, the effect, the rules of the game: the first time tragedy, the second time . . . ? Homi Bhabha has shown that mimicry shifts the balance of the system it performs by performing it, casting it in relief, providing it with a new point of reference.[9] Live action heritage, even if aiming for pure repetition of earlier heritage forms, shifts their meaning and effect in some sense or other through the performance. And most heritage making does not aim for mere mimicry but some mix of that and new access points: My father and his Americana.

This is why genealogy is required: to trace heritage games to their sources in the eighteenth and nineteenth centuries while also understanding them as interventions in degree, kind, and character. Genealogy, the story of how something comes into being, traces continuity and modulation in the game itself. Heritage *morphs* in this way. Since a changed world makes it impossible to play the old heritage game without some kind of intervention in its terms (even if one wanted to play it as it was), just about every heritage act today has some live action dimension. I believe this "doubleness" to be the grammar of heritage: the condition of all heritage making today. Like all abstract grammars, it admits of countless variations as, across the world, ethnicities, groups, nations reidentify themselves (and prepare themselves for the marketplace) through self-applying the terms of heritage to their pasts. They are on the job constructing their villages, temples, monuments into heritage sites, building museums to encase their artifacts in the venerable vitrines of heritage, narrating their origins as heritages. This rewriting of the past that is going on around the world is also a rewriting of the *terms* according to which the past is written. In turning the past into a heritage one also turns the heritage game into something new and contemporary. This is what makes heritage practice uncertain, controversial, energizing, and highly indicative of new times.

III

What then has been the classic formulation of heritage, that practice of heritage with capital *H* which is the uneasy source of contemporary heritage invention? What is the heritage of heritage? How did heritage become a secular church of the past, a static image contained in that secular cathedral, the museum, that secular monastery, the university, that secular monument, the nation-state? When did mere tradition morph into that more exalted thing: a "heritage"? How did the past get to have so much authority? After all, persons have remained wedded to the past through performative rituals, acts of memorialization, loyalty to the dead, through the physiognomic dwelling of the past in the human brain and body. And in many other ways through which every person lives a life with some modicum of continuity, depth, narrative. These are not yet heritage unless specifically named such, refracted through the interpretive lens of heritage practice, identified as heritage by those who hold the past unto themselves and/or by others who are scripting their practices as heritage (chapter 3 is about this with respect to certain regions of Southern African carving traditions inherited from generations past).

Heritage arose in the eighteenth and nineteenth centuries. It is a central cog in the structure of modernity, a way of framing the past and ongoing traditions into an ensemble. It arises in tandem with the nation-state and is totally caught up in the history of nationalism, which remains true to this day—and also with the museum, the university, and the institutions of civil society. Once the concept and practice of heritage comes into being, it has the tendency to generalize beyond the strict realm of nation building, nationalism, and the like to group empowerment, family heritage, church heritage, identity politics, and the like. But to understand how heritage practice spreads is, in the first instance, to understand how it arises as part of the apparatus of the nation-state and its civil institutions.

To repeat thoughts of Anderson already mentioned, heritage is part of the logic through which a nation grafts its future onto a putatively shared past. The event of bringing diverse peoples into a singular fabric of citizenship is, as Anderson says, violent and hegemonic and relies heavily on shared culture as well as aspiration. That culture, scripted as a putative unity at the origin of the national project, becomes a way of bringing citizens together into the shared project of rescripting *them* as citizens.

Heritage is the instrument of this hegemonic process, this minting of groups and persons into the coin of the realm, that is, citizenship, nationhood, *one nation under God with liberty and justice for all* (as I used to recite in school). Heritage takes on the force of destiny; it is an instrument of becoming through which people are minted and an aura or ideology of destiny through which the nation is proposed and imagined. Now established as coin of the realm are values which become national, museums which store artifacts understood as the patrimony of the nation, recitations of history, morals, culture, science through which the modern university recites and interprets "civilization" and so civilizes its young into positions of citizenship. All these processes, and others, are heritage constructing. Without them, without, that is, the great event of nation building in the eighteenth and nineteenth centuries, there would, I surmise, be no rescripting through which the past and its ongoing traditions, performances, rituals, and other ways persons are embodied in and wedded to the past became a heritage. And so, through heritage, what was someone else's past becomes that of each citizen. This is part of the hegemonic process through which new persons called citizens are minted. Naturally, the process gives rise to all manner of resistance, including and especially to the heritage game, within the formation and constitution of the nation-state, just as it does within the colony when this same heritage is "proposed" (that is, offered in the missionary position and in schools of education and in all manner of social training) elsewhere. Heritage is, whatever else it is, a game that arises as an instrument of hegemony.

The process of heritage formation has two relations to the past, not one. At a moment of nationalism, capitalism, and colonialism, of the secularization of religion and the formation of nation-states, the past came to be understood as the gold standard of the modern state and culture, a currency accreted over time, held in trust, assuring the future. In their ritual and religion, museums, courts of law, poetry and politics, ideals, sciences, and liberal arts were the aggregation, the crystallization of European peoples, European nations. These values hold nations together and ensure their future. They are bankable. The past comes to represent the slow buildup of themselves over time, fine and noble, time tested. This inheritance was a sacred trust to grow then gift to the next generation. Heritage was identity through lineage, Gilbert and Sullivan stuff, Winston Churchill stuff, Lady Diana Spencer stuff. Past values, accumulated over time, are believed to be the gold standard of modern life and are cast in the aura of gold leaf religious truth. These values ("Britishness") comprise an aesthetics: not simply a moral bank or a time-tested set of economic and social practices. They are cast in the glow of aesthetics, of religion.

But heritage is equally a vantage point from which modern life could and should be critiqued. For modern life had lost sight of its true origins, its deepest values in the whirl of its getting and spending, class transformations, industrialization, urban blight, Victorian work ethic, taste for conquest. Modern society was, yes, up to a point the accretion of noble values, but it had also lost its way. Foundering in the desert, unaware that it lacked a road map or destination, modern society required reminding of what it really was and where it had gone wrong. This turn to origins/deepest values became the stern stuff of moralizing. Only the return to and appropriation of a people's virtues and ideals would set the people again on its right historical road, supply them their destination: their (think symphonic cadence) destiny. This critique of where the state and society are tending is part of the ongoing cultural corrective mechanism through which the nation is reimagined, its path put (or urged to be put) on a different tack.

Together these scripts entrust the past with the power to ensure national identity and urge or enforce national identity. Both heritage as the idea of a bankable set of values and heritage as the idea of a national origin or destiny arise out of the larger fabric of modern thought and institutional practice, and I would like to briefly survey some of this fabric. First I turn to the side of heritage as a bankable set of values, codified over time into a gold standard for the future. Call this the conservative side of heritage. It has its source in religion and also in scientific practice and thinking, in particular the rise of modern scientific empiricism, the idea of knowledge learned from experience, tested across different persons and over time. Time-tested values become the repository of the best of human experience, the storehouse for knowledge and morals. Railing against the radicalism of the French Revolution, David Hume (who died just before the event) and Edmund Burke (who wrote just after it) set forth this basic tenet as the principle through which societies may remain bound together: Without the conservation of knowledge tested across multiple agents and over time, there can be no knowledge at all, nor morals, nor principles of justice. This collective storehouse is something like *civilization*. It opposes everything radical (i.e., revolutionary) because the revolution junks the very accumulation of values through which civilization lives.

The storehouse of accumulated values is associated with stewardship of estates, favored canonical texts (Bible, Shakespeare), eternalized artifacts in museums, time-tested procedures for generating new knowledge and for doing the right thing, and the accumulation of wealth from the colonies. There could be no storehouse of artifacts and ideas to turn into "heritage" apart from the three great forms of secularization: the museum, the university, and the state, which together exhibit it as patrimony and educate the young. Through these institutions the nation-state recognizes itself as having a heritage and takes pleasure in it, cultivates citizenship through it, symbolizes power by it. Heritage is the internal self-symbol of the nation, the image of its longevity, durability, futurity, accretion over time.

Accretion means buildup: it is a critical part of the "logic" through which nations symbolize themselves. The image of cultural trust is not superfluous, it is essential to an imagination that brings together banking, accumulation of goods, market growth, colonial power, and moral value. Heritage is a bank of values held in trust for the future. It is the capital of the nation's moral fiber, the human capital that will sustain it on the playing fields of Eton, the warpath at Waterloo, the march to Pretoria. In turn these adventures in power bring back goods and chattels which add to the bank. Heritage is part of the ideology of colonialism. Its moral dimension legitimates European hegemony over the very colonies which supply the raw materials and endless trail of artifacts—not to mention sweat and muscle—that allows for the filling of museum, the bringing of cotton to Manchester. Its religious/secular bonding of values and goods, institutions and persons casts culture in the missionary position.

Market economy, as is well known, largely ran on exploitation (of labor) and theft (of artifact). The Greek statue became an English treasure, the Egyptian obelisk part of the glory of France. The museum and the nation-state arose and operated as an ensemble. Without the formation of nation-states in the eighteenth century, it is hard to imagine the great institutions of preservation (museum, also archive and modern university) becoming understood as storehouses for *heritage*. In the long halls of the museum, filled with Italian, Greek, Middle Eastern, later Chinese and Japanese and African masterpieces, the nation could display its power of ownership in the form of a narrative in which the size and scope of these eternalized things offered confirmation of the state's equal claim to power, glory, and longevity. The museological display was a pantomime drama revealing (that is, creating or constructing) the origin of the nation, and singing the praises of its future. The moral perfectibility of heritage has everything to do with this *image,* which was a secularization of religion in the state halls of the museum. The great nations of eighteenth-century Europe (France, England, Hapsburg Austria, Russia of Peter the Great) built the most prominent museums.

The museum became a transport train of artifacts from the contexts in which they were produced and circulated to the place (the museum) where they became encased under glass. Muted of meaning, the artifact in the museum became a cipher for a power of interpretation over it which glorified viewer/citizen/European subject. This power over the muted object is often glossed as contemplation. The birth of aesthetics arose around this museological form of practice.[10] As did the birth of that related practice: connoisseurship. The thing under glass wanted to be dated, labeled, and categorized by genre, style, medium, artist. A vast accumulation of data points to secure knowledge of the artifact by genus, species, and also idiom, the attempt therefore, in the work of Giovanni Moretti and others, to generate objective criteria based on an artist's individual brushwork, use of line, and other gestures so that works could be definitively assigned to the artist or artisan.[11] Connoisseurship is about authentication, the establishment of provenance. Provenance is where the heritage artifact meets the marketplace. Bernard Berenson made a fortune authenticating Italian primitive paintings, often buying a work of art, then using the stature he had accrued in the art world in virtue of his collection, authenticating it, and selling it for ten times the price. And nothing put a higher value on an artifact than its place in a museum. The priceless eternity of the object in that sacred heritage space caused the price to soar. (There is nothing like an object's being priceless to jack up its market value.)

In the lecture halls of the university, the long and continuous march of civilization was recited and imbibed and the liberal arts acquired, which came (in the modern university) to be understood as *Bildung*: character formation, the making of productive citizens who are productive in virtue of their training in civilization. The modern university was conceived in Berlin for this purpose. Recitation of heritage was central to the cultivation of a citizen believed capable of playing a productive role in the state.

It should be said that passing the baton of scientific, moral, and other social values in the "heritage bank" to the next generation was not always believed a matter of rote learning. Matthew Arnold, whose father was a schoolmaster, described heritage as his society's means for: "the pursuit of our total perfection by means of getting to know, on all the matters which most concern us, the best which has been thought and said in the world, and through this knowledge, turning a stream of fresh and free thought upon our stock notions and habits."[12]

Arnold's "best which has been thought and said in the world" has become a kind of motto for this idea of accreted heritage, as the European tradition knew and imagined it. While rote learning is essential, like schoolboy discipline, imagination and rewriting are also central to mastery. This is a hedge on the conservation of knowledge over time, since preservation and innovation to an extent go together. Transmission of knowledge is also to an extent the reinvention of knowledge and values. (It should be noted, however, that this does not imply a reinvention of the *terms* of the heritage game, merely a statement that the accretion/transmission of values is creative.)

Then there is the second side to heritage, the romantic side which poses origin in response to the anxiety that modern life has lost its way. This is heritage the cure for degradations of capital accumulation, brutality of the workplace and work ethic, not to mention the ascendency of new and threatening class interests/demands. This is heritage the cure for everything dull and dispiriting in Victorian life. The proposal is that a lost origin, once retrieved, will set modern life right. This lost origin is the true foundation of nation, humanity, spirit, the path to social destiny.

The concept of origin is a romantic concept, but also one woven deep into the fabric of the way the nineteenth century came to understand the world of the present in relation to the past. Linguistic philology was crucial to this new form of understanding at the core of this side to heritage. Friedrich Nietzsche, heritage's most profound apothecary was professor of philology at Basel before resigning his job, and the philological principle proved central to his and the nineteenth century's concept of tracing the present tense back to its putative origins. Philology, an invention of the nineteenth century, is about finding one's linguistic roots through tracing back the tree of languages to linguistic roots in more ancient tongues. The nineteenth century discovered Indo-European as the father and mother tongue of European (and other) languages and, amazed by this discovery, turned it into a cultural image of Europe's cultural past. The burnished metaphor was that linguistic origin equals cultural origin. To find the roots of one's sentences was to find the roots of one's thoughts, feelings, creativity, culture, self. Linguistics became the royal road to identity. So the full equation was linguistic origin equals cultural origin equals (true) identity. In spite of much confusion within the discipline, the equation of linguistic origins, cultural origins, and human *identity* was resolutely believed to hold.[13] And this was partially to justify racial difference (as difference in origin), partly to justify the Romantic move of Friedrich Nietzsche, Matthew Arnold, and others who believed that return to and interpolation of cultural origins into modern life was the only way to combat the degradations of that present age.

The Greek was invariably origin of choice over the Hebraic. Both Nietzsche and Arnold believed the debasement of modern life had to do with the domination of "Hebraicism" (and for Nietzsche also Christianity); both believed culture would be renewed only through retrieval of Hellenic origins. This was Romanticism pure and simple, which always favored the stone ruins and wine dark sea of the antique world. (It was also a sign of the ambivalence with which Jews were accepted as citizens of modern Europe.)

Classicism was needed in modern life to offset its "disquieting absence of sure authority.... If we look at our own inner world, we find all manner of confusion arising out of the habits of unintelligent routine and one-sided growth, to which a too exclusive worship of fire, strength, earnestness and action has brought us. What we want is a fuller harmonious development of our humanity, a free play of thought upon our routing notions, spontaneity of consciousness, sweetness and light' and these are just what culture generates and fosters."[14]

That is Mathew Arnold railing against the stuffy, rule following nature of Victorian culture (which he thought of as debased/Hebraic). Hellenism would supply modern life with spontaneity, harmony, a sense of authority, the virtues of moderation, risk, and any number of other correctives. At the end of the day, one has the feeling Hellenism was simply being loaded with all manner of correctives under the illusion that they were the genuine virtues of that antique time and land. This too is Romanticism. And so the "heritage" of origins became a way of putting into operation debate about the present and future of a people by reference to its putative past.

And so, through the double perspective on the past provided by heritage society's trajectory into its true future, its destiny was assured. Heritage was the bank of values, accumulated over time, codified as though it were a religious truth that held a nation's future in trust. And heritage was the origin that would set that society right again, attune it to its destiny. Heritage was the cause of modern life and its cure.

This stance magnified European authority over the colonies by asserting the European future over the colonial future. It happened in this way. Recall Frantz Fanon's remark about the "devaluation" of the past under colonialism. It is worth reciting his sentences: "Colonialism is not satisfied merely with hiding a people in its grip. . . . By a kind of perverted logic, it turns to the past of the oppressed people and distorts, disfigures and destroys it. This work of devaluing pre-colonial history takes on a dialectic significance today."[15]

One can now understand the role of heritage in this process of downgrading, taking Fanon's thoughts further and more precisely: The colonies (prior to becoming colonies) had their own ways of keeping the past live. The colonizer introduced a new regime of historicity, a new way of authorizing the liveness of the past. That new regime was heritage practice. The regime offered the gift of European heritage while denying that the colonies were capable of their own heritage practices. By denying the colony its own heritage of origins, the colony was denied its own *destiny*: a future to be lived on its own terms. By denying the colony a heritage of values and artifacts accreted over time, the colonizer denied it a culture that was capable of being passed on to future generations. Deny them both and you deny them the possibility of having their own future. The message was that the future of the colony could only happen through attachment to the colonizer. By denying the colony a fully formed heritage, by devaluing its past into a crypt, the colony was consigned to a state of perpetual stagnation, mortification, a permanent state of living in the what-was. It was given modernity only in the form of European mimicry and servitude. Give India its own heritage and you are providing it with its own origin, destiny, patrimony, its own ability to modernize on its own terms. You are giving it an exit visa from the colonial world. The heritage game denied the colony a *conceptual space* in which to think its own entry into modernity in terms different from those of being an appendage to Europe.

The exception to this proves the rule. In certain parts of Africa, colonialism allowed, indeed cultivated a place for "tribal" tradition or heritage. This happened through indirect rule.[16] Political authority was outsourced to the *amakhosi*, or "chiefs," over strictly contained rural spaces in exchange for peace, labor, and materials. Within the space of indirect rule the chiefs authorized customary law and ongoing social tradition. Customary law and tradition thereby morphed into a kind of bastardized heritage. But this heritage was viewed by the European as lacking authentic origin, destiny, futurity; it was seen to be a degraded heritage form incapable of cultural modernization. Relations between the chiefs and the colonizer were similarly an ongoing act of negotiation—but not on equal terms. The chiefs were finally on a leash, given a wider or lesser berth, depending. The traditions they cultivated remained vibrant on many occasions, but within a controlled, ultimately panoptic space. They were what Mahmood Mamdani calls colonial "subjects" rather than "citizens."[17] It is also known from the work of Jean and John Comaroff that in the actual trenches of missionary work modernity arose in the colonies as a give and take between traditions.[18] But this was not acknowledged in the official ideology of heritage. Colonial heritage practice generated many unexpected results that ran counter to official purpose. But that official purpose was clear: to exalt the colonizer's future while denying anything beyond a debased future to the colony's own traditions.

This is the core reason why decolonizing societies find it essential to enter the heritage game, make for themselves heritages. To do so is a rehabilitating move, a way of self-assigning a future by taking over the ideology which allows them to ascribe origin and destiny to their past, accretion and transmissibility to their "values." And so a central part of the postcolonial dialectic is reconceptualizing the precolonial past as a heritage, finding a way to claim that past as the origin of one's future. Heritage becomes a point of national origin, as I have described earlier in this introduction.

We can now also see more clearly how postcolonial heritage making must be live action heritage. In the dialectic played out between colonizer and colonized, national heritage is both asserted as superior to the colonizer's and as simply *different* (one among others). It has to be. For decolonization may be colonization over disparate peoples in the name of nation building, but it is not, and cannot be, avowedly world power in the sense of the British Empire. Its oppositional stance is partly defined as over and against the relationship between heritage and colonial globalization. In this frame of mind, a Mahatma Gandhi will, when asked what he thinks of Western civilization, famously answer: *it would be a good idea*. India has civilization, the West mere pretense. India's origins are deeper, older, uniquely civilized: superior. But Gandhi can only make his remark as a half joke, because even he knows (former lawyer in England and South Africa that he was) that India cannot be a nation apart from Western culture and heritage, even he knows it cannot assert its heritage in anything like a universalizing stance in the British sense. A decolonizing society like India can never play the colonial game in reverse, seeking to degrade and denature the British past. Indian national heritage at the moment of decolonization has to be a *live action gesture* that veers between taking over the older colonial practice and changing it in accord with these new social exigencies. It repeats the terror of heritage only insofar as it imposes this over disparate peoples in the name of its own national growth. In this way the will to domination is not absent from the postcolony, whose use of heritage is also human abuse built into the processes of nation building.

These words, *use and abuse,* are meant to recall Nietzsche and his famous discussion of the use and abuse of history. History is written, Nietzsche thinks, by and for the present and is written in order to empower the present (individuals, groups, nations, whomever) in this way and that. The question is when empowerment is simultaneously disempowerment of self or others, and for what reasons, and how egregiously, and how much disagreement there is about such matters and how easily (or with what intractable difficulty) disagreement may be resolved. Abuse as a particular kind of use of heritage may come in whatever form the use of heritage may assume: abuse of the details of the past, the instruments of heritage, the archive, the museum, the university, the court of law, the media, the state, abuse of self and/or others. Nietzsche, forerunner of deconstruction, thinks of use and abuse as two perspectives one can and should take on any given piece of history making, which is why I've two chapters that take up Thabo Mbeki's African Renaissance, a postcolonial gesture of rhetoric with terrible disempowerment associated, but also motivated by a genuine project of rehabilitation. And I've another on Sarah Palin and her deployment of the heritage of the American small town, which she turns into a fundamentalist gold standard filtered through the histories of film and television, but in that chapter I also discuss the role of the media in constructing Obama as Lincoln. This chapter too is meant to suggest how intricately the use and abuse of heritage interact.

Nietzsche is of relevance to the understanding of heritage because of his double-edged view of history, considered as a form of human empowerment through writing or narration. For Nietzsche history is both a vital sign of life and a burden (everything in moderation, say the Greeks). The use of history is by and for the present, to deepen present life by enhancing its energy and qualifying its origins. Nothing is worse, he believed, than an excess of history, a fixation on the past, an inability to extricate oneself from its power and burdens. Without the ability to forget the past and dive into the abundant stream of life, human beings are hamstrung, powerless: dead. "Imagine the extremest possible example of a man who did not possess the power of forgetting at all and who was thus condemned to see everywhere a state of becoming,"[19] Nietzsche writes in his early essay "The Use and Disadvantages of History for Life." "Such a man would no longer believe in his own being, would no longer believe in himself, would see everything flowing asunder in moving points and would lose himself in this stream of becoming. . . . He would in the end hardly raise a finger."[20] "He who cannot sink down on the threshold of the moment and forget all the past, who cannot stand balanced like a goddess of victory without growing dizzy and afraid, will never know what happiness is—worse, he will never do anything to make others happy."[21]

Chastening words these, unless heritage is *itself* a route to immersion in the present, perhaps deepening the call to a nation's futurity, energizing its present, giving it pride and vivacity. Nietzsche does not go into the relation between history and heritage in this essay (although "preservation" is part of what comprises history, and that certainly is a function of "heritage" today, as in the World Heritage Sites of UNESCO). An excess of history, Nietzsche moans, is part of what allows a people to believe its age is morally superior to all others, the pinnacle of whatever processes have happened to lead up to it. The urge to superiority is the same kind of urge as the exultation of heritage. And so the Afrikaner heritage of the Great Trek, enshrined in monument, spoken in church, "derived" from biblical chapter and verse, was meant to confirm the unique presence of that tribe within Africa as *originary*. They were the ones who built the country by trekking into the interior and defeating the Zulu horde, not the English, nor the Portuguese, and certainly not the African. It is their country, belonging to no other; they have established the right to sole dominion. This aura of religion applied to the past suffused the Nationalist Party in a haze of paranoid Afrikaner omnipotence, all others being a threat to this heritage biblically derived. And when prominent Afrikaners spoke out against the myth, they were punished with particular vehemence. If the twentieth century has taught one lesson, it is that obsession with heritage can be a license to terror. We know it from American doctrines of manifest destiny, we know it through Voltaire's oft-cited remark that if one can get a man to believe an absurdity one can get him (or her) to commit an atrocity; we know it through Germany, Serbia, and Pol Pot.

Heritage is territory of use and abuse and also of Nietzsche's double consciousness. On the one hand it is here to stay, a basic route to recognition, profile, capitalization in contemporary life, a way of bridging local with global languages, a way of remaking identity and positioning a group within neoliberal markets.

This is a philosophical book about heritage as well as a study of twentieth-century and contemporary cultural changes especially pertinent to the postcolony that go under the name of heritage making. There is a vast and lively literature on heritage management, museum studies, heritage, memory and nationalism, and particular heritage sites analytically/critically unfolded. This book seeks to draw out moral/political dimensions to heritage practice by attending to the double action of heritage making. At the same time, it seeks to demonstrate by example that the logic of heritage I have called live action is at the core of heritage making. The book is in that sense dialectical. In the chapters that follow I choose three postcolonial sites, India, South Africa, and the United States, and aim to show how heritage games are live action (veering between old heritage sources and newly grafted/morphed aspirations) in each case.

India is chosen because its moment of decolonization and heritage construction is about recovery of its own devalued past. The chapter on India unfolds just how difficult it can be to find representations and structures which regain access to that past, which rescript it as nonalienated heritage.

South Africa is chosen because the politics of heritage are so controversial and robust in that transitional democracy. South Africa is a country in search of a single national narrative, a shared national consciousness, and yet its problems and prospects of heritage making point away from that into a whirl of identity politics, historical arguments, and market forces, setting it as an entry point into the prospects for national and local heritage making in the twenty-first century. South Africa is also of interest because it has morphed in some complicated and less than complete way from a settler society (dominated by a settler state and values) to a society set on reclaiming a precolonial past repressed by that very settler formation. South Africa is a postsettler society and a society set on discovering the way forward for itself through return to its (idealized) precolonial culture, complete with indigenous ways of knowing. These competing narratives are the topic of chapters 4 and 5. South Africa occupies a hybrid place in the postcolony in virtue of its diversity of kinds of population and its specific kinds of national heritage construction (postsettler, precolonial). This hybrid position is perhaps shared by certain Latin American countries such as Mexico and Guatemala.

The USA is included because it is the first postcolonial nation and because it is a settler society writ large, therefore a perfect case study in how settler societies construct terms of heritage differently from those societies which, like India and South Africa (after 1991), turn to a rescripting of the past. Chapter 2 will be about that graft in the case of India, with respect to museum culture and art, chapter 6 about America and its ability/liability to graft settler heritage onto contemporary politics through the vehicle of the media.

My book aims to demonstrate the logic of live action heritage, but does not seek consensus about the stories it tells. Should it succeed in stimulating debate half as lively as the heritage practices it discusses, I will be delighted.

Chapter Two

Recovering and Inventing the Past
M. F. Husain's Live Action Heritage

I

Early modern Indian art is a drama about recapturing a past repressed under colonialism, *museumized*, alienated from Indian elites as an effect of colonialism, and yet living on each and every street corner. It is this paradox, along with a deep split in late colonial society between modernizing elites and nonmodernizing "subalterns" that generates this drama. The nationalist impulse is deeply connected to this desire to reclaim the past. To reclaim the past is also to invent it, invent it as a unified, precolonial form. This is an artifact of colonialism.

Edward Said and others have detailed the many ways in which this museumizing imagination treated entire cultures. Great cultural moments were petrified in translucent preservatives for the Western gaze and consigned endlessly to replay the past in a series of exact repetitions.[1] These ideas are now familiar. The picture of the Indian past, indeed the totality of Indian traditional life, as a timeless artifact under glass, comes through clearly in the eighteenth- and nineteenth-century paintings and watercolors composed in India by British painters. Painters like Thomas and William Daniell, William Hodges, Sir Charles D'Oyly, and George Chinnery went to India, in the words of Daniell, "to transport to Europe the picturesque beauties of the favored regions [of India]."[2] They ignore the boundless energies of millions and represent India as if were nothing but an eccentric cousin of Constable's *Wivenhoe Park*. They did not merely drain India of its life and vibrancy, but blended their concept of the picturesque with a kind of pre-Raphaelite romanticism of the ancient. They fixated on the ancientlike ambience of India, typified by its decaying temples, eternal pagodas, and half-empty palaces, as images of their own past recaptured. Let me explain by way of illustration.

An Anglo-Indian landscape painting might contain animals or Indian laborers in its forefront. These will appear to blend into the landscape, as if they are part of it. The viewer's eye might be led along a road or a winding vista from the painting's foreground (where the figures are relatively small and insignificant) to its background, where in the distance (but occupying a central place in the pictorial composition) will be a hill station, a picturesque valley with ancient banyan trees, or the fragments of a ruin. Or these figures might appear in the back, part of the endless presence of landscape itself. While the colors, asymmetries, and foliation in these pictures proclaim the presence of the picturesque, the compositional style also signifies something closer to the style of Claude Lorrain, that is, a painter of the classical ruin. It is therefore instructive to glean the difference in mode of conception between a Lorrain and a British landscape of India.

The seventeenth-century French painter Claude Lorrain creates artificial, Arcadian worlds painted also foreground to background. He places farmers and cows in the compositional foreground and presses the eye along a winding path into the background of his pictures, where invariably a classical ruin is to be found. Lorrain's landscape paintings, watercolors, and etchings treat the nature of this ruin somewhat differently from the custom of the British painter in India. Lorrain isolates the ruin, making it barely visible yet pictorially central, as if a nearly infinite gap of space must be crossed to return to it. Space has become the metaphor of time distancing us from this ruin, the distance between the ordinary and mundane present and the eternal world of the classical past that is no more. In a Lorrain the past exists simultaneously with the present. The tranquility of the eternal, signified by the ruin, is poignant in its silent separation from us. The obliviousness of those cows and farmers in his pictorial foregrounds forces us to witness our own remoteness from the ruin. As our eyes traverse this pictorial distance, our urge for connection with the past is intensified as if that inexorable gap between foreground and background, which is nothing other than time itself, might be overcome in a leap of vision that would abolish the laws of transience and recreate the eternal. Yet this desire to erase the gap between present and past quickly gives way to melancholy, since the ruin, while tangibly part of the landscape's "presentness," is there only in the form of an unapproachable shell: it is no longer capable of animation. Our sadness is, however, matched by a special pleasure afforded by the beauty of the ruin; this derives from its inapproachability.

In this poetics the ruin is stained with the patina of the classical world, whose traces are indelible but whose memories are faded. The ambiguity in the dwelling of the shepherd and the cowherd is that they are and are not part of this landscape of eternity. They live among these ruins blessed with a special proximity to them and yet are also the eye of the present leading toward the evaporating past. Sometimes Lorrain does set the entire landscape in the antique—including the figures in the front that he casts in the ancient garb of classical shepherds. Still the poetic is that of a canvas suffused with a lyricism of the *past*. His soft aura impressed onto the past signals a culture in the beginning throes of modernity, for the other side of modernity is always a recognition of the loss of traditions, forms of life, and images of the eternal. Lorrain's world is one where proximity to the classical past can no longer be taken for granted—even for the peasant living in harmony and spatial proximity to its monuments. It is a world that has discovered the inexorability of time.

This is a break with the thinking of the Renaissance, which had presumed to dwell in complete continuity with that past. The Renaissance is convinced that classical ideals still command complete authority over the dignity of representation. Thus in the architecture of Brunelleschi, in the city planning of Alberti, and the design books of Serlio, and most self-reflectively in Raphael's *School of Athens*, the point is to remake the beautiful in accord with these ideals. With Lorrain, that classicism begins to appear a ruin, a piece of the past no longer inhabitable, except in the nostalgic imagination of the poet. Romanticism will, as modernity rapidly progresses, exaggerate this desire for return, as if the anomie endemic to modernity were intolerable to the modern poet, for whom progress could only take place through a cultural injection of that classical past which it was the task of the poet to recover in imagination.

This gap between past and present, between tradition and invention, between continuity and disruption, is a common feature of modernities. It is the counterpoint to an awakening sense of historicity, incipient nationalism, growth in technological forces, capitalism, and rapid changes in the social fabric. The symbolic forms of modern cultures express or encode something about the way in which the past has become problematic for modern subjects. For some the past will now appear as the guarantee of continued identity and integrity, while for others it will be that lodestone of the archaic which must be cast off in order that a glorious historical future may be realized. Many cultures of "the West," but also those of India, will have ambivalent and contradictory attitudes toward the past, viewing it as both a site of authenticity and a burden to be cast off.

Things are quite different in the Anglo-Indian representations of the colonial period. The British colonial painter (along with the company school "native artists" he taught) does not approach the ruin as the uncanny presence of an evaporating past. Nor does the British colonial painter seek to evoke nostalgia. His representation is rather one of a fascination with an ongoing exoticism in which the entire culture strangely but happily exists—as if for eternity. He approaches old Indian monuments and ruins just as he approaches the fakirs, holy men, and workers who live among them—as an unbroken stream of stilled/timeless life.

FIGURE 2.1. William Hodges (1744–1797), *View of Part of the City of Benares*, circa 1781. Gray wash with brush and brown ink over pencil squared for transfer, on laid paper laid down on nineteenth-century wash mount, 23 ⅝ x 40 ⅛ in. (60 x 101.9 cm). Yale Center for British Art, Paul Mellon Collection.

This is the attitude of one who luxuriates in a cultural museum whose people and ruins are all of a piece: together timeless. No irreparable loss attaches to the Indian past because it is not gone but is instead everywhere alive. Indeed Europeans found in the Indian world a living image not simply of the Indian past but of their own. Bernard Cohn has argued that

> the major interpretative strategy by which India was to become known to Europeans in the seventeenth and eighteenth centuries was through a construction of a history for India. India was seen by Europeans not only as exotic and bizarre but as a kind of living museum of the European past. In India could be found "all the characters who are found in the bible" and the "books which tell of the Jews and other ancient nations." The religion of the Gentoos was described as having been established at the time of Adam and Eve in the Garden of Eden, and preserved by Noah. . . . The Brahmans were Levites or Nazarites; Jains Rehabites. Indians were, for some Europeans, the direct descendants of one of the ten lost tribes, for others the manners and customs of Indians derived from the ancient Egyptians who were the descendants of Ham, the son of Noah.[3]

This mode of assimilating India as a preserved fragment of the Western past allowed the Westerner to preserve his conceptual scheme intact. Thus, according to Cohn, the link between India and the European past was a requirement of interpretation as such. Europeans knew the world through its signs and correspondence to things known. The exploration of the terrestrial world was being carried out at the same time that Europeans were exploring their own origins in the pagan past of Greece and Rome. Hence another way of knowing Indians arose through looking for conformities between the living exotics of India and their ancient counterparts in Egypt, Greece, and Rome. The exotic and the antique were one and the same.[4]

This early moment of European self-mirroring becomes in the nineteenth century explicitly museumized. James Fergussun's lecture from 1866, "On the Study of Indian Architecture," is a perfect illustration of these attitudes: "The European past can be seen in India as in a museum. Builders in India have been doing the same thing since time immemorial, which enables the British to understand how their own great religious buildings of the middle ages were constructed."[5] Note that equally ancient lineages were attributed to Africans, who were believed to be equally lacking in the capacity for development. Christopher Miller points to

Charles de Brosses, a friend of Voltaire, parliamentarian, and student of the primitive writing in the 1760s, as an example of such thinking:

Civilizations and religions all follow the same evolutionary path, once they get started, but that some are "stuck" at the zero point, outside of progress, for, "their customs not changing at all, two thousand years bring no alteration in practices." . . . Black Africa provides de Brosses with a happy crossing of the temporal with the spatial, for in its perpetually arrested state it presents (makes present) a condition identical to that of ancient Egypt; to go to Africa, spatially, is to travel backward in time to a point of "pure anteriority." This conflation of space and time is so much a part of our current assumptions about non-European cultures that we may not even recognize its metaphorical basis.[6]

Even Hegel, that arch glorifier of the West, refers to Africa as "the land of childhood."[7]

Now if Indians were the sons of Ham, then the Bible was still alive and well. If India was a world where everything was reincarnated on a daily basis, then nothing could ever be lost. Thus there is in the British painter's sensorium no perception of difference between the Indian laborer and the ruin. India could hardly be conceptualized by such persons as a place where ruins ring of transience, for nothing in India was in the end ever ruined. India was rather an exotic flower whose every petal, every building and every place was timelessly existent as a piece of the past replayed forever, as a living monument. No need for nostalgia here, for the painter, traveler, or poet had arrived at a world where nothing dies, where everything stays the same because nothing is ever new.

The colonial painters could paint India in the style of Lorrain, but in a way that defeats his ultimate point. Their landscapes may meander down visual paths toward old hills or ancient ruins, yet everything in the character of their paintings conspires to defeat the poignancy of ruins as such, because this place was in their minds timelessly picturesque. India could out-romanticize romanticism by showing it how to recover what modernity could only yearn for: the premodern past now rendered golden through the weeping eyes of modern nostalgia.

To represent India as a luminous exemplar of the romantic picturesque (not to mention the biblical past), it was necessary to keep its representation pure. Needless to say, that involved repressing the representation of its poverty, disease, and scars of exploitation. As Pratap Pal and Vidya Dehejia put it: "[even the] British photographer's perception of India was in many ways remarkably similar to that of the early British painters. The realism that was made possible by the camera rarely emerges except in a certain limited category of news photographs. The photographer certainly saw the poverty and squalor of certain parts of India, but he chose not to record them; he was a photographer in search of the picturesque, much like the eighteenth century landscapists."[8]

Indeed colonial photographers mostly recorded an India of snake charmers, maharajas, British officers at the half-tilt, and monuments.[9] This mortification of living traditions was connected to the imposition of a colonial regime of painting on India, not without its own charms and surprising idioms, but one that in essence repressed the spirit of Indian painting and redirected it into a sensibility of color use, modeling of form, pictorial organization, and subject matter that was constantly at odds with "instinctive" Indian ways of picturing. This produced a kind of fascination: paintings in which a fight is always going on between regime and internal aspiration or sensibility.

When the J. J. (Jamshetjee Jeejeebhoy) School of Art was founded in Bombay, its first report, written in 1857–58 by the English art teachers who were imported for the task of this reeducation, stated the following: "our native students have much subtlety of the eye and finger and will probably make excellent copyists, engravers and mechanical draughtsmen."[10] The report went on: "Their tendency is to repeat traditional compositions which have come down to them from a distant age without refreshing or even glancing at real life. Hence they degenerate instead of improving. The grotesque images with the shapes of men and animals in all parts of the Hindu temple are unredeemably bad. Their sculptured foliage is purely abstract in character."[11] And: "It seems that the safest way of attempting to regenerate this defective and artificial manner of design without destroying what it has inherited from European Schools of Art is to set the students to copy faithfully the objects of nature, men and women. . . . Thus a school of design would in time arise, native in the best sense, owing its accuracy, truth and natural beauty to European inspiration but moulding its material into purely Indian types."[12]

A more concise statement of the remaking of the "Indian type" into an essentially imitative identity (into a colonial type) could not be found, since Indianness, robbed of its traditional values (which are, in that laconic style of the English put-down, "unredeemably bad"), most now be recreated as a type that owes its values ("accuracy, truth, and natural beauty") to the European type on which it is modeled. Indianness is heritage debased then remodeled by the colonial, European lens.

The castigation of the Indian sculptural past into a set of "monstrosities" is the subject of an entire book by Partha Mitter, and the topic will not be pursued here.[13] By a dual logic the Orient is at once consigned to the status of that which must repeat the past in an eternal way and be robbed of its own past, whose values and forms of authenticity are viewed as degenerate.

Even these imitative Indian colonial works betray cultural continuities with traditional Indian ways of seeing, thinking, and modeling, for example, the sense of flat space, crowded figures, posture, and hierarchical sizing. The past is there even in its moment of greatest repression. There is a difference between English and Indian colonial works, but one that the English consider a sign of "hopeless inferiority" and ill-organized thought processes. This denies neither the force of the repression nor the related element of rupture between traditional art and colonial Anglicisms. It simply shows that even in "prison" people can only be "themselves." Partha Mitter has written brilliantly on such late colonial/early modern precursors as Ravi Varma, whose works span the gamut from classic company school to Indianized pre-Raphaelite to Art Nouveau advertisement, in every case revealing complex inflections of Indian space and pictorial mood within an essentially imitative and Anglicized framework.[14]

Through the early history of modern Indian art, these repressed or chaotically organized dimensions to "Indian" experience will again flourish in more creatively posed, self-expressing forms. It will only happen gradually. And, as we shall see later in the chapter, it will take an historical sea change within India itself, namely, independence.

Since in both English and Indian colonial representations the Orient was consigned to the status of the past, it followed that it was hardly in a position to remake itself in a modern way. Where there is no loss of the past, there can be no modernity. Turned into a museum, it was robbed even of its capacity to lay claim to its past cultural productions as its own, for they now existed for the viewer rather than for the Indian whose ancestors had made them. The Indian was reduced to the status of a slave in Alexandre Kojève's famous sense (loosely adopting Hegel): one whose capacity for self-recognition in the field of cultural labor is taken over by a master who now assumes the recognition and ownership of the slave's productions as his own. Objects of the colonial past were therefore freed for the West to take over and "modernize" in any way it wished. For, if the Indians had ever been capable of producing these objects for their own ends, that day had passed. India, China, and Africa were no longer capable of producing the new. They had lost both self-consciousness and humanity, the capacity for producing the future on their own terms and for using the past. If modernity represents a break with the past, then for colonial cultures this break is imposed from without and exists in the manner of a wound.

Their past had ended up in somebody else's heritage game, on somebody else's playground.

II

Various domains in the late colonial world are shaped by the desire to return to and recover their pasts. The recovery of the past is connected to a decolonizing, nationalist instinct, but also to an attempt to heal the scars of what Homi Bhabha, taking up the thread of Franz Fanon, called a "split" subjectivity.[15] It is a natural aspiration for subjects split between modernizing and traditional selves, and whose traditional selves have been subject to disfiguration. These aspirations are complicated by the desire to recover the past in contact with the ordinary persons on the street corner and in the rural areas. To the eye of the elite, half-modernized painter or writer, the lives of ordinary people on the street corner (where a great deal of life takes place in Indian society), in the temple and rural area are a living wellspring of traditions: proof that the signs of the past are alive in the present, that, in spite of colonial disparagement, the old ways remain alive. This is a mixed blessing, since the also modernized Indian elite believes, in his or her Anglicized voice, these to be quaint, archaic, unmodern, and worse. But this elite person also feels that on the street corner the living wellspring of tradition can be found in what is a society otherwise mortified for its past.

This wellspring of tradition the elite knows also to dwell within: but in fragmentary, confused, and ambivalent form without integration.[16] The elite knows on a Sunday he or she will not serve roast beef, put away the Charles Dickens, change from three piece suit to dhoti and sandals and pray at the temple like those ordinary Bengalis, Rajasthanis, and other locals whom he or she sees there every day. Split between "bipolar" forms of dress, performance, identity, the elite longs for simplicity of perspective held by a nonmodernized "subaltern," even if the elite also has contempt for that person's class, caste, and limited experience of the world at large. The nameless person of the street corner is romanticized; proximity to the past is projected onto him. He or she becomes the bearer of tradition, a living legacy or heritage with all due aura floating above, working, sleeping, praying: he or she is the royal road to the crypt of the precolonial past, proof that it is alive and well in the here and now. Such people, with their dhotis, unmodified beliefs, and nonmodernizing ways, are invested at the time with an essentialized property of "Indianness." The rumination of the late colonial Indian world is full of discussions about what is "Indianness," who has it, how can we recover it? It is in this context that the ruminating elite find themselves drawn to the subaltern onto whom they project this magical fountain of identity. In the aspiration of recovering the past from colonial castigation, alchemical traditionalism is found—and projected—onto these folk. They become a mirror of the elite's fantasy of reauthentication: the elite's fetish.

A royal road to the past through contact with the man on the street corner (from whom the elite is also alienated by virtue of his modernity). The alienated thing in the museum, dormant or lost tradition and the nonmodernized person *blend together* in a fantasy of recovery, as if each could be used to restore the other to elite colonial Indians, thus giving these persons a heritage, point of origin, common set of transmissible values: a way forward. It is almost as if the fantasy is that the artifacts in the museum, vivified by the living traditions of the street corner could now get up, walk and start singing in the present, participate in the noisy communalism of the street corner. This transference of *proximity* onto the past, this conflation of people and artifacts, is as illusory as it is instinctive.

This double alienation (from artifact and ordinary person) and fantasy of double connection (to each through the other) is the crux of the problem of early modern Indian art. What the attempt to reconcile the elite with the subaltern, the modern colonial subject with the nonmodernized one, through representation reveals is just how wide the gap really is. To revivify the self through a double return to the street corner and cultural artifacts is a kind of dreaming. Both the past and the street corner are like seawater to a person dying of thirst on a boat: omnipresent and undrinkable.

I would like to call this moment of dilemma the split between encrypted heritage from above (the museumized precolonial past that has been robbed of ongoing relation to the present) and ongoing live tradition from below (the life on the street corner that is fantasized as proof of ongoing tradition). Merged together, these would produce authentic Indian heritage and the piston for nationalism (one's own national future).

The first move in this game of making the two merge may be conveniently dated to Jamini Roy and the Bengal school at the turn of the century. Roy's paintings and watercolors have absorbed canons of Western painting and Christian myth. Some have a Romanesque use of tapestry that flows around the women like saris. No doubt Roy has seen the Romanesque through books, which merges in his poetic imagination with the stories he heard from his grandmother as a child. The pictures also derive from Indian miniature painting, specifically of a type found in the area of Bengal and Orissa. And they have as their source Indian folk art traditions, possibly even late-nineteenth-century popular Calcutta "street" painting like the Kalighat. In Roy's pictures one can detect a break in consciousness between painter, past, and folk tradition that gives rise to the nostalgic aim of reconnection with what is experienced as a displaced present and past. This is partly why the figures can appear to be princesses while also standing as folk icons: they are invested with the pictorial royalty of the museum and the simple charm of ordinary people. And so princess and folk icon, Western garment and Indian sari are hybridized into single forms.

Similarly, a drama over the person on the street corner, the ordinary person is, to the early modern Indian artist, a sign of living tradition opposed to the museumized way in which the Indian past has been propagated. Moreover, that person is taken to represent an aspect of the artist's own divided self, invested with essentialized authenticity because in danger of disappearing and already existing under colonial disfigurement. It is this "excess" or wild element of significance that turns into a type, a sign, a "subaltern figure." The ordinary Indian becomes the living sign of "Indianness," that property of cultural origin which the elite painter desperately seeks. Now the drama of the subaltern is also based on the reality of those who are in dire need and lack voice. However, the construction of these persons goes far beyond that powerful social reality or realism into a melodrama, and it is the melodrama that is internal to the early modern art historical shape.

The subaltern, a figure introduced and made famous by postnationalist Indian historiography,[17] is the being constructed by larger social reality— by a shape, if you will. Early modern Indian art invests this subaltern figure with immense ambivalent meaning that endures well into the history of modern art. This construction takes on monumental proportions in the early history of Indian art when, in the 1950s, Indian artists wished to reveal the intensity of the poor, the untouchable, the one who knew little of the complexities of modern life but was simply burdened

FIGURE 2.2. Maqbool Fida Husain, *Kumhar (Potter)*, 1947. Private collection.

by that life. A drama is played out in the early work of M. F. Husain, Ram Kumar, and others in which the subaltern appears in the guise both of object of sympathy and of nostalgia: sympathy in virtue of his terrible poverty and incapacity to help himself; nostalgia because the simple life of the subaltern is romanticized as the bearer of an authentic "Indianness" (lost heritage, identity) uncorrupted by hybridity, fragmentation, or colonial ambivalence. The artist is in the impossible predicament of wanting the subaltern to become modern, and yet keeping him or her in a lost precolonial past so that the artist may return to the fantasy of origins by drawing close to his or her inscrutable, auratic being.

However, the very gesture of painting the subaltern in a modern style confirms the unbridgeable gap between painter and painted. For the painter's style is certainly neither the subaltern's own, nor one that the subaltern could finally even understand or use. Within the circle of this representation, the subaltern cannot, in Gayatri Spivak's words, speak at all.[18] She remains dumb.[19]

III

How then does the next stage of modern Indian art work through this predicament in which the past remains an inaccessible, museumized form of nostalgia and the ordinary person from the street corner (aka the subaltern figure) is invested with the artist's desperate desire to find again the depth of these traditions by drawing close and idealizing him/her as the authentic bearer of the Indian essence?

Only when the nation came into place could the past suddenly appear a potentially live Indian heritage rather than a colonial and mortified property. The nation created the enthusiasm for rewriting the past in the name of the future because with, the nation, all of a sudden India *had* a future. From the confidence that India was a thing capable of inventing its own future came the opening of a conceptual space for rewriting the past as the *origin and source* of this future. Indeed the process of differentiation from the British colonizer and then nation building required a heritage formulation through which the Indian subcontinent could remove its jewel from the royal crown and take it back (into its own, newly created museum), differentiate itself from England, and script an ancient/venerable, unified origin for its diverse peoples. Nation building demands

(I suggested in the previous chapter) this kind of heritage instrument. It was left to the live action activities of arts, letters, and speeches, and museums and other institutions, to (variously and in tandem) find the terms to articulate destiny (the future of this new nation) in relation to origins. It took nation building to provide the change in perspective allowing the past to be rewritten as an Indian heritage. There were various versions of course, and the history of India has been about their competition.

We must turn to 1947 and the formation of the Progressive Artists' Group: during the year of India's independence. At that time Maqbool F. Husain, Sayed H. Raza, Francis Newton Souza, K. H. Ara, S. K. Bakre, and Hari Gade, associated with Bal Chavda, K. K. Hebbar, and, later, Ram Kumar, formed themselves into the Progressive Artists' Group with the declared project of forging a modern Indian art. The British had exerted powerful pressure on Indian artists during the eighteenth and nineteenth centuries, training them in the style of the Company school, a transposition of faintly disordered British portraiture and landscape painting to the Indian subcontinent. Some Indians had indeed become quite accomplished representatives of this school. Husain calls this style the ultimate example of *nature morte*: it killed off India's dynamic topography by reducing it to still life, as if Calcutta in all its gritty urban density were but the pale imitation of Constable's Wivenhoe Park.

While the progressives turned to India's own past, they also wanted to discover what modernism in the West might offer a newly independent India, as Husain put it: "I was one of a group of painters who thought we must find our own roots. . . . In those days the dominant style was the academic school of Britain . . . Royal Academy and all that. . . . We revolted against that school of painting . . . we just wanted to find the language. . . . We adopted the Western technique . . . but not in concept. . . . I have a very definite goal . . . I must find a bridge between the Western technique and the Eastern concept."[20]

The earlier Bengali modernist school of painting was seen to be too romantic, unmodern, and merely nostalgic about Indian tradition. Initially, while many studied from the reproductions of Picasso, Klee, Braque, German expressionism and other modernists, the Progressives were determined not to enter into mimicry. Their aim, one shared by modern art generally, was to find influences that would reflect and help shape rather than obliterate their own burgeoning voices; to appropriate influences from the West on their own terms just as Picasso had done with the

African mask and Matisse with Islamic art. The time was one of a vast experimentation, which made Souza say: "Today we paint with absolute freedom for content and technique, almost anarchic; save that we are governed by one or two sound elemental and eternal laws of aesthetic order, plastic coordination and colour composition. These artists knew there was no turning back. India was modern, and must forge a new identity for itself."[21]

Crucial to Husain and the progressives was a fundamental change in how the past came to be negotiated. Rejecting the "nostalgic" Bengali view, they arrived at the idea that past traditions were only recoverable in new ways that must inevitably alter the fabric of the past and test its ability to transform itself across historical time. No longer would the move be to place nostalgic versions of a museumized past onto new canvases by dressing beautiful/simple people (locals) as fantasies from the *Arabian Nights*.

The progressives burned with the idea that their work would be a significant gesture toward a new India and the creation of its new national subjects. Implicitly they understood the importance of symbolic and institutional forms for the creation of national consciousness, and their goal was reflected in their great game of reclaiming the diversity of India as a whole. The subcontinent's past had to be rewritten as *Indian*, the property of the nation available to all citizens, a vast world of origins found in artifact, religious epic, and edifice. Just as the newly created "Indian" museum allowed each cultural agent the experience of reimagining his or her relation to the past, so the modern canvas went through a similar experience. For the modern canvas was *like a museum* in this respect: the museum extended its range over India's entire past culture in the guise of collecting and exhibiting patrimony; the modern Indian canvas ranged over India's entire culture in the guise of reclaiming its styles. Husain is a Muslim, but painted as a secular artist for whom the Hindu epics were as much his thematic material, the Chola bronze his stylistic field, as Mogul painting and Islamic rug design or textual ornamentation. The key was to lay claim to the whole of the past as *his*: his in virtue of his newly wrought position as an Indian citizen.

A unified field of the past was thus set in place through the modern Indian canvas, and in the museum in accord with the demand for a heritage instrument. Rajput painting, Chola bronzes became understood as the cultural origin of the self, lost or eclipsed under colonialism, whose interpolation back into culture would set India again on its feet. The museum set forth these culture forms/artifacts as patrimony, high heritage with glowing pride. The painter reactivated then into a second life through the collision with Western modernisms. Both the museum and the painter thereby shared in the invention of citizenship. By constructing a unified field of the past in the sense of a heritage of lost origins, deep patrimony, a set of representations came into place which could (in principle) encode each and every citizen into a shared condition of belonging, bring them together into a shared historical trajectory. Each person would, in this idealized experience of the unified past, find themselves the same as all others in the claiming of it. A culture of citizenship was to arise around this new formulation of the past. No longer Hindu versus Muslim, Bengali versus Rajasthani, the goal was to produce a new form of national belonging through shared pleasure in the same, universal patrimony of origins. And so the past took on a vital role in the construction of the Indian state and the modern Indian citizen who would inhabit it. Heritage played the role of nationalizing individuals, played the role of national politics.

In chapter 1 I suggested that heritage making in the twentieth century is a tradeoff between thin and thick content. On the one hand, heritage must be broadcast, profiled, and to a potentially wide/global audience. On the other hand, it must serve the deeper, less evident purpose of return from alienation in a whirl of *self-becoming*, which pushes it in the direction of complexity, and a smaller audience capable of grasping the heritage role. I suggested this problematic may be best addressed through a distributed array of heritage products, some thinner, others thicker in meaning and innovation. And so in India the museum served the purpose of heritage making, easily profiled for a wide audience, the modern art movement that of intensity and complexity. In the galleries of the national museum, the stuff of the past became immediately broadcast as "Indian heritage." In the modern art movement, heritage valences were less evident but more innovative, singular, deep. While the museum constructed a heritage of artifacts and their stories, modern art constructed an amalgamated heritage of past artifact (celebrated and transformed through the act of painting), cultural tradition (prayer, washing, eating, marriage, etc.), and, crucially, the ongoing life of the street corner. The visual rhythm of the street corner was the place where ancient and modern life collided in an endlessly renewing dance whose visual rhythms and shifting visual patina were a jazz riff soliciting innovation from visual art. Painting was privileged because of its representational capacity—because of its ability to picture this dance on the street corner.

Until the 1980s these worlds of the museum and of modern art were pretty much restricted in actual practice to a small number of Indian elites and a few sympathetic internationals. Only when India achieved a new, wealthy, and globalized business class did these systems develop into a significant art world. At that moment the expanding art world of India merged with global art systems, and Indian modernism became an international silver (even if not gold) currency. The growth of Indian art markets, the global prestige of Indian business, and a global turn in the postmodern art worlds of Europe and America finally dislocated a longstanding neocolonial prejudice which prevented Indian modernism from being taken seriously. Until that time, Europe and America all too often prejudged the very *idea* of a modern Indian art project as hopeless: derivative, dependent, incapable of achieving its own terms of innovation. Noting the presence of Western source modernisms in modern Indian art, it was immediately assumed the signs of difference which are the clue to innovation in Indian art were simply signs of bad imitation: of a painter trying to speak a language he or she could not quite master. Indian painters were seen as what my grandmother would have called seconds, throwaways you buy on discount because of all the "flaws." Modern Indian painters were written off as bad Picasso, bad Matisse, bad everything, yokels endeavoring in the manner of New York City taxi drivers to speak good English, but always with a funny accent. When difference is downgraded as bad mimicry, neocolonialism is writ large: the judgment that modernist traditions in the global "satellite" regions of the world are incapable of paving alternative paths to modernity and are instead repeats of the Company school, that school training Indian subjects as (second-rate) Western painters. The West (Europe and America) could not, until India arrived on the international financial stage as a global player in a globalized and more decentered world in the 1980s, begin to rethink the "funny accent" or the damaged cotton as instead a pattern stitched of complexity and innovation. It took some doing for the West to even begin to accept that India could use Western source modernisms as *material* for its own adventures, rather than remaining in the stylistic schemes set down by those modernisms. It was only when Indian wealth at home and abroad became sufficient in the late 1980s to generate a robust Indian art world that India passed beyond the status of satellite into that of art center (China would follow a decade later). There is nothing like a rise in price (in Indian art markets) to raise Western consciousness.

The modern Indian canvas celebrates Western source modernisms (treats them as iconic, retains significant parts of their stylistics) and subjects them to its own stitch. This double relation is one of genuflect and transformation. Western source modernisms are not only appropriated to globalize Indian art, they become the material through which Indian art can approach its own past artifacts and traditions in a way that morphs them into something new and experimental. Picasso and German expressionism, surrealism, and abstraction become the route to retrieving and remaking the Indian past, setting it into experimental motion by amalgamating it with these modernist styles rather than just copying it or approaching it with nostalgia.

It should be noted that, even though the museum and the modern canvas were part of the invention of the Indian state heritage project, in fact the Indian state and significant sectors of Indian society were from the start antagonistic or at least ambivalent toward this secular heritage project. I speak of Gandhi's purified Hindu culture set against the "heritage" of the West and proclaimed as the essence of everything Indian, its true self. There was hegemony in this: it deleted from the unified field of culture Rajput painting and many other elements which the museum and painter wished to incorporate. It deleted from the nation of India a subsegment (many Muslims). Hinduism was played out as a national heritage and became a piston of partition and violence and, hundreds of thousands of deaths later, led to the creation of Pakistan. Ambivalence about the secular project was there in the Indian state, and widely in Indian society, from the start. I shall return to this.

IV

The point of innovation in the art of the progressives was to transform the past into new amalgamations of representation that could present India as part of the modern global stage and send the past reeling into a whirl of modernism which had its own self-confirming fascinations. But, at the same time, as these artists aimed to genuflect toward precolonial forms, treat them as iconic. It is this double regard for the precolonial past, as model, prototype, and origin, on the one hand, and material for utterly free appropriation/remaking, on the other, that is the basis of their live action heritage game. They morphed past artifacts and styles, while leaving them sufficiently intact, that they might remain celebrated in their canvases as the source of all, the point of origin, the referent for cultural return. In this way the past became the starting point for a modernism that would be about Indian difference, Indian modernism, Indian heritage, rather than dependency on source modernisms and heritage forms from Europe (as if those source modernisms were colonial heritage again imbibed in the passive voice). Husain and his compatriots wanted their art to stand as an experiment which touched the multiple realities of (then) contemporary life in a way that celebrated artist-centered freedom. But they also wanted source artifacts to stand as strong signs of identity and purpose. Husain would have called the museum the ultimate place where culture is stilled (as if a butterfly under glass). He wanted to make the ancient Chola bronzes in its galleries dance right out onto the street and merge with the people there. But he also wanted to celebrate them in his paintings as distinctive originating *types*.

The choice of past artifacts and styles was a choice guided by two things. First, these had to be iconic and, second, formally amenable to transformation in the whirl of a modernist canvas. The Chola bronze, the Rajput miniature painting, and other such artifacts were chosen because of the cultural authority flowing from their status in past tradition, but also because they are so amenable to transformation when set in that whirl of experiment. The experiment melded three domains into one: past artifact, source modernisms from the West, and the rhythm, texture, and color of the street corner. Innovation in the modern art of India is about this triple melding. Source modernisms from the West free Indian artists to rediscover their own past traditions through a new lens; conversely, past tradition and street rhythm ring changes on source modernisms, making their appropriation innovative rather than imitative. That was the project goal anyway, making the rewriting of Indian heritage truly live action. The progressives reached out to Picasso, Matisse, German expressionism; and this free interpolation of European modernisms freed them to transform traditional Indian styles (Chola bronze, Rajput painting) into the mix. European source modernisms, chosen by elective affinity, gave Indian art the distance on its own traditions and the stimulus of radical remaking, which allowed these artists to return to the past and meld it with what was imported from Europe. At the same time, the key was to complete this triple appropriation by injecting into the canvas something of the rhythm and vitality of the street corner, thus melding past styles, European source modernisms, and daily life. By melding source modernisms with traditional styles and the rhythm of the street corner, all elements were changed, becoming visually kinetic. Transformation became the signature item of Indian modernism. The work became icons celebrating *remaking* while also genuflecting toward source icons which carried the authority (now) of a heritage past, a global modernist point of departure.

The key was to turn a passive existence of subjection (colonialism) into a self-generated gesture of agency and to avoid the pitfalls of incoherence and/or slavish imitation of the West (its source modernisms). These things were none too easy to accomplish. But, insofar as they were successful, the progressives overcame the old drama of the subaltern on the street corner and the past bottled in the formaldehyde of the museum through this unbottling of the past and this capturing the rhythm of the street corner. And both could be freed to happen through the newness of what Indian painters brought back from France and Germany. Only in this way could imitative interpolation of European modernism be overcome. It wasn't always overcome.

This revision of the relationship between the contemporary Indian canvas, street corner, and past became a way of resolving the problem of *style* in modern Indian art on the basis of what Goethe called elective affinity. The lens of Western modernism allowed for free assimilation of the Indian stylistic past; the forms garnered through return to that past, and the rhythm and energy of contemporary Indian life, allowed the appropriation of Western modernism to avoid imitation. However, not every modernist style can be melded with every Indian tradition. The creative work became that of synergy. What was celebrated was the achievement of an elongated process of becoming.

This expansion of agency in the whirl of becoming is a classic condition of modernist art. Indian modernists felt a close alliance with those artists in Mexico whose heavy, leaden past was brought to the dreamlike, knifelike vision of the Mexican future through their cross-pollination of pre-Columbian and colonial forms with cubism and surrealism. Tamayo, Rivera, and Orozco were considered compatriots by many Indian modernists. Diffusion and melding is a story also told about the Haitian painter Wifredo Lam, who worked in Paris with the surrealists then imported their style back to his own culture to picture it with surrealist density and mystique. Lam melded African-like sculptural forms from surrealist source modernisms with the tropical rhythm of Haitian ritual/religious culture, representing it close up but also from the distant otherness of the surrealist gaze. It can be told of Cecil Skotnes, and his idealized woodcarvings of southern Africans are deeply rooted in cubism and surrealism; they turned the African figure and form into a universalizing modernist principle while also being highly attuned to local inflection. It can be told of Gerard Sekoto, who found his genius in the winding streets of Sophiatown—that chaotic para-city grown up with the city of Johannesburg and at its edge—by attending to the brilliant refractions of color and hard shadows which the dry, transparent light produced on corrugated iron and crumbling plaster, bringing to the representation the colors of fauvist painting he saw in picture books. The point here is that diffusion of source modernisms and their melding is a standard way modern art is globalized in the twentieth century.

In India diffusion became the middle term allowing Indian art to achieve contact with the street corner and also the past. On the one hand, the past is treated as iconic (a heritage ideal), on the other, the object of transformation. The progressives wished to break through the heritage crypt of the museum (British and Indian alike) by transforming past artistic traditions through contact with source modernisms and contemporary Indian realities. But they also wished to retain in their canvases the aura of a past scripted as heritage. There is a reason why (for example) Husain endlessly painted the Ramayana and Mahabharata: these Hindu, now, in the secular imagination, "Indian" epics, were the heritage signs of India, the epic stories transposed to the register of a nation and its "glorious past." In scripting the epic as the screenplay for the new nation, the epic was itself conscripted to a modernist paintbrush in space, figuration, and color.

Thus did the progressives aspire to the double logic of live action heritage outlined in the introduction to this book: preserving, indeed creating, heritage legacies while also seeking to intervene in the *game* of heritage.

The project emerged only gradually. At the pictorial level, Husain and some of the progressives began to charge their modernist spaces in certain central ways, growing partly from the soil of Indian life and partly from old Indian artifacts. Husain, whose work went furthest in this regard, dynamizes and completely fills pictorial space, casting the planar

FIGURE 2.3. Maqbool Fida Husain, *Ganga Jamna or Mahabarata 12*. Painting: oil, canvas, 70 x 120.5 in. Gift of the Chester and Davida Herwitz Collection, gift of the Davida Herwitz Fine Arts, Trust, Peabody Essex Museum, Salem, Massachusetts, reproduced courtesy of the M. F. Husain estate.

geometry into motion. He employs brilliant colors to envelop space with symbolic and expressive value while modeling the human form in distinctly Indian ways, in accord with lessons learned from his study of the Gupta period of sculpture and what he knows of Indian postures generally. Husain's tendency to activate and completely fill pictorial space is a response to the Indian environment that he has internalized and finds natural. The Indian street or village is a place of overwhelming, overcrowded activity, where people wash, work, take counsel, feed children, sleep, or pray—in fact, experiencing every possible facet of living—oblivious to the thousands of cars, bicycles, and passersby. Buildings disintegrate and are recycled for every kind of use; shops spill into the street where people and animals live side by side. All this is cast in searing light and brilliant color. Space in India, moreover, evidences strong juxtapositions and contradictions. Slow-moving animals are counterpoised with the flow of traffic; modern streets abruptly give way to dirt paths, cars to bicycles; ancient temples display their garishly painted upper stories, representing multiheaded and multilimbed gods and goddesses. Indians construe this surface chaos as exhibiting certain deep internal divisions. Some animals or men are taken as holy and others not; persons belong to specific castes or religions. Deep splits between persons Westernized or not, rich or poor, are painfully obvious. It is this structure and scope of space that Husain has internalized, in which he feels at home and indeed which define for him what home is.

A great deal has been written on the construction of space—the spaces of work, of privacy, of play, of nature, of city life, of crowds and silences, of inner and outer, of time and eternity, of representation and activity—to the point that Foucault has declared that ours is "the age of space." But what may seem natural to an Indian painter might not be to a Westerner whose sense of spatiality is dramatically different in certain respects. What feels crowded to a Western eye and uncomfortable to a Western kinesthetic sensibility will not be experienced in that way by a person whose internalized spatial grid is that of an Indian city. Near chaos will be rather read as a complex and relatively well-defined cultural geography, tightly filled spaces will not feel claustrophobic but rather active and alive. The wall, which Leonardo told the young painter to study, will be a wall not of white and gray Italian stucco cracked with the sinewy lines of time but rather a wall plastered with layer upon layer of paint, dung, graffiti, drawing, film poster et al. For a Westerner to appreciate Husain's project requires an adjustment to their grid.

Husain not only energizes his spaces but tends to split them in accord with street and society. This formal device activates the pictorial space by elaborating simultaneous layers contrapuntally. Husain's splits, which directly reverberate with the many fissures of Indian life, are achieved by reconstructing cubism in Indian terms, turning cubist planes into dancing, dynamized juxtapositions. For example, Husain's *Cage* series takes the stilled masklike intensities of Picasso and sets them in motion, while also rigidly containing figure within overlapping spatial planes. It is homage and riff. The series is Husain's paean to the role of women in traditional India, a role that is melodramatic in its containment, active without exit visa. Woman is in traditional culture the shakti of man, her energy is for him, his. She is cast into a motion within prison walls: caged.

Husain's figures retain motion even when vertical and without any immediate task. *Maya* (1977) splits the figure of Maya (the mother of the Buddha who dreams she is giving birth to the Buddha, only to find it true) along multiple vertical planes. This split energizes the figure even while she

FIGURE 2.4. Maqbool Fida Husain, *Cage V (possibly Cage IV)*, not dated (circa 1974). Oil, canvas painting. Gift of the Chester and Davida Herwitz Collection, gift of the Davida Herwitz Fine Arts, Trust, Peabody Essex Museum, Salem, Massachusetts, reproduced courtesy of the M. F. Husain estate.

remains statuesque. Another way to put this is that the type of statue referenced in the work is itself a dynamic statue (classical Indian sculpture).

Husain has rejected key Western modes of portraying the figure:

> One reason why I went back to the Gupta period of sculpture was to study the human form.... When the British ruled we were taught to draw a figure with the proportions from Greek and Roman sculpture.... That was what I thought was wrong.... In the East the human form is an entirely different structure.... The way a woman walks in the village there are three breaks ... from the feet, the hips and the shoulder.... They move in rhythm.... The walk of a European is erect and archaic.[22]

FIGURE 2.5. Maqbool Fida Husain, *Maya or Tribal Girl*, 1977. Painting: oil, canvas, 76.5 x 44.5 in. Gift of the Chester and Davida Herwitz Collection, gift of the Davida Herwitz Fine Arts, Trust, Peabody Essex Museum, Salem, Massachusetts, reproduced courtesy of the M. F. Husain Estate.

RECOVERING AND INVENTING THE PAST

In many of Husain's paintings, one will find that the female figure twists to her left or right from the shoulders, but slightly to the opposite from her hips. Maya bends independently from the knees, hips, and shoulders while also assuming a sculptural pose. This mother of the Buddha shares with the Chola bronze its taught/flexible lyricism. Referencing both Indian

FIGURE 2.6. *Shiva as Lord of the Dance (Nataraja)*, circa tenth/eleventh century. Tamil Nadu, India, Chola period, bronze, 27¼ x 24¼ x 9½ in. (69.3 x 61.8 x 24.1 cm). Kate S. Buckingham Fund, 1965.1130, the Art Institute of Chicago. Photography copyright © the Art Institute of Chicago.

sculpture and Western modernism, the painting reduces to neither by resisting the hard closure and stillness of a Picasso figure and the overall design of the Chola bronze.

In her stylized yet relaxed pose, Maya is both person and iconic work of art. She is a figure naturalized while also offered as a tributary icon. This image of woman both naturalized and sepulchral suspends her between person and persona in a patriarchal gesture.

The role color plays in India has been important in engendering Husain's chromatic conception, as Husain himself explains: "Color . . . [in India] is not light but a symbol of certain emotions [or deities] . . . a certain mood . . . if you find a piece of stone and you apply orange colour to it you don't have to make an eye and nose . . . the villager will think it is the god Hanuman."[23] This use of color envelops a pattern of details with mood and texture, rather than as a way of opening the picture to a light source. Husain's treatment of color is closest to German expressionism, to which, for many reasons, Husain and some other Indian painters feel instinctively close. The employment of color as an opening medium is fundamentally foreign to the Indian conception, not only because in India natural light is so hard and brilliant that it seems naturally to enclose space, but even more because Indian paintings do not open through perspective to the world. They establish melodramatic or symbolic worlds. In Indian miniature painting, for example, color is employed both musically and symbolically. Delicate and poetic rhythms are set up in the miniature through combinations of color, theme, and details. Color articulates space as mood and symbolically suggests emotion.

To return painting to its sources in the past while also opening it up to the street corner is for Husain the test of his art. He is not simply a modernist, he is a populist. Husain was once asked in the 1960s by a gallery owner in New York why he did not paint abstract art. "You could make it here if you did," the gallery owner said. "There is nothing abstract about a billion people," the painter responded. All through his career Husain has believed that the very proof of authenticity in his art has been in its ability to be recognized by "the people on the street and in the village." That villagers could look at his pictures when he would bring them to villages and say, there is Siva, Parvati, Arjuna, there is the story of the chariot or of Hanuman was demonstration of its connection with sourced origins and cultural roots, so he believed. This vision or illusion of painting certified as genuine by vox populi is the nationalist impulse writ large. I paint the nation, and it recognizes itself in my paintings, Husain would say. And he has taken delight in the fact that villagers recognize the gods in his pictures while also finding their own characteristic gait, posture, movement there. This merger of the human and the godlike into one form is exactly what heritage culture accomplishes in its canonizations of origin and values. Heritage culture is patriarchal insofar as it naturalizes and deifies at once: the case of Maya.

VI

The canonization of a culture has other flaws. It mythologizes culture in a way that abstracts it from politics. In 1976, the year of India's emergency, Indira Gandhi subverted the constitution and assumed a position of direct authoritarian rule. She did it to secure national power against spirals of violence and disintegration, to combat corruption and secure personal power. The state, incapable of exerting control over a boisterous subcontinent, made the decision to do so through tougher, more violent means. Husain made what was to many the morally and politically disastrous decision to paint Indira Gandhi. Husain claimed to be working purely as an artist: capturing the historical intensity of the mother-times, without laying claim to any particular party, ideology, or views on the torture of dissidents, the imprisonment of alternative voices, and the spiraling black market due to draconian controls. He was purely showing the country itself. But the very gesture itself of painting a leader assuming the authoritarian and repressive throne could not be other than an authorization of the institutions of power by an institutional painter who was already a national icon in virtue of his setting the past to work as live action heritage.

It was proof that he had become a national figure. Soon after the emergency, he was appointed an honorary member of the Upper House of Parliament—along with the writer R. K. Narayan and small number of others. For Husain, it was an excellent opportunity to draw the parliamentarians up close, and he took full advantage of the free cabling and faxing he was allowed (these were the days before e-mails). Mr. National Treasure, himself now a heritage item, ceaselessly moving about the country in flowing gray beard, chiseled biblical head, bare feet, and a three-piece English gentleman suit, a man who could easily pass for Charleton

Heston or even Moses (with a little help from Hollywood). He'd often been asked if he would act in films; clearly he had the screen presence; and, with his national heritage status assured, the ensuing decades of his life became the stuff of celebrity, the scandals with underage film starlets, the fleet of Bentleys, an equal number of children, grandchildren, muses, always surrounded by a crowd of live action Bollywoods, international art curators, hangers-on, and let's not forget his collectors.

That same decade later, in 1987, Indian art was catapulted to the world commercial stage. The British auction house Christies decided that India's wealth, at home and abroad (in Bombay, London, Silicon Valley), was sufficient, and its art world robust enough, to hold a major auction of Indian contemporary art. This took place in Bombay, the first of many, with Sotheby's quickly following suit. Overnight, the prices inflated a hundredfold. Indian art became status currency for the corporate giant, the advertising firm, and the bourgeois collector.

Modern Indian art had paradoxically been freed to invent itself by exclusion from global markets as these. In the 1940s and '50s a few national institutions (the Museum of Modern Art in Delhi and Lalit Kala) had offered support to this part of national culture, a few dedicated collectors and perspicuous friends (old Indian maharajah wealth, German Jewish refugees to India, the odd intellectual, and a small number of collectors from abroad like my parents). Absence of a market allowed the project of modern art to proceed in all its complexity and spontaneity, without the need for constant branding and attunement to the global cultures of museums and exhibitions and auction houses. This absence of markets caused careers to tailspin, artists to take second and third jobs, and consigned some to impoverishment, bitterness, stagnation. There is no romance in exclusion from the forces of capital despite the charms of *La Vie Boheme* in the opera theater. No, making art without a robust art world to circulate it was no party. But the upside was freedom to pursue a complex project, even if it was not immediately comprehensible in international heritage-speak or biennale-speak.

However, with age, iconic status, celebrity value, and a lot of people paying a lot of money for a Husain, his work gradually became a branding logo. Not entirely, but in some serious part. The story of Picasso, Husain's hero, is instructive. At the risk of total self-indulgence and impropriety let me quote from an earlier book on the star icon where I wrote this riff on John Berger's story of Picasso's celebrity:

the result of his appearance in a thousand newspapers, magazines, art journals, photo shoots, [which occasioned the] . . . Picasso logo as he began to repeat himself, plate after plate, bowl after bowl, posing for the art photographer—bare chested with his piercing eyes, drawing in the sand for the camera, eating raw fish, living in neoclassical eternity in the eyes of millions. Visiting him there was, one supposes, rather like visiting Grace Kelly as he churned out yet another south-of-France azure ceramic bowl or painting of night fishing. You got your two hours of genius on display and went home to publish it in the magazines. The genius of his endless innovation ended up in this assembly line of individual creations and endless poses, each reeking of the name PICASSO, so that the cardiologist or lawyer who read the magazine and then purchased the plate would be assured immediate recognition value for self and friends. This price of the Picasso object was set by the cult around his genius, the aura of the work, but also by the marketing logo of the product. With Picasso (and after) genius took on an aura beyond all commodity value and in so doing set the value of the commodity, the price of the assembly line of art items.[24]

The same story can be told of Husain, pursued by his bevy of collectors, corporations, and nouveau riches who all wanted a piece of his work with high recognition value so they could publically profile themselves as having "a HUSAIN." This artist, never one to scoff at money, delivered with aplomb in a command performance of horses, horses, horses, an endless array of quickly painted items which everyone could recognize as a "Husain" without very much effort and which, hanging on their walls, loudly proclaimed, I too own this, I too fit the collector profile. What they were buying was status, image, a mirror to reflect their success, a calling card for their publics. And the work increasingly catered to this market, reducing itself in innovation and content to a language of buzzwords, that is, a parade of horses, bold strokes, elements there for recognition value as a "Husain."
And so the celebrity painter produced and sold a train of Husain-products, leaving him rich and giggling all the way to the bank. The public particularly loved his rags to riches story, motherless child of a poor tailor, artist run away to Bombay to paint, living hand to mouth on Bombay street corners, surviving in the early 1940s by painting cinema hoardings (big hand-painted billboards advertising Bollywood films), holding the status of an art so intense as to be indifferent to money, a story which in

every way enhances the modernist genius in the three-piece suit, beard gray and flowing, barefooted. It freed him from caring too much about wealth, while dazzling the public into offering millions.

Husain was my friend, and I tell this story not without difficulty. Markets energize and also corrupt, especially when genius has allowed the painter (Husain, Picasso) to become mythological and is now the myth giving credence to the artist's brand (setting its price). Sadder still is that celebrity made Husain the fiercely secular Muslim painter uniquely vulnerable: vulnerable as an object of Hindu backlash during the Hindu-Muslim violence that gripped Bombay during the early 1990s with the Shiv Sena riots and has continued since. At that time Husain was attacked personally, his apartment bombed, his art slashed. It is well known that terror and celebrity form a circuitry: terror seeks visibility on national and international stages, and the media is what delivers it. Attack a media figure, a celebrity icon, and you gain just that. Indeed terrorism seeks celebrity, presence before the TV camera through threat and act which bring the stalkarazzi, embedded with their American forces and CIA agents, hunting them as implacably as they hunted (and finally bagged) Lady Diana Spencer, Princess of Wales. Of all the living artists from the original Progressive Artists Group, Husain was uniquely targeted: targeted because of his celebrity, his status as "National Treasure," because he took the secularist project further than any other of these painters, some of whom turned abstract, others social realist while Husain adamantly and creatively claimed the panoply of the past as his for appropriation, and that of any Indian citizen in virtue of citizenship—especially goddesses and especially erotically. His appropriation of the Hindu goddess, merged with a succession of muses, inamoratas, film stars pursued publicly and transposed effortlessly into paintings, works on paper, films, incensed right-wing politics. And he carried out his erotic life in the public arena: it became part of his status as celebrity artist when he followed film stars and then cast them into paintings and movies. All these factors made him a highly visible/vulnerable target for Hindu fundamentalist claims of "desecration."

And so Husain's being picked as a prime object of fundamentalist violence, his paintings slashed, apartment bombed, an old man under constant threat of death. There is currently a Web site dedicated to proving that Husain's paintings, and the text of an earlier book I wrote on him, celebrates the copulation of nude Hindu goddesses with beasts of the field.[25] Whatever one thinks of his Picasso-like appropriation of women, there is neither rape nor bestiality nor any similar degradation in it.

Husain was also attacked because of his free, self-inventing enjoyment, the abundant eroticism of his gaze on India that anthropologically merges woman and animal, animal and god, god and thinker. His celebration of the fusion of modernity and village life brought him close to Picasso (in the best sense). Both were born into societies where human and animal lived in proximity (and still do). Out of this fusion Picasso produced *Guernica*, Husain his epic cycles. The presumption of Husain's free gaze, its pleasure taken in all things Indian, challenges the fundamentalist's claim to control and parcel out enjoyment on the basis of ethnicity, religion, caste, language, or whatever. What right have you, you Muslim (it was said), to paint our Goddesses in the nude? We own them, you have stolen our enjoyment (here I follow work of Thomas Blom Hansen): and so reprisal, violence, exile.[26]

And so Husain, the arch-secularist, the man who hated being referred to as a Muslim painter despite his ongoing affiliation, the man who did more than any other artist to create a national, secular heritage for a newly forming Indian citizenship ended his life away from his homeland, living between Doha and London until his death in June 2011.

In this Husain's story and India's are one: in enthusiasms and malcontents.

Chapter Three

Sustaining Heritage
Off the Road to Kruger Park

I

They sold their wood sculptures by the side of the road winding from Johannesburg to Kruger Park, sitting patiently on rusted oil drums under a burning dome of sky. Tourists on their way to tented camps stopped to survey the carved pieces of marula wood and asked, "How much?" "Fifty rands, boss, but for you twenty-five," might come the reply. Perhaps haggling would ensue, and if luck was with these roadside merchants they would return to their scrappy villages, pockets bulging with money for beer, tea, paraffin, mealies. They were part of the informal economy the way others were who rushed to the windows of cars stopped at the corners of Johannesburg streets to offer leather bags, handmade brooms, windscreen washing. Few would have called them artists.

That they were selling their wares from the dirt off the side of the road already meant momentous changes from their past, for things made originally within the systems of their culture were now being exported as something others called craft. But the objects were still being made more or less as they'd been for generations, perhaps centuries (although who can know for sure?).

Then in the 1980s, as apartheid crumbled and townships burned, interest in African arts became strong in South African art departments and museums. The desire was to know, and dignify, black traditions, to find better ways of describing them than words like *quaint* and *craft*. Cultural acknowledgment sometimes precedes civil and political rights in a changing, democratizing society and serves as a first pass at respect. And there was much to respect about the celebration of knotted wood and rough-hewn edges, the intensely expressive rhythm, the sense of spirit in the material sold by the side of the road to Kruger Park.

This desire was central to the cultural politics of the national transition, the way it was being imagined as a transition of justice.

The first exhibition of fine art made by black Africans took place in a South African museum in 1986, at the Johannesburg Art Gallery, organized by curator Steven Sack.[1] From 1940 until 1973, hardly a single art work by a black artist had been collected by the Johannesburg Art Gallery, the most significant South African museum of the day.[2] In light of this neglect a conference called "The State of Art in South Africa" was organized in 1979 at the University of Cape Town, and "much of the first day was spent debating why no black visual artists . . . were presenting papers at the conference."[3] "What I have heard [said sculptor Gavin Younge] is there is the feeling that nothing important would change as a result of the conference."[4] In a society dirempted by the rules of state terror, a central goal was simply to open the institutions of art to excluded populations. Thus, on the final day of this Cape Town conference, "the artists present pledged to no longer allow their work to be sent overseas to represent South Africa until all state funded art institutions were open to black as well as white students."[5]

And so it became an urgent intellectual project to find terms to acknowledge black traditions in their own right. This brought about the heritage turn for Vha-Venda and Va-Tsonga art.

Vha-Venda and Va-Tsonga sculpture is among the most prominent and longstanding traditions of black sculptural carving in the southern African region, and while it has absorbed all manner of influence over the centuries, its legacy has remained continuous, passed on from generation to generation. This is why it was a particularly fine candidate for "heritage": the accretion of worthy artistic and spiritual values passed on (and, yes, of course also gradually changed) from generation to generation. Its point of entry into the South African art world came when visionnary aficionado and gallery owner Ricky Burnett visited one millennial settlement composed of sculptures and small buildings by Jackson Hlungwani, pronounced it apocalyptic, and began to bring Vha-Venda and Va-Tsonga sculpture to his gallery. This is what he saw when he arrived at that place called New Jerusalem, a settlement composed entirely of sculptures and buildings by the artist as an act of devotion, perhaps of preaching, perhaps of transubstantiation, now sadly collapsed and in ruins. To understand the scope of this New Jerusalem, where Hlungwani and his extended family have lived (located at Mbhokota in Gazankulu, Northern Transvaal), the story of Hlungwani's life needs to be told. Working for a builder, Hlungwani developed ulcerated legs. Arrows were shot through both of his legs by traditional healers to drive out the evil spirit, for he believed he had been taken over by the forces of Satan. After this "healing treatment," one of the legs went from bad to worse, to the point where Hlungwani could no longer walk, nor could he stand the pain. Determined to commit suicide by poisoning himself the next day, Hlungwani had, that night, a vision of Christ and two companions, who told him that he would be able to walk again. God had, he so believed, appeared to him. And so it apparently was, for he soon walked again.

Hlungwani's spiritual village of New Jerusalem is a place where daily life—his and that of his extended family's—takes place under the sign of millennial religion. It is a place of art and of home, of artifact and of temple, where art is of spiritual use—as it was in European medieval times. The "central spatial concept of is ... the negative 'outdoor room.'"[6] Hlungwani has a scrapbook into which he has pasted pictures of everything from the City of Heaven to the Globe Theatre and the amphitheater of Epidaurus. Images of Zimbabwean and Pueblo Indian ruins also figure prominently in his repertoire of world historical forms.[7] These images found a second skin in Hlungwani's passion of Christ, appearing in all manner of spontaneous combustion in the sculpture and architecture of the village. According to Peter Rich: "His building activity at the New Jerusalem site can be seen as the articulation of an architectural landscape. . . . By a process of intuitive, organic and incremental growth he burrows, carves out, cuts away, as well as builds up the land. Through dry-packed stone walling, raised platforms, ramps and retaining walls, he articulates outdoor rooms—open to the sky."[8]

Hlungwani refers to the plan of this site as "The map of life."[9] From the steep incline of the small village (New Jerusalem) past the house where his son lives, which is also a studio workshop and gathering place—for his sculptures and for people—one ascends to the healing rooms, of which there are four for different kinds of sicknesses. The entrance is next to the "acropolis area," the left side of which is "Christ's Office," an area with one- to two-meter thick walls. This room is for "viewing rather than entering." The entire site is stamped by the Old Testament while also a New Testament route of Pilgrimage.

The design of this site might seem a far cry from anything having to do with modern life and art. For Hlungwani seems nothing if not early Christian, millennially transformative, and his site seems nothing if not a repetition of the earliest churches—carved out of rock in the canyons and craters of Palestine, hybrid in their recruitment of multiple traditions to the task of worship, indifferent to the worldliness of Catholicism, the work ethic of Protestantism, the system of urban articulations of the Renaissance. His is a traditional community overlaid with the born-again character of the converted. (Except that there is also nothing more contemporary than the recurrence of millennial tradition.)

When he caught his breath, Burnett was determined to bring Hlungwani's sculptures back to his Newtown Gallery and display/interpret their intensities. Located in the Market Theatre district of downtown Johannesburg, where Athol Fugard was writing/performing plays, Peter Dirk-Uys performed his famous hostess, "ambassadoress," and madam of National Party kitsch, Evita Bezuidenhout, black performers were routinely performing with whites onstage in direct contravention to apartheid legislation and were also members of mixed audiences; where leftist anti-apartheid people were brewing the future and intervening in the present, or just plain venting over beers, Hlungwani's art joined the mix.

The Univeristy of Witwatersrand had begun acquiring sculpture from Venda and Tsonga carvers in the 1970s. A decade later Burnett introduced Vha-Venda and Va-Tsonga sculpture by Hlungwani and others into the gallery system in the mid 1980s. Burnett understood that this sculpture was difficult to place in the larger scheme of modern and contemporary art; neither quite modern nor quite traditional, it was art with a difference. He understood that to respect its particular voice, room would have to be made in concepts of modern and contemporary art for it. Intuitively groping his way toward a limning of its voice, Burnett stressed the rural experiences of the artists.

Anitra Nettleton and other art historians had begun working on this region in the 1970s. By the mid 1980s they were already rethinking categories of black art in a number of related ways.[10] In relation to Vha-Venda sculpture, Anitra Nettleton published a fine explanatory essay in 1989: "The Crocodile Does Not Leave the Pool: Venda Court Arts."[11] This essay details (along with earlier writing by Burnett and others) how

Hlungwani and other carvers recruit traditional styles of carving in the service of deeply felt belief systems. The guiding belief is that at death the ancestor's spirit passes into a great lake, where it exists as a carbon copy of what it was. Snakes and fish also live in this lake, hence their importance as religious or metaphysical elements in the carving. The great lake (Fundudzi) is seen as a mirror of the kingship and society itself, with the crocodile (a central Venda sculptural form) being also the name for the king, and the python being linked, among other things, to creation: "when the python within the primordial pool 'created' animals and people by vomiting them from his stomach . . . and, on the other hand . . . to the perimeter of the pool, where he 'writhes' while lying in wait for his prey."[12] The python has multiple associations, including fertility. It is a mediator between the living and the dead (this is an ancestor-worshipping society).[13] The crocodile and the python together symbolize fraternity between key groups in historical times: they are signs of history and unity. Such traditional beliefs are layered with ideas from missionary Christianity about Christ,[14] prophecy, healing, sin, and resurrection to produce an intense, hybridized religious mysticism.[15]

And so the end of the nineteen eighties is the moment when Vha-Venda and Va-Tsonga sculpture becomes an object of wider gallery circulation and intellectual reflection, brought into university and art gallery, into acknowledgment and circulation beyond the contained world of Vha-Venda and Va-Tsonga communities, beyond the side of the road to Kruger Park. New terms are required for its interpretation, new ways to spell out the continuities and evolutions of its traditions. And the intellectual project becomes to begin to think that through. For the old binary oppositions between art and craft, artist and artisan, modern and unmodern do not seem adequate to doing the sculpture justice. Nor indeed does the very distinction between art and artisanship or craft or religion. For this work is neither produced out of dialogue with the system of modern arts nor is it, one presumes, made under the concept of art, if by the concept of art one means that history of consciousness and intentionality originating in the Renaissance of which these artists are at the time unaware. In order to mark the particular terrain of this powerful work, South African art historians and critics hit on the concept of "transitional art" in the late 1980s. Transitional arts were theorized as neither primitive nor modern but betwixt and between. The goal was to dignify a wide variety of artifacts produced by (then) contemporary black Africans living in townships, rural communities, and urban peripheries by vesting them with this in-between theoretical space. Indeed the art historians were right as far as they went. For none of these objects seems either to be modern art (in the way Picasso or Kandinsky is) or "primitivist." Primitivism is itself a construction placed on West African sculpture, the heads of Easter Island, Pacific Northwest totemic poles, and ancient Egyptian painting by modernist culture, turning these various artifacts into universal/erotic fetish items abstracted from their contexts of life, muted of voice, formalized, interchangeable, so as to bless its own modernist project with the aura it places on them. The category of transitional art was articulated at the end of apartheid, in anticipation of and in the inaugural days of political transition, and its deeper use was to assimilate a wide variety of black African arts to the project of democratic acknowledgment. But therein it was a category that ranged over too wide a domain. Township and peri-urban art are quite different from their rural counterparts; arts springing from recent history differ from organically evolving and intact traditions; major differences disappeared in the category which simply lumped all this work together in virtue of what it is *not*. The binary opposition primitive/modern so central to modernist culture remained intact in this analysis, which is really where it failed. Criticized from the start by fine art theorists like Colin Richards, by the mid 1990s the category was dropped, and no further conceptual work was done on Vha-Venda and Va-Tsonga sculpture by such persons.[16]

I want to pursue the conceptual stakes of its acknowledgment beyond their very fine start. Now, twenty years later, it is timely to return to their project of acknowledgment and push it further. A good way to begin is to consider how Vha-Venda and Va-Tsonga sculpture is in its own way modern, even if not, in the 1980s and 1990s, produced in dialogue with the modern system of the arts nor under any related consciousness of maker-as-artist. How then is it modern? The sculpture is in its own way a response to modern life, and modern art is in some deep sense that art which inhabits modernity and is, as Baudelaire put it, a response to modernity's conditions. These are for the French poet conditions of transience, the fleeting, ephemeral, contingent.[17] In Parsian modernity of the nineteenth century these contingencies are associated with the dazzle of urban life and the creation of that new urban being, the flaneur, who morphs into something far more in Baudelaire's image of the modern artist. Vha-Venda and Va-Tsonga art are hardly modern by virtue of celebrating the dazzle of modern life. But they respond to their own conditions of contingency and transience. The sculpture is traditional, yes, but also the product of intense South African colonial and apartheid modernity. Its artists are the heirs of longstanding traditions and remained, as of 1990, rural persons, filled with the passions of traditional society and millennial inheritance (which is itself a part of the long arc of colonial modernity!). These artists have been the subject of apartheid regulation, although they are not disenfranchised of community like so many black African workers whose apartheid experience was of exiting their rural areas of Natal, Eastern Transvaal, Transkei to sweat in the mines, occupying grim single-sex hostels, visting wives and children once a year, sending home rands so families may survive. And Vha-Venda/Va-Tsonga sculptors excel at speaking to the modern life they have been of. They have seen newsprint, television, and magazines and their creations are sometimes ironic social gestures in wood. They've a keen eye for colonial, white, English, Afrikaans absurdity and they are charmed by silly innuendo. Owen Ndou carves from wild fig a work called *The Gentleman's Game,* a carving of a man in plus fours who is playing golf; we see a master at work with a totally comic/ironic gaze on white privilege, the privilege of the colonial. Golf is not exactly your basic sporting pastime in Vha-Venda—nor is watching golf on TV—and Ndou had, at the time of his making of this piece, never actually seen a golf game. Yet the golfer's gait and the golfer's swing are so much there in the sculpture that one can see a master observer at work.

This tendency toward parody in Vha-Venda and Tsonga carving may be found more generally in contemporary African societies and has been wonderfully discussed by Achille Mbembe in relation to Cameroon, suggesting a shared condition of modern address to what Mbembe calls the state that commands (rather than including) and does so through the aesthetics of vulgarity, through excessive display of spending, eating, fornicating, genuflecting, self-adulating, in short, the carnivalesque. Now it has to be said the apartheid state was not exactly one of the carnivalesque, nor one keen to celebrate excess, unless considered from the perspective of monument building, religion, and communal kitsch, in which case perhaps it was. At any rate, the stakes are a loosely shared set of modern responses to authoritarian politics played out in the form of this kind of spectacle or that.[18]

Their work can also be a composite of nerve ending vibrating with the anxieties of modern life. *Job Seeker,* by an unknown sculptor from Vha-

Venda, is a single piece of wood from which a running man is carved as if caught in a moment of extreme tension. His entire body impels itself toward an unknown destination. The figure is seeking a job, but the existential anxiety with which the knotted character of the wood and its long, sinewy lines are used to animate his comportment, the sense of his plunging toward an uncertain future, bespeak knowledge of modern life and its crushing anonymity that goes beyond the particular event. The sculptor has felt the pressures of modern life, the social anomie of apartheid, the infusion of modern technology into Vha-Venda, the need to participate in a modern capitalistic system with limited job opportunities (40 percent

FIGURE 3.1. *Job Seeker.* Collection of Daniel Herwitz and Lucia Saks. Photo by Peter Smith.

unemployment and more underemployment even today). These experiences of a system and a history exist in his nerve endings like anxious, unwanted threats.

So their work, both traditional and of modern life, defies the easy opposition between modern/unmodern or modern/traditional. Indeed, and this was the most telling point of the analysis of the eighties, it is not quite art either, if by "art" one means work produced within the modern system of the arts and the related consciousness of maker-as-artist that is a legacy of the Renaissance. On the other hand, in its artisanal bravura, expressive intensity, and power of engagement with rural South African apartheid conditions of modernity, it is too close to what that system calls art and modern art to dispense with either term.

II

To recap: the nature of the instability is that, on the one hand, the work is rural, continuous with tradition, organically emergent from generations of carving and religious life; on the other, it speaks within the system of modernity these rural black apartheid dwellers (sculptors) have lived. It seems to inhabit a place just adjacent to that which the modern system calls art. What concepts, categories, genres of modern art, or nonmodern art, should be used to place it? Into what cubbyhole shall it go? Should this work be called modern/art? Should the appellation be denied? Where does it fit on the received map of art historical/art critical concepts? Vha-Venda and Va-Tsonga sculpture is, as it were, a new continent or land mass that does not easily fit on the existing map of the received globe.

The genealogy of this representational map of the modern, according to which the binary opposition modern/unmodern or modern/traditional was framed, originates in a picture of the modernist and avant-garde art movements of the West: of Paris, Berlin, Moscow, Rome, Milan, London, New York et al. This picture or map is drawn to pinpoint art movements which

1. break from the past in a vast act of experimentation aiming to reestablish core geometries of the medium by new means (analytic cubism),
2. plumb the depths of the medium to its core, evacuating all else as extraneous (Mondrian, de Stijl),

3. experiment in new technologies in the name of bringing about the utopian future (constructivism),
4. place works of art in dialogue with theory, critique, utopian vison (constructivism et al.),
5. convulse the imagination by juxtaposing irrational elements in montage (surrealism),
6. beat the bourgeois over the head with his or her comfortable world (just about everyone),
7. smear acrylic onto unprimed canvas then submit hand prints, cigarette butt, spittle as artist's signature (abstract expressionism),
8. silk screen into multiples the system of celebrity in which dollar bills, soup cans, star icons, most wanted men turn into images and are consumed by Americans along with their breakfast cereals (Warhol),
9. morph avant-garde utopianism into identity politics by staging earthquakes along the fault lines of gendered, racist, neocolonial representations (Barbara Kruger, Cindy Sherman, et al.),
10. produce an assembly line of new/salable art products seeking to undermine the commodity form of art (20 percent of artists, some of whom can now, thanks to the market, afford an apartment in New York),
11. preserve sharks in formaldehyde, Disney cartoon characters in gold leaf, stone in Utah, undergarments in underground galleries (everyone with a Duchamp for a Dada),
12. join unexpected media into marriages which produce children full of haunted memories too old for their years (William Kentridge, Kara Walker).

These points on the map are well known.

The map of the modern is also a map of global diffusion: diffusion of source materials from modern and avant-garde art across the planet, into Mexico where Diego Rivera and others meld cubist planar construction and surrealist irrational intensities with pre-Columbian physiognomy to produce public and private art worthy of a society carrying its past like the blade of a knife and its future like a violently held dream. It diffuses into southern Africa where Gerard Sekoto, having visted France and drunk deep of the early modern still life painters and the fauves, paints his beloved Sophiatown in dry, oversaturated, slow, yellow light, his men arching forward in a single rhythm of pick work in purple, orange, brown. The previous chapter was about diffusion into India; it could have equally been about Latin America. The globalization of modern art is a story of late and postcolonial modernity wherein diffusion takes place through a sustained act of appropriation from source materials (the modern arts of Europe). These materials are melded with local intensities, as in the example of India discussed in chapter 2.

Finally the map now pictures contemporary trade routes through which art production buzzes in increasingly homogenized ways. Like the heritage and human rights language discussed in the introduction to this book, this circuitry of biennales, auction houses, installations has given rise to a new global art-speak, a neoliberal language of buzz-styles and buzz-critique that packages art products in globally standardized formats while allowing enough local twist for product variety to appear in art markets. Contemporary Chinese art is the current darling of this system, since the global image of China carries the magic combination of newness to the system, fast-rising economic power, and high-profile visibility, and this image brands Chinese art products before they are even seen. Like the discourses of heritage and human rights, profiling is purchased at the expense of thinning of content. This does not mean everything in a biennale or auction house is boring; far from it. The point is rather about profiling pertinent to neoliberal art markets.

Vha-Venda and Va-Tsonga sculpture does not fit well on any part of this map. It is not a kind of sculpture created through diffusion and absorption of source modernisms. It has not, when Burnett brings it to Johannesburg, appeared in the global circuitry of the biennale or auction house. At that moment it has remained rural, its gaze on modern life evolving from within, its framing of the life of which it is part continuous with longstanding spiritual beliefs and forms. It has remained a tradition: organically morphing without definitive stylistic break or rupture into modernity. This is what prepares it (along with its evident power of expression) for the appellation of a "heritage" by those seeking to discover in the new South Africa a diversity of such, thus dignifying all ethnicities with an appellation formerly restricted to the settler. But the price of calling it a heritage is that it remains traditional, does not sit easily with the modern arts of the world according to the map/picture which art history and criticism have created and inherited. At stake is the acknowledgment of this work as both heritage (if that is what it wants to be called) and complex, modulating work which is also part of modern life. But that acknowledgment requires addition or revison to the picture/map of modern art that can provide it with no location. The stakes of acknowledging Vha-Venda and Va-Tsonga sculpture are an intervention in concepts of modern art as such.

To summarize: the work looks modern, shares sinewy, broken, nervous sculptural intensity with German expressionism, Rouault, and many others. It speaks to the exigencies of modern life, existing within that frame of modernity to which its rural creators are subject. The work is not generated through encounter with/appropriation of source modernisms from Europe, nor is it created out of a break with tradition; it is not urban but rural. It seems to neither quite fit on the map of modern art nor fit entirely apart from it. How then to change the map to accommodate this uneasy form of belonging?

I find it useful to recall one of my favorite passages from the philosopher Ludwig Wittgenstein in thinking about the sometimes uncomfortable fit between this sculpture and the concepts which don't manage to find a place for it: "A main source of our failure to understand is that we do not *command a clear view* of the use of our words.—Our grammar is lacking in that sort of perspicuity. A perspicuous representation produces just that understanding which consists in 'seeing connections.' Hence the importance of finding and inventing *intermediate cases*."[19]

It was a technique of Wittgenstein's teaching to try to find and invent examples of items about which it was too simple to say either that it was or was not a number, human being, computer, or object or natural or artificial kind.[20] Such examples, he tells us, allow for the seeing of "connections," connections between ranges of concepts which occur in a similar range of language games. They afford purchase into how our concepts are constructed and into their terms of framing the world. Intermediate cases are about exposure, the exposure of the inner grammatical systems which have been hidden from view, tacit, received, circulating without understanding of their construction and limits.

One might think of Vha-Venda and Va-Tsonga sculpture as an intermediate case, about which it is too simple to say either that it is modern art or that it isn't. Such an example would, on this line of reasoning, tell us something about the network of concepts through which modern art is framed, about the hidden genealogy of the map. That map of modern arts from Paris through Berlin, from Picasso through the avant-gardes to Josef Beuys, Fluxus, Warhol, Kiefer, and, centripetally, through diffusion, to Rivera, Husain, Sekoto is a capacious one. But it leaves certain other objects unable to find clear points of entry. And so relative to this map, it is too simple *either* to say Vha-Venda and Va-Tsonga sculpture is modern or that it is not. It remains, within the system of the map, an intermediate case.

To call Vha-Venda and Va-Tsonga sculpture an intermediate case, about which it is too simple either to say it is or is not modern art, would be one way of marking its special characteristics. It would be one fair, possibly excellent way of acknowledging the art so long as the binary opposition between being on the map and off it were revalued. Being half on and half off, or marginally on, would not and should not mean devaluation (as craft, unmodern tradition). But, even with this revaluation, the map is a particular system of representation privileging source modernisms in the "West" and their diffusion. It pictures a Eurocentric story.

A second approach would be to say that the acknowledgment of Vha-Venda and Va-Tsonga sculpture requires a new and improved global map of the moderns which makes borderline objects also central, finds them a nice cosy place on the map of the modern. Call this rearticulating the shape of the map to include the Dark Continent. This project wishes to retain the commitment to a single system of representation, a standard model for modern art—but of a more inclusive sort. And yet Vha-Venda and Va-Tsonga art seems to represent a genuinely distinct route for how art becomes modern than anything on that map. Neither the result of avant-garde activity nor of global diffusion from source modernisms, Vha Venda/Va-Tsonga sculpture seems to be of modern life in a way that causes the term *modern art* to change in meaning if applied to it. The term *modern art* becomes a sliding signifier if extended to the Dark Continent. It slides into something not as yet illuminated. It is therefore hard to imagine how this work from Africa could be placed in the same, singular, representational scheme as source modernisms and their diffusion without losing its special characteristics. The idea of a *single map of the modern*, a single kind of story, art gives way to a multiplicity of such.

When it comes to multiplicity I am fond of another idea of Wittgenstein's, his famous image of language as a set of overlapping games. This is the antiessentialist Wittgenstein eschewing essential definition of concepts, words (representations). The *locus classicus* of his thought is in these passages from the *Philosophical Investigations*: "Consider . . . the proceedings that we call 'games.' I mean board-games, card-games, ball-games, Olympic games, and so on. What is common to them all? . . . You will not see something that is common to *all*, but . . . we see a complicated network of similarities overlapping and criss-crossing: sometimes overall similarities, sometimes similarities of detail. 'I can think of no better expression to characterize these similarities than 'family resemblances.'"[21]

There is no essential definition to a language game, no single set of features which make all the things we want to call games into games. Rather, there are strands of similarity and difference between the kinds of games played, the kind of things we call games. The stability, integrity, use of the word *game* is a matter of how these various games "crisscross" to form a web of rope. The interesting question becomes: how are these strands of similarity related? How do the various games overlap? What is the nature of their crisscrossing? What kind of "complex system" (to use more recent language) do they form?

What is invited (but not pursued by Wittgenstein) are a set of different answers about complex system, power, interaction, circulation, autonomy, hegemony, history: a study of the world, in short, which addresses the manifold of relationships between kinds of games, between individual games. This set of stories will go far in limning the terms of life.

If one pictures modern art as a set of language games, one is invited to question the way various kinds of modern art form (and do not form) strands of similarity and modes of overlapping. The result of picturing modern art as a set of language games would be to eschew the idea that there is a single genesis of modern art, a single map of it adequate to the globe. The Eurocentric story picturing modern art as originating in Europe (and diffusing globally) would give way to a more variegated approach to art in relation to modern life. Arts enter the fabric of modern life through tradition, break, experimentation, circulation, economy, in a number of distinct ways, some of which are perhaps yet to be discovered or theorized. Wittgenstein's image invites one to ask how these various strands of modern art might relate. And the answer will be: not in any single way but in multiple kinds of ways. Baudelaire tells us, I have said, that modern art is the art of modern life, of modernity.[22] Ergo there are various kinds of modern art because there are various kinds of modernity. Out of respect for multiple kinds of modernity, a new approach to modern life has arisen in the literature of the humanities and social sciences in the past twenty years, one that goes under the name of *alternative modernities*.[23] This literature approaches global modernity not as a singular thing sourced to Europe and globalized through diffusion (through the history of colonialism) but rather as a system of overlapping societies, beliefs, cultures, all in some sense related through the long diffusing arc of colonialisms, yes, but also marked by profound differences of history, tradition, culture, state politics, and so on. These differences in real places are mirrored by the need for multiple kinds of stories of modernity rather than a single arching narrative of modern life. Real differences require changes in the heritage of stories of the modern which theory has inherited. And so the philosopher Charles Taylor distinguishes two kinds of theory of modernity: "acultural" versus "cultural." Acultural theory pictures modernity as a set of changes in human belief/reason/agency resulting from institutional transformation, the rise of the state, the growth of market economies, science, instrumental technologies, and the great forces of modernization generally. Cultural theory pictures modernity as the rise of a new kind of culture or set of cultures.[24] It is most natural to think of modernities as variously shaped by systemic interplay between "acultural" and "cultural" factors.

Dilip Gaonkar speaks of cultural factors in this way: "It is generally assumed that the lived experience and embodied character of modernity vary vastly from site to site. This is not entirely correct. . . . Difference always functions within a penumbra of similarities. . . . What is common to these strings of similarities is a mood of distance, a habit of questioning, and an intimation of what Baudelaire calls the 'marvellous.'"[25]

But even as fine a postcolonial theorist as Gaonkar is somewhat too Eurocentric in his formulation of the terms of modernity. For "distance," "questioning," and an "intimation of the marvellous" are aesthetic\ philosophical categories framed in the Paris of the nineteenth century and carried into the long history of European modernity. Do they pertain to Vha-Venda and Va-Tsonga modernity? Or does a somewhat different lens need to be put in place to understand what is modern (and also traditional) about those societies? Let me dwell on the question for a moment. Vha-Venda and Va-Tsonga modernity is, I want to say, missionary/apocalyptic Christianity fused with older spirit beliefs; it is a modernity of subjection under colonial and apartheid regimes. It is not that of city, new science, modern university, art world. It is not that of Paris, capital of the nineteenth century, revolutionary Russia, or the Chicago exhibition. And so the Ndou brothers are whimsical and ironic, which is, yes, a kind of "questioning" in Gaonkar's sense, questioning of colonial figures in plus fours. But it is not sustained critique in the way the source-painter of modern life Eduard Manet is: I speak of the Manet who turns rag pickers into philosophers, placing them in gray enclosures of Spanish portraiture, spaces which flatten out by their shoes and empties, at the bottom, refusing clear/coherent visual entry on the part of the spectator, who is visually alienated from the figure. This confusion of visual entry is meant to subvert the easy omnipotence according to which the bourgeois expects the world to conform to his grasping eye and is paralleled in the permanently obscure expression on the faces of Manet's figures. In an exact reversal of the history of painting to his time, the more you look at them the less you feel entitled to know of them. Are they philosophers like Diogenes, cynical to the point of refusal? Are they possessed, mad, indifferent, bored? Or simply drunks, brain wasted, dessicated, like some homeless person (*Bergie*) selling magazines on Orange Street, Cape Town or in the Mission District of San Francisco, people who have always lived in the dark otherness of a society which doesn't give a damn? Manet's wizardry as a painter is to invite through his twists of figure, perspective, brushwork, etc. . . . this pervasive questioning that evaporates the certitudes through which painting, art viewing, and the culture of the museum were framed. Ndou is simply not of this philosophical world. His questioning remains ironic fascination, I think. As for Jackson Hlungwani, he is Dostoyevskian in his Job-like questioning of life, but his messianic belief in salvation speaks of answers in the realm of miracle, not questioning diffused (perhaps temporarily) into marvel. Nor does Hlungwani dwell in contingency like any Parisian artist/flaneur. His contingency is colonial/apartheid subjection before an authority not of his own will, also contingency before God.

Even a first-rate postcolonial thinker like Dilip Gaonkar remains within a European frame when he privileges *modernism* and its aesthetic characteristics as the common thread to the culture of modernity. This is why Africa is an excellent place to explore alternative modernities. It opens the field to variants and differentials (without denying the importance of the ParVaan philosopher/artist to the story of modern cultures).

The concept of alternative modernities allows Vha-Venda and VaVa-Tsonga sculpture to be thought of as modern/art in its own way while neither standing as part of the modern system of the arts, and the modernity that system is of, nor of the urban world and developing art markets which create a Manet and supply his art with content. Put another way, the concepts both of "modern art" and of "art per se" shift in accord with the *kind* of modernity they register, even if in one specific sense these terms are restricted to the modern system of the arts where they arose. Both modern art and art per se must be rethought as family resemblance concepts, defined by various overlapping games where they find their meaning and use, the original game being that of modernism and modernist culture, but by now in the twenty-first century, with its recognition of globalization, in a number of other domains of play. Vha-Venda and Va-Tsonga are one.

Now to open the field to diverse stories of modernity, to open correspondingly modern art and art per se to a family of domains in which they have play, is not to deny that there is also a global/neoliberal system which renders certain of these domains central and others peripheral. There are axes of concentrated power buzzing between America, Europe, China, Brazil, and India, say, which dominate in the production of media, state control, market growth, and cultural diffusion: including modern arts. Other locations are peripheral in the sense of being *subjected to means of production from elsewhere* without having *equitable access to this circuitry of production*. Emmanuel Wallerstein has discussed such inequality of access and dependency upon production from elsewhere within the world economic system, and this pertains also to the art world (art markets).[26] There is domination in this inequality of global position, but also, ironically, freedom in being under the radar screen if you are far enough from the circuitry, a kind of protection from the system. One might think of Vha-Venda and Va-Tsonga art as a minority art culture whose autonomy was sustained, even protected, because the work fell under the global radar: having been consigned to the impoverished South African informal economy by the side of the road to Kruger Park.

Until that work enters the global gallery in the mid 1990s. What happens then?

III

First, the work is dignified into a heritage, and a search is set in place to find better ways to frame and acknowledge the art than the received binary oppositions from art history and criticism. I have taken this project of interpretation further by destabilizing concepts of modern art and introducing concepts of alternative modernity. South African art historians and art critics, however, took this project far enough back then to prepare the work for gallery and circulation. For, in the system of modern/contemporary art, interpretive innovation always plays two roles: acknowledgment and branding for entry into the global market. There is no way around this; it is how the market works. Interpretation aiming for acknowledgment also prepares product value by profiling new or undiscovered or marginalized work. And so the second part of the story is how Vha-Venda and Va-Tsonga heritage changed once the work began to circulate within the commodity form of the South African and international art worlds. It is a story about what happened to the relative continuity of tradition once the work hit the marketplace. This is a story with a beginning but not an end.

Now we are into the mid 1990s, and Vha-Venda and Va-Tsonga sculpture is regularly appearing in galleries. It is collected, written about, sent into wider and wider circulation. It is shown in Europe and America. Hlungwani becomes the darling of the corporate lobby and office park, which in South Africa wishes to legitimate itself by highlighting an iconic black African presence. Hlungwani's jagged sculptures become a poster image for the new South Africa at home and abroad. Here is work whose exultation is astonishing, whose fierce intensity of line is immediately recognizable as having modern expressive currency. For some it has the uncanny property of recalling the sources of modernism, those Africanist origins of jagged line and planar construction found in cubism and German expressionism. Yes it is art produced half a continent away from such West African sculptural sources, but the global art world is not big on exact location. Through a chain of intuitions, Vha-Venda and Va-Tsonga sculpture is simultaneously placed at the origins of modernism and in a luminal/outsider location. Global art markets are relentlessly in search of new products and latch onto this chain of significations with delight. Here is a new item which refuses assimilation to standard prototypes while recalling both source modernisms and the very sources *of* modernism. And which stubbornly refuses assimilation. The delight is compounded by the rapt gaze the world has on South Africa during the brief moment of the 1990s. These are the Mandela years, the days of awe. This aura is cast onto southern African sculpture. All these market perceptions increase the desirability of the product.

And here is the irony. Once the global market embraces Vha-Venda and Va-Tsonga sculpture, all the hard questions about its place on the map of modern and contemporary art vanish. Circulation within the global art world confirms, indeed establishes, its provenance as contemporary art and does so without further rationale than its profiling and the fact of its circulation! Because the sculpture appears in all the galleries, suddenly this sculpture earns the status of contemporary art. All sense of its uneasy relation to the modern system of the arts disappears under the profiling, a profiling whose cannibalization of southern African sculpture to the category of contemporary art rivaled early modernist misreading of West African sculpture as formalist by Picasso and other geniuses. Philosophical implications about the concept of contemporary art beg to be drawn from this.[27]

There are a number of ways in which new objects achieve the status of contemporary art. One is through interpretative acts of recognition (here performed by South African art historians and curators). Another is by this kind of fiat: through entry into art markets with their own forms of profiling. Profiling and circulation produce status, but so also does recognition. Together profiling, circulation, and recognition interact to define or at least brand an object as "contemporary art." Recognition seeks to carve out a place for new and liminal art by rearranging received concepts and theorizing new exhibitions. These critical and scholarly acts which acknowledge are part of the larger art world, part of how art markets bring in and brands new commodities. But the market also brands in ways less about acknowledgment and more about mere preparation for circulation. Circulation confirms stature and generates celebrity.[28] For Vha-Venda and Va-Tsonga sculpture, the profile that counted had to do with the South African moment. Anything cast in the glow of Mandela and the Truth and Reconciliation Commission became desirable within the system of the art world, especially if it was an object redolent with a certain outsider status, which the art world then interpreted as new, unusual, even avantgarde. The result: a winner was struck, at least for awhile.

As a result of all this, Vha-Venda and Va-Tsonga art had their fifteen minutes of fame within certain European (as well as South African global) art markets in the mid to late 1990s. How did fifteen minutes of fame ring changes in artists ill suited to the public eye, persons who might have formerly sold their work to passing tourists?

At first, this change from artisan to artist *semi-celebrity-cum-noble-outsider* status seems to have done little to Vha-Venda and Va-Tsonga artists, apart from giving them some cash, commissions, and recognition. However, before long, contact with the gallery system caused artists who have never seen modernism (except in magazines collected into scrapbooks) to see these firsthand, in European museums. Rural artists who had never traveled to the great cities of London and the like drench themselves in the strange intensity of cities, who had never talked about art except in the terms of their Venda or Christian belief schemes must learn to communicate in broken English with artists and gallery people from across the globe, people who wish to compare their sculptures to Joseph Beuys and other visionary modernists. These rural sculptors have been thrown into the cosmopolitan world by fiat. They reel, dislocated, amazed, revved into overdrive.

I had the chance to meet Owen Ndou for a dinner in Johannesburg in the mid 1990s. It was his first trip to the big city and he had arrived by taxi-bus, wandered, and seen a great deal of art he'd never seen before. No longer selling by the side of the road, he got in another minibus and took it along the road to Kruger himself: to see the animals firsthand he'd been sculpting only through magazines: rhino, lion, Cape buffalo, and leopard and traditions of carving. Soon he would be in London, sketching in the museums.

After awhile this art ceased to be flavor of the month, after awhile nothing much sold, the Market Theatre became crime ridden, Ricky Burnett's gallery closed. He stashed a large amount of the work of Jackson Hlungwani in a container parked outside his Johannesburg house. One day the container was stolen. A dispirited Burnett made his emigration to America. The work still has its German, English, French, South African collectors. It remains in circulation (museums, galleries, corporate lobbies) but its place in the art world is uncertain.

Change in consciousness is a more permanent result for these artists, although variably. Jackson Hlungwani has passed away, and we shall never know about how he responded exactly. Noria Mabasa, another of the fine sculptors in this tradition, has apparently learned to live well enough with the gallery, continuing to work more or less as she always had, letting all the changes in status and experience bounce off her when she buries herself in her work. These artists were always about money; they were desperately poor. She's happy to sell. The Ndou brothers appear to be a different story. Their earlier forays into plus fours evolved organically from within their traditions, which they did not call into question. Now they explicitly wonder at the limits of those traditions, at what they do not know and cannot do from within them.[29] This self-questioning means ironically they are more modernist than they used to be, more centrally located on the map of the modern than they once were. For the first time, they themselves view their legacies as that distant, partly eclipsed thing called heritage. The global system which declared their work "contemporary art" by fiat has, to an extent, won out. This is why the modern system of the arts is hegemonic. Alternative modernities are under constant threat of assimilation by it, their genuine differences from hegemonic modernity giving way to its forms of consciousness.

The Ndou brothers are now working out new ways to carry their tradition/heritage forward—or not. Call this the condition of live action heritage. Who knows where their children may choose to live, or what they will be influenced by, perhaps the Internet, perhaps text messaging and computer graphics? And what will this mean for the compact village traditions that for centuries have generated Vha-Venda and Va-Tsonga sculpture? Will these traditions be reformulated for a new (art world savvy) tourist trade?

There is a point of irony here. Recall that the rise of heritage practice in the nineteenth century served to fill a perceived gap between modern life and its past. Modern life had lost its way and required restitution of lost or obscured origin to set it again on a path to its proper destiny. Heritage was that construction which diagnosed and "cured" the gap. Here, in the case of Owen and Goldwin Ndou, the re-construction of a tradition into a heritage ends up *opening* the gap between (their) contemporary practice and earlier tradition.

The South African art historians and gallery owners who so impressively "discovered" and acknowledged Vha-Venda and Va-Tsonga sculpture performed the *live action gesture* of rethinking those traditions as heritages. Ironically, the very act of recognition has put the tradition acknowledged under a question mark. Recognition is not simply interpretative, it is about profiling new work for circulation in the art world, about circulating it so that it commands attention, collection, more circulation and interpretation, and exhibition. Entry into this commodity form has caused Owen and Goldwin Ndou to stand for the first time apart from their past. Is this a good thing, a bad thing, will it lead to wonderful innovation or alienated stagnation? I do not want to be nostalgic for their richly spiritual but also economically impoverished past. That would be paternalist and also Luddite; we live in an age of the commodity form which whirls artists off the road to Kruger Park. In such a world acknowledging a tradition, indeed bringing it into representation as a heritage, challenges the continuity of the heritage brought into being.

Recognition always comes with a price tag attached.

Chapter Four

Monument, Ruin, and Redress in South African Heritage

I

South Africa is a country in search of a national narrative that can articulate and bind together official state culture and citizenry. There have been two that have come close and remain in play. The first narrative was the driving ideal of the democratic transition in the 1990s. Essentially an artifact of transition, it stressed redress, acknowledgment, social flexibility, and building a culture of human rights. Actively opposing colonial and apartheid heritage, the narrative demonumentalized, which is what this chapter is about. The second narrative, of African Renaissance, was an older artifact of Afro-centrist history, deriving from the discourses of Afrocentric return in the late nineteenth century, the formulation of the African Renaissance in the 1930s. It was adopted and written as the official ideology of South Africa/Africa by State President Thabo Mbeki. Mbeki developed policies designed to build the African Renaissance into state institutions—with uneven success. The ideology preached renewal for South Africa and the African continent through a grafting of precolonial heritage and indigenous ways of knowing with neoliberal thinking for a rapidly globalizing, democratizing country—and (putatively) continent. This narrative hit the wall of science policy during the HIV/AIDS crisis. Since it intersected in fascinating ways with the demonumentalizing script of the country at a moment of transition, it will be introduced in this chapter, although it is the focus of the chapter following.

Each of these narratives was articulated in response to the inheritance of colonial and apartheid cultures of monument and ruin, terror, violence, control. Each drew on the diverse cultural dynamics of southern Africa, the ways of life of Indian, Indonesian, Khoi-San, Zulu, Xhosa, Portuguese, French, German, British peoples braided together and also artificially separated by the long arm of South African history. Each scripts (and eschews) South African heritages differently. For the one responds to South Africa's sense of becoming a postcolonial nation where the monumental forms of past power (colonial/apartheid) must now morph into templates of equality, where morals have to be understood in terms of an ongoing memory of past injustice. The other responds to a desire, especially on the part of black South Africans, to empower new African selves by reterritorializing the state through an idealized image of precolonial life, thus taking back the colonialist's devaluing of that so-called precolonial past (and the black Africans, not to mention indigenous peoples who lived it). This has been called the African Renaissance, and it is the subject of the next chapter. The point here is that South Africa is comprised of diverse people with profoundly different experiences of shared history, persons who find they cannot agree on any single formula for the scripting of the past into a shared heritage. Some require both (and others too), others the one or the other. What these diverse peoples, up to a point, share (for I do not presume to include all South Africans in this) is the desire for a larger and more luminous national story that would cast their own more local heritage adventures (whether in museum work, tourism, reenactment, preservation, storytelling et al.) centrally under its wing, thus including them. For so many were not included in the stories of the past (colonial/apartheid), except in some subservient/distorted position, that it is not simply that they want to tell their stories or market their pasts to European tourists; they want their ways of telling and even marketing to matter nationally, to be central to the script of the new/emerging nation. Not everyone wants this, and some indeed actively do not, preferring that their heritage making reflects their own province, or affiliation, or poetic selves. But many (and this is admittedly vague) do want their heritage making to concur with larger national positions, for it allows them the sense of equality and power that comes from believing the nation is in their interests, speaking in their name. Perhaps it does not (in terms of job creation, human rights, whatever), but perhaps the will to find in its current representations a mirror of their own activities and desires remains forceful nonetheless. These people, all too often formerly excluded from state power and story, want their own adventures to matter for the state, and matter by resonating with a larger national self-representation or picture that would include them. I cannot prove this, but I can at least try to make this claim compelling by pointing to a texture of something between anecdote and fact throughout this (and the next) chapter.

To begin, one can learn something of the desire in South Africa for a shared national narrative, a mode of consciousness that unifies/includes and enthuses, by focusing on the recent FIFA World Cup hosted by South Africa in June-July 2010. That spectacular event was the occasion for a month-long party, a grand and theatrical celebration that was as spontaneous as it was orchestrated. Nowhere was this clearer than on the final night of the World Cup. It is July 11, 2010, the moment of victory for the Spanish team. Spain has put unrelenting pressure on the Dutch goalie with elegant passing across midfield and up front and shot after shot on goal until a 116 minutes into the game Andres Iniesta scores. By midnight 20,000 youths are dancing down Long Street in central Cape Town, glowing in midnight illumination of moon, star, and flat screen TV. They spill from bar, café, restaurant in a river of unfurled flag and vuvuzela. The street that has hosted the fan walk, that ritual approach to Green Point Stadium from the Company Gardens prefacing the Cape Town games, is tonight medieval, its mosques, government buildings, old bookstores disappeared behind courtiers draped in the colors of Spain. French hug Ghanaians who down beer with English who carouse with Mexicans who sing with Senegalese. South Africans of every color are merged into the crowd, for an instant reveling in this international suspension of human division as a metaphor of themselves. Tonight social strife and division have been red carded. There is only the shared splendor of success, the euphoria that the country has pulled it off, neither glass nor bones have been broken, nor tourist assaulted, the games have proceeded like clockwork in beautiful stadiums, the best World Cup ever, some announcers have said. South Africa has declared itself safe and orderly as New York or Berlin. It has profiled itself as capable of pulling off a major signature event, branded itself for the global marketplace. By some irony it has taken the gaze of the world and a global congregation in stadium and city to get South Africans to dance together. The last time South Africans occupied a unified space with this degree of pleasure was when the entire country stood in line to vote in the first democratic election of 1994 and then the year following when they won (against all odds) the Rugby World Cup. The Rugby World Cup was widely experienced as an event in a long corridor of national wonder. Few could believe it; many took pride in it. The FIFA World Cup has offered them a second chance at the miraculous. They are happy to fall into a dreamlike belief that their fellow feeling is sustainable and their future assured. A taste of the Cape and every European will want to invest in property and tourism, even if it has been raining during many of the games and the glorious Table Mountain has been invisible through the fog. After a ten-year hiatus, the Cup has reactivated South Africa's national narrative, which, in the 1990s, South Africa inhabited as if in a trance.

Cut to 1994, to the first trancelike experience of miracle which this world cup reactivated in spirit, a miracle which took place out of a spiral of economic collapse and increasing violence that had accompanied the demise of the apartheid state. The signal year for apartheid's demise was perhaps 1985 when then State President P. W. Botha (aka Old Crocodile) got on the South African television and, instead of announcing major reforms (as expected), vowed in his most resolutely biblical voice that South Africa would never "cross the Rubicon." Almost immediately, the South African currency—once among the strongest in the world—devalued by 300 percent vis-à-vis the dollar. Violence escalated in the townships, where resistance was growing in proportion to an increasing spiral of human rights abuses by the South African police and security branch. War intensified between the armed wing of the African National Congress and South Africa at its northern borders. By 1987 South African business knew apartheid was bankrupt and began secret negotiations with the African National Congress about what would happen after, as did various other sectors of South African society. But it was only with the collapse of the Soviet Union in 1989, which had crucially supported the ANC, that this struggle organization realized it could not win in an all-out war with the National Party of South Africa. Especially since its Marxist allies Mozimbique and Angola were sinking along with their Titanic, Soviet Russia. This collapse of communism eased the National Party into the realization that it would be better to negotiate than fight until it too exhausted its resources in an endless spiral of conflict everywhere in the country. The importance of

1989 cannot be overstated for the South African transition. Had the events of 1989 not happened, apartheid's end would have taken a quite different, more violent trajectory.

South African transition to democracy proved the miracle that nobody believed could have happened even while it was happening. Apartheid was formally ended in 1991. Nelson Mandela and F. W. De Klerk entered a formal state of negotiation/power sharing to hammer out the terms for a new state. The CODESA (Convention for a Democratic South Africa) talks between them and their parties (1991–92) were fraught with instability but continued on. Mandela succeeded in getting his party to drop their demand that the mining industry be nationalized; the National Party agreed to rights which two years earlier they would hardly have imagined thinkable for the country. These talks took place in a climate of fear and conflagration: Zulu nationalists (the Inkatha Party), aiming for provincial autonomy, fought the African National Congress with thousands dead in the Natal Province (KwaZulu-Natal), aided and abetted by the Third Force of the South African Security Branch. Key ANC figures were assassinated. And yet the talks led to an interim Constitution (1994). That interim Constitution, with its preamble about reconciliation, mandated the first free and democratic elections in the history of the country, the terms of the Truth and Reconciliation committees, and the pathway to the writing of a final Constitution. Even with that document completed, it was widely expected that the elections of 1994 would fail to come off. Some whites bought long-life milk and hoarded canned goods in expectation of anarchy, the Inkatha Party boycotted the elections until a week before they took place, the Pan Africanist Congress refused to participate at all. And yet these elections were a milestone in South African history, a setting of the wheels of democracy in action, the beginning of national democratic process. Madiba (Mandela) was voted the first state president of the new country, and so an international moral icon assumed power.

This miracle of beginning continued into 1996 with the proceedings of the Truth and Reconciliation Commission. Above the commission each and every day was their banner: Truth, the Road to Reconciliation. The TRC was the first commission of inquiry into human rights abuses that offered the unlikely feature of qualified amnesty. Qualified amnesty emerged from the CODESA talks as a compromise formation: the African National Congress wanted outright punishment for crimes, the National Party wanted blanket amnesty (as in the Chilean Truth and Reconciliation Commission, which was in certain other respects a model for the South African one). Qualified amnesty was so controversial that it was added only as a postscript to the 1994 interim Constitution. What was offered was amnesty in exchange for two things: complete and true testimony by perpetrators (something hard enough to measure) and proof of "proportionality." Proportionality is, in one sense, an absurd criterion, since gross human rights violations are by definition out of proportion to their motivating circumstances. But the idea was to refuse crimes clearly adjunct to the "war" between the apartheid state and those desiring its downfall, such as the rape of children, the killing of old people who happened to be nearby, and so on. Most applications for amnesty were turned down, although major torturers did manage to secure it, including Jeffrey Benzien, the famous waterboarder (who might have had a future working in Guantanamo, although that is another story).

What qualified amnesty allowed the TRC to do was formulate itself as a proceeding motivated by forgiveness, reconciliation, and nation building, rather than the sterner stuff of retribution. The banner of Truth, the Road to Reconciliation could not have been raised above the podium in an aura of the miraculous. This aura was central to the entire working of the South African Truth and Reconciliation Commission. In the TRC the best of Anglican and black African religion merged, as if a utopian motto for the future of the country, a moral model for future citizenship.

The year 1996 was also the moment when the final Constitution of the country was adopted. Beginning from a concept of the dignity of the individual, that document goes on to flesh out what human dignity means in terms of among the richest panoply of human rights as yet offered by any state constitution. The rights mandated by the final Constitution include a panoply of civil and political rights, but also substantive rights such as the right to health care, a job, and housing. So that all South Africans may achieve the right to an education, the Constitution prescribes primary education in all the eleven official languages of the country. This emphasis on linguistic diversity institutionalizes cultural diversity as central to dignity and therefore preservation through language as a right. There is also a place in the Constitution reserved for "customary rights," although these are eclipsed by individual rights when customary law comes into irreconcilable conflict with individual rights. Perhaps most important, Article 39B mandates that each and every constitutional judgment be taken out of respect for the spirit of the Constitution as a whole, thus prescribing a regime of continuous philosophical and social reflection on what dignity means and how that notion is to be cashed out in terms of shifting human circumstance. Put another way, Article 39B prescribes that each judgment be a new beginning, rewriting the terms of justice in however great or small a way.

These events were refracted in a radiant play of images over the South African media and in a radiant set of performances by State President Mandela. "Rainbow Nation" was the catchphrase of the day; "One nation one station," the ad for the South African Broadcasting Corporation's Channel 1. Mandela's wildly coloristic shirts made him look like David after the defeat of Goliath wearing Joseph's coat of many colors in a vast biblical extravaganza restaged in Africa. This was how it felt being there at the (then) University of Natal, Durban, at a moment when universities were rapidly transforming their European heritages, opening themselves to a mass of formerly excluded populations, rapidly globalizing for the knowledge economy, caught in a frenzy of debate about what it was to be an African and also a university in Africa. While Africa became a joyous question mark, Mandela was busy taking tea with Betsy Verwoerd (widow of the architect of the apartheid state Hendrik F. Verwoerd), declaring his entrance in Afrikaner life by throwing out the rugby ball, busy being feted by the likes of Lady Diana, becoming moral exemplar cum celebrity.

Tremendous positive energy was released in South Africa through the rapt gaze of the world upon it. For in a six-year period South Africa had gone from global pariah to the Mandela years, from security forces to truth and reconciliation. South African images circulated everywhere, and the country was quick to attempt to capitalize upon that profiling. In 1996 a television commercial was widely broadcast during Cape Town's bid to host the 2004 Summer Olympic Games. That commercial featured a former prisoner from Robben Island recalling the importance of intramural games for prisoner morale during the terrible days of his imprisonment, while a camera lovingly lingered on the now empty site of the prison, the point being to sell the idea of having the games in Cape Town under the banner of South African liberation. The point of the commercial was to recruit painful history and its moral achievement to the twin purposes of nationalism and global branding, to persuade the world that the high moral road deserves recognition in all forms, especially that of the Olympics with its roots in the birth of civilization and its avowed purpose of game-driven civility. But even moral recognition is a matter of global competitiveness, and the birthplace of the Olympics won out: 2004 was awarded to Athens.

Recognition is also a business decision; profiling and branding are capital in the complex system of neoliberal marketplaces. Hence the bid for the 2008 Summer Olympics went to Beijing. South Africa during those years conflated global recognition on moral grounds with global competitiveness in the marketplace, assuming that the Mandela brand could bring business. That and structural adjustment: 1996 was the year the neoliberal turn was codified in South African economic policy by Treasury Minister Trevor Manuel in the form of GEAR, the Growth, Employment, and Redistribution Act. GEAR artificially tailored the South African economy to fit the stringent suit of structural adjustment in order to achieve target goals of an annual GDP growth of 6 percent or more by the year 2000 and the creation of four hundred thousand new jobs each year through foreign investment and internal economic efficiency. What happened instead was that the global market turned to China, leading to little foreign investment and the real loss of two million jobs in South Africa. Even South African manufacturing began to outsource to China as well as other regions of Africa (Malawi) where employment could be had cheaper. Instead of economic and job growth, close to 40 percent of the country's workforce found themselves unemployed (depending on who did the measurement and what was counted as "informal work"). While Black Economic Empowerment broke the boundaries of race, the goal was nothing more than to generate a small elite black African industrial and banking class. South Africa's Gini coefficient (differential between rich and poor) remained among the highest in the world.

Then the moral capital began to depreciate in value through a number of global and internal recognitions. These included: 1. that crime was out of control, policing a failure in the newly weak (that is, no longer authoritarian/fascist) state, 2. that no public works programs were being properly instituted that would drive the country toward the noble human rights goals set forth in the Constitution, and 3. that "racialized" practices were deeply ingrained in the new regime, including some which had been subdued during the apartheid regime between black, Xhosa, Zulu, colored and so on.

Nineteen ninety-nine was the year that the country found it could also no longer hold off acknowledging the ravaging presence of HIV and AIDS. The province of Kwa-Zulu Natal (then the AIDS epicenter) was by that time 39 percent HIV positive. The rate of infection there had skyrocketed to between 12 and 20 percent. The first deaths were beginning to happen on a mass scale since the gestation period before HIV infection manifests as full-blown AIDS is shorter in Africa than for the American strains of the virus. In response to this crisis, State President Thabo Mbeki articulated and held to the policy of AIDS denialism, leading to significant depreciation in South Africa's global image and a crisis of governance. Opposition groups of scientists, the Medical Research Council, and others engaged in fierce debate against the government, whose stance became increasingly recalcitrant. Postcolonial rhetoric took on the guise of irrationality; the so-called African Renaissance disappeared from view. South Africa quickly became rebranded as AIDS capital of the world rather than moral capital of it.

And so by the end of the first decade of the South African transition the experience and narrative of the miraculous had collapsed. In real terms the society began to marshal its resources toward addressing at least some of its problems. The power of the Constitution was invoked as corrective to both the crisis of housing (in 2000) and of health (in 2002). In a pair of landmark decisions taken by the Constitutional Court against the government, rule of law was established and confirmed. The first decision concerned a Mrs. Grootboom who had been living in a shack on the Cape Flats, a flimsy lean-to built on sand without electricity, running water, or sewage. As one among millions in the same condition, she chose to sue for her right to housing in the Constitutional Court. The court ruled in her favor: that the South African state had failed in its constitutional obligation by not as yet making a "reasonable effort" to institute her right to housing, meaning the rights of many like her. This decision prompted a program in which more than two million houses have been built, with electricity introduced into informal settlements, running water. The results have been as dramatic as they remain inadequate (Mrs. Grootboom died a decade later, still without a house).

The second case against the government was brought in 2002 by the Treatment Action Campaign, an HIV/AIDS activist group which successfully sued in the Constitutional Court on grounds that the government had failed to make the reasonable effort mandated by the Constitution to institute the right to health. The government was forced to roll out antiretroviral drugs which became affordable by the country on account of a second lawsuit won by the Treatment Action Campaign against two pharmaceutical companies producing the drugs, which forced those companies to cut cost.

The Treatment Action Campaign was led by activists who had to shed their old "loyalty first" code of conduct leftover from the struggle days, when solidarity without dissent was crucial. This was not easy to do, this break from a government composed of former African National Congress cadres, but it led to the formation of a culture of grassroots democratic dissent in the new South Africa. The Treatment Action Campaign deployed hard-learned "struggle expertise" (from the anti-apartheid struggle) in mobilizing heterogeneous populations in protest against government policy as well as pharmaceutical price. Anthropologist Steven Robins describes their technique, following work by Arjun Appadurai, as "grassroots globalization," "globalization from below."[1] "TAC activism straddled local, national and global spaces in the course of struggles for access to cheaper AIDS drugs. This was done through the courts, the Internet, the media, and by networking with South African and international civil society organizations. Widely publicised acts of 'civil disobedience' also provided TAC with visibility within a globally connected post-apartheid public sphere."[2]

The work of the TAC reconvened what (to stretch a point but not break it) might be called South Africa's struggle "heritage" as grassroots opposition democratic/community organizing politics. This reframing of dissent is an excellent sign for the future, but it succeeded too late to prevent the massive scale of deaths which a half decade of AIDS denialism produced. At this moment about a thousand people a day are dying of HIV/AIDS in South Africa. Over three hundred thousand have lost their lives to the disease; no one can say how many would be alive today had the government acted differently.

The crisis of governance around HIV/AIDS in the Mbeki regime was connected to a larger failure of multiparty democracy in the country. State President Thabo Mbeki had been free to act as he did in part because of the failure of South Africa to achieve a political alternative to his party, the African National Congress which at that time still legitimated itself through its legacy of anti-apartheid struggle. Had a serious opposition party been on the scene to speak loudly against Mbeki's state policies, he might have been forced to ameliorate his position. At least he might not have been reelected for a second term. But the African National Congress was—and remains—the only party in town, all others being marginal to the population. With this failure of the country to achieve multiparty democracy, the African National Congress has in the past ten years morphed into a kind of Peronist party, a catchall of communists, trade unionists, corporate CEOs, moderates, and the like, which is unified not by policy and position (how could it be?) but instead by its role as a conduit between government and big business. The ANC is increasingly the route to tender, corruption, gravy train.

But the pages of history show that South Africa had hardly lost all its moral and economic capital. The South African Rand remained a reasonably stable currency throughout, and the country won its bid to host the World Cup in 2010. This would be the first time these games took place on the African continent, which put South Africa in the position of continental exemplar. South Africa would be put back into GEAR: through the World Cup it would reestablish its claim on foreign investment, this time investment in the form of tourism (if not more). A successful World Cup would demonstrate state efficiency, thus reestablishing trust in this African state; it would demonstrate that South Africa could offer safe travel for international fans and players, journalists, celebrities, and dignitaries, and it would prove the world-class character of landscape, hotels, spas, game parks, cities, cuisine. The World Cup is an elaborate tourist opportunity for hundreds of thousands and, through the eyes of the media, for millions around the globe: a unique profiling/branding opportunity. The 1996 version of GEAR was about exploiting South Africa's moral capital and structural readiness (according to World Bank/International Monetary Fund criteria). The 2010 remake of GEAR would be about exploiting its *aesthetic* capital and doing so visually by beautifying cities, building hotels, readying roads, offering world-class trips to desert, sea, and game park. The point was to create a *visual encomium* in which circulation, board, cuisine, city, point of view, face to face contact with locals would generate future capital. The world would be convinced that South Africa had first world status, yes, but in particular that its beaches, sunshine, game parks, mountains, wineries, and condominiums are competitive with Costa Rica, Tuscany, Phuket, Sydney, and Rajasthan. The country would be profiled through journalist, TV camera, and eye witness of French, German, Egyptian, Mexican tourist. This emphatic set of lenses meant that new airports and infrastructure had to be efficient and also carry the visual splendor of world-class sites. The stadiums had to gleam with newly wrought beauty. The roads must be free of potholes, chaos of taxis, the ugliness of violence and impoverishment.

That the world (or parts of it anyway) wanted to remain within the frame of the South African miracle, reveling in the magic and moralizing it as true grit, national will power, and democratic providence is clear. The 1995 Rugby World Cup victory lived a second life on the American screen with Morgan Freeman as Madiba (Mandela) and Matt Damon as Francois Pienaar (then captain of the South African rugby team), directed by the high-minded poet of grit himself, Clint Eastwood. Well after the Truth and Reconciliation Commission had passed from the foreground of South African consciousness, it was dreamily replayed by a spate of academics, poets, filmmakers, state officials (including me it has to be said), all of whom wanted to retain a taste of the power of this example before the feeling of miracle, the sense of ideality faded.

And so the Green Point Stadium in Cape Town was designed by the German architectural firm GMP Architects and built by South African construction firm Murray and Roberts Construction at the cost of 4.4 billion ZAR (approximately 650 million U.S. dollars).

This major expenditure represented a gamble on the economic future since this amount could have been used otherwise to solve the problems of housing or education in the Cape province. Many critics pointed this out at the time of construction. Why was Green Point chosen for the site of the stadium? Many thought it was to break the ghettoized nature of

FIGURE 4.1. GMP Architects, Green Point Stadium. Wikipedia.

Cape Town by opening up a rich, cloistered enclave of the city to the general South African population. Perhaps, but I believe the choice had to do with ensuring that the Cape Town games take place in visually superb and socially cloistered ground. Green Point is among the most elegant spaces of Cape Town, its location fronting the Atlantic Ocean and next to the (world-class) Victoria and Albert Mall. In preparation for the event, the Green Point seafront was also remodeled. Where international visitors were forced to pass townships, for example, along the main arteries from the Cape Town International Airport to the city, government housing was strategically built so that international tourists would arrive and depart with a rosy picture of South African social development. Were these World Cup visitors to have slowed their taxis and studied the government-constructed plots more carefully, they would have noticed the lean-tos: for lack of employment has caused recipients of government beneficence to rent them out while living in the shacks they've jerry-built at the back of their properties.

And so the fan walk served the purpose of merging congregants/fans together in an ecstatic ritual prefacing the games; but the fan walk also controlled their circulation within strict visual/urban parameters. These parameters were efficient, safe, and a matter of visual profiling in the hope/expectation of future investment. From fan walk to the finale on Long Street the city was treated as a strict tourist container; large, anarchic taxis were disallowed from entering except at controlled points, police and then the army (when police went on strike) closely monitored relevant urban space; the fan walk was designed to highlight Cape Town's best urban experiences. It is not that these goals were devious or even inauthentic. They were about bringing the World Cup off well, with safety, and in a way that would reactivate South Africa's earlier goal of foreign investment: this time through the sensuous branding of the country as tourist/property owning destination.

In the sweep of the spectacle, all criticism disappeared. The pleasure of finding again a shared national consciousness (*we did it, we are up to it, we can blow vuvuzelas together, the world again notices and loves us*) was overwhelming. But the day after the finale on Long Street this "we" woke to a hangover, unsure how to return to the banality of ordinary life, the disillusionment of their problems, the discarded remains of the unfurled flags and broken vuvuzelas on the streets and in the doorways. Within one week there were massive strikes as employment tanked after the blip of World Cup occasional labor. Unemployment again descended to around 40 percent (depending on how one measures this). The World Cup had been a genuine achievement, the approbation of the world real: it was something to be proud of. But the world quickly moved on as it always does in neoliberal society, and there would be, it was soon realized, no dreamlike fix to follow, no immediate payback for the cost of the stadiums through investment in property, increased tourism, or anything else. The European Union is at the moment in (or close to) economic crisis. The price of housing in the Cape continues to fall. As of 2011 the fate of stadiums like Green Point is undecided. No one quite knows what to do with them.

The year 1996 was about the fantasy that South Africa's *moral* capital would translate (with the help of structural adjustment) into economic development; 2010 was about the fantasy that its *aesthetic* capital would translate into a second tier of same. Both may yet happen, however the fixation on such alchemical forms of panacea ought to be reconsidered. The next site of the World Cup is in Brazil (2014). Perhaps South Africa ought to follow the lead of Brazil and learn to go it economically alone far more than it currently does, taking greater responsibility for good governance, employment, development, and the like. Given the capriciousness of markets, the strategy of readying the country for foreign investment is not sustainable. Growth must also be internally stimulated, equity internally mandated. And there is a related point about national consciousness and fellow feeling. What the Rainbow Nation and Finale on Long Street showed is that South Africa's sense of imagined unity is dependent upon a shared experience of the miraculous. The miraculous is always temporary. Hence the sense of national unity and purpose is insufficiently articulated; the country has yet to discover—or create—more sustainable forms of national consciousness.

II

This national consciousness of the miraculous transiently revitalized around the FIFA games arose, I said, around the great events of the transition: the TRC, writing of the Constitution et al. Above all, I have described that consciousness as *demonumentalizing*. Naturally then it was played out around monuments and, more generally, the "monumental."

The monument is a flash point around which group and national narratives get articulated, gaining power and claiming authority. The monument turns the past into a living symbol, a central predicate in the assertion of heritage. The ashes of the past, acknowledged as irreparable, become symbolically reconstructed into something else: the hard currency of stone. Around the physical solidity of the thing, the ensuing process of mourning becomes a process of *solidarity*, of resolution. The logic of monuments is to articulate group origins, implicate group destiny. The monument is an essential element in the formation of heritage practice. The power of the stone is the occasion for the genesis of group power.

Without the monument (and museum and church and university), it is hard to imagine the practice of heritage ever arising. The colonial monument in South Africa bespoke Rhodes on horseback, framed by lions at the Rhodes memorial above his estate in Cape Town, surveying his rightful dominion, Cape to Cairo (Cecil Rhodes's prophesy and project of control over the entire African continent in the name of England). It bespoke King George V on horseback laying claim to the port harbor of Durban, Natal. Such monuments were the object of William Kentridge's shortest film in the Soho Eckstein series, a film called *Monument* (1990). It is a riff on the opening scene of Chaplin's *City Lights*, where the mayor of the town (here the benefactor Soho) is making a speech before the unveiling of a monument erected by the city. Chaplin's film famously sticks it to sound film (Chaplin made it a few years after the talkies came into being) by having the mayor speak in a parodic jumble of nonsense words. Kentridge follows suit in his. In Chaplin's film the unveiling becomes the occasion for comedy when the tramp is found nesting in the monument's armpit with a chase scene ensuing. Kentridge's humor, more acrid to the taste, comes when what is unveiled is the strong body of a black African at work, with the weight of stone pressing on his head. Hardly the stuff of monumentalization: rather the stuff of people struggling under the weight of "monumental" and painful tasks, struggling to endure.

Kentridge's second film demonumentalizes by revealing ruination in the social system which monumentalizes at the expense of black labor.

During the apartheid period the colonial monument singing of Cecil Rhodes's Cape to Cairo or King George's Durban harbor gives way to Afrikaner identity politics cast in a different currency. Had there been no Boer War in South Africa, it is likely there would have been no apartheid state. That war took place because Cecil Rhodes rode in on his fine horse to claim England's share of booty from the poor Afrikaans farmers who, by chance, had unearthed a boundless treasure of gold and diamonds. The Boer War, fought between 1899 and 1902, was the opening act of the twentieth century. Already going full force when the champagne bottles of the new century were uncorked, it proved a model for the bombs, bunkers, ruins, rubble, and wrecks that were to follow. It featured the first concentration camps: Lord Kitchener, furious that a ragtag group of Afrikaners carrying tattered Bibles could stump his best commonwealth troops, burned the Afrikaner's farms so that nothing could grow again and placed their women and children in concentration camps where many died of disease. The Afrikaner population never forgave his humiliation or that the English had started the war for the sake of gold and diamonds. Their radicalization took place around the memory of ruined farms, ruined earth, and ruined people. They grew more racist, more xenophobic, deeply attached to rising German fascism. The Afrikaners' own experiences of English concentration camp led to the master plan for apartheid. Like concentration camps, apartheid is a way of concentrating and controlling people, of regulating work, leisure, circulation, and dwelling. And so one architecture of humiliation becomes another. The Afrikaner, once the last apostle of colonial rurality, becomes the new master of state power.

When the apartheid state came into being with the National Party's rise to power in 1948, the monument was built in the town of Valhalla, between Johannesburg and Pretoria, to celebrate it. The monument, unveiled in 1949, was designed by the architect Gerard Moerdyk, himself imprisoned in the Standerton concentration camp during the Boer War, to commemorate the "Great Trek": that event of the early nineteenth century when a band of Afrikaners drove their ox wagons into the interior of the country and established themselves in the Transvaal, fighting off Pedi and Soto, cowboy style. These settlers drew their ox carts into a laager, a tight circle through which the Zulu enemy could not penetrate and from which they could fire their muskets from positions of relative security. It is because of the great trek, the mythology goes, because of what the brave and simple Afrikaner did, that the great nation of South Africa was founded. We and not you, the monument declares, are the originating moment of the nation.

Origin indeed means destiny in this heritage game, which according to the terms of the Voortrekker Monument emerge exclusively from

FIGURE 4.2. Gerard Moerdyk, *Voortrekker Monument*, 1949. Wikipedia.

Afrikaner culture and history. The monument's encircling outer wall is covered with ox wagon reliefs. On the inside a series of paintings depict the trekkers. An inner circle cut out from the first floor allows the visitor to "witness" a cenotaph of fire and funereal stone below, emblazoned with the words "Ons vir jou Suid Afrika" (We for you, South Africa).

There is a marriage of male and female in this monument, with its rings of encircling "maternal" spaces and its rising, phallic forms—the shaft of the building, the upright flame within. Safety and force, nurturance and power converge in a religious gesture. This is heritage (origin and destiny, male and female) with a capital *H*.

Moerdyk drew his inspiration for the building from Bruno Schmitz's Völkerschlachtdenkmal in Leipzig, and there is a special "dialogue" between these two monuments around ruination. The Leipzig monument was built at the beginning of the twentieth century to commemorate Germans fallen during the Napoleonic wars. Its construction at the time of the Boer War allowed Afrikaners to fuse their gesture of memorialization with its own. I would call the German monument the architectural unconscious of the Afrikaner one. Through identification with the passion of the Leipzig memorial (with its *Leidenschaft*), the monument claims a double origin for the new state, in the great trek and the humiliation of the Boer War—thus converting hardship into resolve, indeed victory at the moment of the National Party's ascendancy. Something between an art deco radio tower and a Romanesque church, the monument proclaims this in a pro-German voice, right at the end of the Second World War, as if taking over the mantle of the fallen Third Reich. And so the monument makes the origin of South Africa reside in a uniquely Afrikaner identity and through the operation of heritage proclaims the destiny of the country to reside only in Afrikaner hands.

Afrikaner identity politics on the right (and note that a significant Afrikaner minority refused this persuasion) built a series of monuments to its language and history, in Paarl there is the monument to the "Taal" or language which soars phallic above the earth like a Washington monument, but in the modernist style of Le Corbusier. In Burgersdorp, where the National Party is said to have been born (or held its first meetings anyway), a battle took place over the monument erected in 1893 in honor of equality between Dutch and English and for the colonial Parliament. In 1901, during the Anglo Boer War this statue was damaged by British troops and removed from its base. After the war the citizens of Burgersdorp pressured the British government to pay for a replica which was unveiled in 1907. The original monument (decapitated unfortunately) was unearthed in King William's Town in 1939 and returned to the town square, where it now resides (headless) next to its replica. Such is the story of monument versus monument, that clash of trashing and replication.

FIGURE 4.3. *Völkerschlachtdenkmal.* Wikipedia.

The monument is a heritage call which in every possible way does *not* seek to intervene in the Eurocentric formula of identity politics sublimed as destiny. Like its Leipzig source, it speaks from the position of historical victim at the hands of a stronger European force. If the monument is *live action heritage*, it is because within that formula it speaks of a settler culture which has endured ruination at the hands of another, stronger settler culture (call the stronger the culture of Cecil Rhodes and his project of control over resources from Cape to Cairo). Where it departs from the classic heritage model and becomes *live action heritage* is in its self-positioning of *settler sovereignty* understood as *rightful historical redress*. Our suffering purifies us, proves our worth, and entitles us, the message goes. The form that this conversion of victimhood into sovereignty takes is the apartheid state.

There is a more general point to be made here, which I shall pursue in chapter 6. Settler societies claim sovereignty on the basis of suffering at the hands of another, but also through the pain and triumph of settling itself. It is in and through the act of settling (in this case codified as the Great Trek) that the group believes itself purified, ennobled, and bonded with land. It is in and through the act that a settler society finds its origin, and destiny. Endlessly recited and enacted in ritual after the fact, the act eventually becomes magnified into something biblical. The act is (thus ennobled retrospectively) theirs, the thing that confers exclusive right if not ownership over land and peoples. This right can only come to fruition when sovereignty, dominion over land and people are achieved. In other words, the apartheid state is the final chapter in the long act of settling, it is the destiny prescribed by the settler origin: the Great Trek. Or so it is told through the monument, the state plan, the instruments of heritage. This destiny, now achieved, is what the monument confirms and celebrates.

There can only be one South Africa and it is theirs. The Great Trek, relived as heritage, is that enunciation. While directed at the English, this heritage myth also targeted the "African races." And any claims they might have to dominion in the nation in virtue of being "first peoples." Over time the anti-Englishness of the myth gave way under a pragmatic need for alliance with English power within South Africa (especially business). At this point state heritage contruction shifted to a more inclusive figure, one admired by both groups (Afrikaner Nationalist and English): Jan van Reibeeck, first governor of the Cape Province (I follow work of Leslie Witz here).[3] But the myth of the Great Trek was never abandoned (nor ambivalence toward the English), in spite of the need for pragmatic rapprochement.

Official heritage culture was particularly egregious in refusing to admit prior peoples, black African, indigenous, into its circle of origins. African peoples could have no role in the founding of the country, nor its destiny, and belonged properly, according to the vicious logic of apartheid, in another set of countries: the Bantustans. These "heritages," so constructed by the apartheid state, were a debased regime of folkloric, naturalized origins ascribing to them destinies of menial labor and minor administration. And this brings me to a deeper way in which the apartheid state generated *live action heritage*. The Voortrekker Monument converts suffering into sovereignty, relying on suffering to justify such rule. But the larger project of official apartheid heritage is an example of what Michel Foucault called biopower. Sovereignty is, in Foucault's thinking, distinguished from biopower in that it is rule of law, the power to judge, to condemn to die, and, conversely, to pardon. This is the power of constitutions and legal systems. Biopower is the power to control life, to produce and shape it in a particular way, within a particular domain of disciplinary constraints. Official apartheid heritage follows from the structure of indirect rule (see chapter 1), wherein chiefs were given their own domains of authority within circumscribed limits. What happened within such rurally established chiefdoms was a matter of negotiation between chiefs and colonial authorities, and the negotiation was unequal although flexible. Codify this system of colonial control into a more inflexible system of legal and police controls and a colonial system turns into a modern penal-panoptic formula. It becomes Foucault's biopower: offering the power to live within a specific identifiable future to each people that is subject to the constraints of racist/legal inequality. The political "architecture" of apartheid is a system actively dedicated to generating, shaping, and sustaining these differential/unequal futures. Separate and unequal domains of heritage production were the symbolic/cultural aspect of the apartheid state's exercise of biopower, along with separate and unequal education, law, living conditions, civil and political rights, places of dwelling or "nations."

It is not for nothing that one generation later Thabo Mbeki will seek to rehabilitate African heritages by taking up the mantle of the African Renaissance for post-apartheid South Africa with its celebration of "precolonial," indigenous traditions, its legacy of Negritude, Afro-Centrism, and "presence Africaine," its belief that everything great in the African postcolonial future somehow resided in the African past. His heritage turn aims to empower those sent by force into the Bantustans by gifting them the central place in the origin of the nation and, by the logic of heritage, in the destiny of South Africa and the African continent. Mbeki's African Renaissance is the attempt to generate a national ideology for the country. It is the second of the two narratives which these chapters aim to explore and will be the focus of the next chapter.

III

By the mid 1980s it was clear to many that the monumental "architecture" of the apartheid state and the national narratives conveyed in these stones were in ruins, the plan of apartheid unraveling. By the plan of apartheid I mean its division of populations on the basis of race and organization of them into distinct nationalities, its forced removal of entire populations from their entanglement in cities, its setting them down in godforsaken Homelands, its restrictions on movement and circulation between the races, its surveillance structures, plans for state and economic growth within this form, racist/unequal apportionment of resources and opportunities. This architecture of modern life was tottering. Economic collapse and increasing violence had accompanied the demise of the apartheid state (as I have detailed at the outset of this chapter).At this moment (1988) of tumbling architectures (buildings and state plans), Penny Siopis painted her *Patience on a Monument—a History Painting*. It features a black woman who is bronzed in the manner of a piece of monumental sculpture and who sits on top of a monumental load of cultural detritus. The woman's features are mock versions of Nazi/Deco art: she is cast in the Teutonic build and athletic physique beloved by the Nazi artist and celebrated in Leni Reifenstal's "masterpiece" in the mode of the fascist aesthetic, *Olympiad*.

Sue Williamson refers in her book, *Resistance Art*, to this woman as "anti-heroic, an inversion of liberty leading the people."[4] And so colonial and apartheid history spills out of her work like a genealogy of wastes, a vast junk pile of heritage, "the thickened artifice behind the façade of a faltering regime. The spoils of Empire . . . mountains of affluence blotting out the horizon,"[5] as Jennifer Law puts it. One might add that the reddish gold can only suggest the gold dumps and dust (waste) surrounding the city of Johannesburg, signs of empire, affluence, and detritus. Siopis's paintings from this time are vast images of the archive, the museum, the history of colonial decay unearthed, monumentalized. One could imagine Soho Eckstein standing in the corner of the painting, impassive and sweating in his heavy middle European three-piece suit, standing on the broken back of the monument he gifted the city, unable to determine how to take his next step without falling on the broken glass where his corporate offices once were.

FIGURE 4.4. Penny Siopis, *Patience on a Monument*. Photo and rights courtesy of Penny Siopis.

The ruination of the monument, or the monument standing on ruins, means the collapse of two things: nationally asserted heritage, the terror of one group over all others, and, related, the fact of a singular national narrative, an official national consciousness or ideology, widely believed, which links people together under the shared banner of truth, aspiration, identity. Such narratives are better lost than found, but in their place? What loss is experienced for a nation which finds it difficult or impossible to grow into existence without such a shared way of speaking the world?

Apartheid ended in 1991, but its monuments were still standing. And so the question for the new government, brought to power in the first democratic elections in South African history, (1994): What to do with them?

A number of alternatives were possible.

There was the Budapest model, which gathered all the communist monuments into a theme park at the edge of town, where they immediately turned into Disneyland.

There was the Berlin model, to let the population tear them down and keep the pieces as souvenirs, painted reliquaries. My wife was there when it happened and brought me a jagged piece of the wall covered in red and yellow graffiti, which we then brought to South Africa when we emigrated in the 1990s, only to find it was stolen when we moved house.

There was the French model, to place them in palaces of national culture so that, cleansed of atrocity, they could become French.

There was the Romanian model, to line them up against the wall and shoot them.

There was the American model, which was to privatize: build hotels next to the site, erect billboards on the highway which read "You Are Now Approaching the Famous Site of Whatever," hire guides to explain to everyone why the site is so famous, how expensive it was to restore, and which celebrities have recently had their photographs taken at the site, import expensive granite to erect a wall of the donors in front of the site, obscuring view of it, engage tour companies to schedule the site as part of package deals, allow for product placement.

South Africa followed none of these models.

As archeologist Nick Shepherd tells it:

[in post-apartheid South Africa] heritage has been reconceptualised around notions of redress. . . . Aspects of this programme include an ongoing public process of renaming of sites, towns, cities, streets and public amenities, and the introduction of the Legacy Projects. These include the Chief Albert Luthuli Legacy Project, the . . . Nelson Mandela Museum, the Constitution Hill Project, and the Khoisan Project. At the same time, a decision was made not to expunge the memorials of Afrikaner National History, but rather to retain them as a record of apartheid, and to set them in dialogue with newer, more critically inclusive sites. . . . Perhaps the most powerful realization of this approach has been the Freedom Park Project on Salvokop outside Pretoria, opposite the unreconstructed Monument.[6]

This was the official state position, anyway. For Annie Coombes has shown in a fine book, *History After Apartheid*, that all manner of shenanigans took place by individuals and groups to reduce, ridicule, stand on its head, and in general denature the power of the apartheid monument.[7] The apartheid monument converted the experience of settler victimhood into an exclusive claim of sovereignty. Now a parade of spectacles took place to lessen the effect and take the mickey out of the monument. State culture and policy however makes the Boer monument the object of redress at this moment of transition to democracy. Crucial to the celebration is the undoing of the separate and unequal heritage formula of apartheid (apartheid cultural biopower). How this happens is the gesture of live action heritage. The question is whether it happens monumentally or rather through the undoing of the culture of the monument per se. Another way of putting this is to ask: does the live action heritage gesture of the post-apartheid state place the very idea of a monument (and the power vested within) under "erasure"? How does the culture of the monument change? There is no easy answer.

Consider the Freedom Park Project which specifically designates itself a "heritage destination" on the homepage of its Web site,[8] http://www.freedompark.co.za/cms/index.php, where its vision and mission are articulated in these terms (and photos of the park may be found): "[Freedom Park's mission is] to be a leading icon of humanity and freedom; To provide a pioneering and empowering heritage destination in order to mobilise for reconciliation and nation building in our country; to reflect upon our past, improving our present and building our future as a united nation; and to contribute continentally and internationally to the formation of better human understanding among nations and peoples."[9]

This is a language of redress, reconciliation, and nation building that can be found, more or less word for word, in the Preamble to the Constitution of South Africa (1996) and the report of the Truth and Reconciliation Commission (1998). It is a language authorizing the site to exist as a heritage form with such noble purposes. The home page of the Freedom Park Web site is filled with changing images that have included photos of Nelson Mandela at the site, of State President Jacob Zuma (sans wives) and other dignitaries there, of diverse cultural "heritages" such as African dancing, singing . . . The Web site is a way of taking back the nationalism of the monument and morphing it into the diverse, state-driven cultural politics of post-apartheid South Africa. Instead of telling the story of apartheid (something far more difficult to do), icons congregate in the space celebrating themselves and exalting the site with their presence: these icons from former struggle days include Che Guevara (his daughter at the site). It is both populist (the dancing, choirs) and highly orchestrated as a national image. The Web site contains a chat area where reminiscence on the twenty-year anniversary of Mandela's release from Robben Island and other such topics become forums for blogging.

I begin with the Web site rather than the site because I think this heritage site is as much a matter of Web creation as it is of actual place. Indeed the contemporary heritage site is as often as not a thing built in actual place but also through its calling card and point of circulation: its Web site. The Web site actualizes the heritage dimension by naming it as such in the standard branding language of the twenty-first century. "This is a heritage site; you are now entering the Web site of the heritage site, which tells you the site is a heritage site in case you didn't realize it." But the site does far more than simply brand itself. It actualizes freedom in the new democracy through its populist, participatory blogging around key national moments in an exalted national spirit. It also exalts the actual site of Freedom Park by circulating information about the icons that have appeared there. The key is that the site be registered widely, *seen* and this is the function of the Web.

In other words the heritage game morphs partly into virtual space in order to create an environment that might actualize the promise of popular participation. The Web also plays a crucial heritage-creating function by demonumentalizing the obsession through built sites of stone, granite, or concrete, with their cenotaphs and ritual status. It is hard to have a religion over the Internet, you need a temple, a mosque, a church, a holy city, or sepulcher. The Web site plays a role in this process of demonumentalization while also carrying the aura of revolutionary holiness (Che and Madiba).

The actual site in physical space is evidently also crucial; without it there could be no spatial dialogue with the monument. The actual site is circular in composition. This new circle retracts the closed circle of the Afrikaner laager of ox wagons and replaces it with the circle of the African kraal, that village space of thatch huts arranged around a communal area for solidarity, friendliness, security, and the keeping of animals (village "capital" of cows, sheep, goats) within bounds. The site itself is as user friendly and low key as a heritage site could be. Made from local sandstone, site materials refer back beyond apartheid concrete and stone to the more landscape-friendly work of Herbert Baker, whose Johannesburg houses were about blending the Englishness of the mansion into the local landscape of place. Sandstone is a quiet material that blends with veld rather than seeking to dominate landscape. Its function is to blend rather than interrupt, dominate, enclose. The site is built at ground level; the buildings are low and unobtrusive. The site has something of the feel of an oasis or waterhole where animals might freely wander in the late afternoon when the sun is cool to drink. This flexibility to come and go frees the visitor from the bounds of ritualized belonging, tribal affiliation, or worship. The image is that of traditional deliberation or justice taking place in ancient society under a banyan tree. It is a free space for the multiple offering of lectures, dances, gatherings, a place for a diversity of events or heritage mixes. As such, the site seeks to foreclose on monuments with their power to impose domination, replacing them with conviviality under the awe of democratic high-mindedness (a more "friendly" form of authority).

This overall scheme for participatory democracy, with its special deference to vintage African heritage elements (the kraal, the banyan tree), is what makes the site a gesture of live action heritage at a moment of nation building. The goal is to turn the high-minded language of the Truth and Reconciliation Commission and the Preamble to the Constitution into a heritage before the fact, a newly invented heritage for a new democracy. Key moments in the history of the anti-apartheid struggle are set forth as "our national heritage," old African traditions of court and justice are subtly proclaimed "our new origin." Dignity, right, and redress aspire to the status of a cultural template, as if the heritage were one of words rather than the currency of concrete.

There is a useful point of reference for the Freedom Park in the writing of James E. Young on Holocaust memorials. Young proposes that such constructions should be understood as "counter-monuments" seeking to "return the burden of memory to visitors themselves by forcing visitors into an active role."[10] The Holocaust countermonument shares much in common with the kind of construction central to the South African transition, enough anyway to allow Young's work to sharpen the difference. For the South African object (aka the Freedom Park) does not seek first and foremost to return memory to individuals in the manner of a Holocaust memorial, whose purpose is that one shall not forget, one shall never forget, and whose task is to force the act of memory when the event remembered is one which for all intents and purposes breaks the bounds of ordinary human imagination, hence ordinary human memory. The South African object is a transitional object aiming to build social networks, create and reorient communities around utopian regimes of redress, not simply a complex mnemonic. The South African object idealizes a culture of dignity through acknowledgment. Acknowledgment involves intensities of memory, but also forgiveness and restoration. The kinds of justice which are meant to converge in the mission of the Truth and Reconciliation Commission are truth (testimony, the construction of an archive of the past), social dialogue, and restoration. All in some sense converge in the Freedom Park through the intended relationship of design and spirit.

These goals of participatory redress constituted something approaching a national narrative at the early moment of transition, a shared aspiration which in some significant way suffused national and local consciousness. This narrative of redress, memorialization, and dignity informed the big events of transition described earlier: the 1996 moment. It was a narrative with a popular reach, not merely state driven but pertinent to a larger culture of acknowledgment. The most well-known example of local culture's engagement with the gesture of participatory redress has been the District Six Museum in Cape Town.[11] That little museum memorializes a Cape Town community bulldozed into oblivion in the 1960s, structured in the form of an interactive map of the old streets of the community that once was. This map, on the floor of the museum, takes up the largest part of its space. The space is otherwise circulatory (allowing visitors to move around the map) and archival (allowing them to enter its open plan archives. Former residents of District Six or their familial descendants map place markers denoting "I or my parents or my grandparents once lived here, here was our house." This gesture of self-inclusion is one of public acknowledgment as well as private and public mourning/memorialization, foregrounding loss of a once vibrant and mixed community, but also, through the intimate interactive nature of the museum, retrieving some reparative shred of the community.

The District Six Museum is local heritage in the process of being assembled. It does not seek any grand narrative of that community. Rather it seeks relinquishment of the haunting, restoration in symbolic form of that which was lost, archiving of its fragments for the future, mapping of the old geography. Annie Coombes describes the District Six Museum project as motivated by "Reminiscence, excavation, and reconstruction."[12] If one adds to these motivations the performative intention of symbolically replacing self or family back on the map, one has a working sense of the museum. District Six has lived two lives, first as a place, second as an icon. Its second life is more whole than its first, since an icon is a singular, burning thing while a place is a differentiated set of events held together on a map. The museum accentuates this second life, the life of the icon, but refuses religious aura by remaining more interactive and ordinary in its archival collecting. It does not pretend to canonize the district in the manner of a heritage church. The gesture is live action heritage.

What the District Six Museum (and other related sites) show is that redress, and its related poetics/politics of demonumentalization, were in the 1990s not just a national policy, a program of heritage from above, the product of a transitional state's thinking about its cultural landscape. These poetics/politics had an urgency which captivated diverse groups of ordinary people. At this moment of political transition the consciousness of people and the gestures of the state were (in this way) aligned. This concordance was crucial to the power of the moment, to its consciousness of unity, its shared sense of purpose.

Central to the poetics of redress was the opening of the site from monumentalized ritual to more fluent/free forms of participation. Public participation was, let it be noted, mandated by the post-apartheid state as official culture. The "two main current pieces of heritage legislation, the National heritage Resources Act (NHRA) of 1999 and the National Heritage Council Act of 1999 . . . [place] an emphasis on public participation in heritage management," Shepherd writes.[13]

But public participation was also a populist historical legacy deriving from the anti-apartheid movement within South Africa. Popular front politics in the struggle wished to mobilize broad sectors of the population by engaging them in street art, performance, on-site art, art that would also speak in opposition to the white/Eurocentric position of museums in the country. Popular participation became, during the anti-apartheid struggle, an ideology of popular culture mobilized for the struggle.

Popular culture was posed against the culture of the Eurocentric South African museum. The South African art museum did not mount its first extensive exhibition of black South African "fine art" until 1987–88.[14] From 1941 until 1973, hardly an art work by a black artist had been collected by the Johannesburg Art Gallery even though, unlike the National Gallery in Cape Town, no government law prevented the Johannesburg Art Gallery from doing this.[15] Where the black African appeared was in the museum of craft, while his cohort the Bushman could be found grazing by the waterhole in the museum of natural history: his home was the diorama, not the gallery, he was object of nature, not *Homo faber*.

This separation of black culture from the art museum and placing of the black body in the museum of natural history with animal and landscape has been explored by various South African authors and artists, among them Pippa Skotnes.[16] Skotnes's exhibition and accompanying book *Miscast* (at the National Gallery, Cape Town in 1996) is an excellent example.[17] The underlying principle of *Miscast* was

that knowledge is powerfully embedded in the visual . . . the drive by science to describe, measure, record, and dissect Khoisan bodies in the nineteenth century found expression in diagrammatic drawings, anthropometric photographs, casts and collections of body parts. The image conjured up by the term "Bushman" is generally not one which is contextualized by a specific history, or by heroic acts. . . . The image is one of physical type or specimen, defined under the rubric of science and of physical anthropology, and then rendered immutable through photography, museum exhibits, popular films, advertisements.[18]

Skotnes's own artistic homage to the Bushman are her Bone Books, huge skeletal horses she polishes to the consistency of vellum, then covers in a skin of writing in part from extinct Khoisan languages whose traces can be found only in the dictionary and grammar of the Lucy Lloyd and Wilhelm Bleek Archives in the Cape.

These books of iteration (as she titles her installations of them) illuminate bone and script in haunting diaphanousness, religious in incantation.[19] The spine of the horse is the book's vertebrae, its rib cage the pages. The writing also multiplies quotations from the diverse parts of

FIGURE 4.5. Pippa Skotnes, *Book of Iterations*. Institute for the Humanities, University of Michigan exhibition, December 2009. Photo by Peter Smith.

European civilization; these horses speak the book of history where it can be read that all Europe contributed to the extinction of the Bushman, his language and culture, his naturalization. Naturalization indeed, for the history of the museum has placed Bushmen within the book of nature rather than civilization.

The book of nature has its remnants in the dioramas and vitrines of colonial and apartheid days. Then what to do with these old representations in a new museum? A similar question to that asked of old monuments and eloquently raised in an exchange Skotnes had with then State President Thabo Mbeki over a Bushman diorama which had been removed from exhibition at the National Museum, Cape Town into storage in 2001.

In that diorama a noble male "specimen" of the Bushman "species" stands arrow ready in a well-wrought encomium of grassland, tree, and burnished sun. The figure is romanticized; the mise-en-scène Adam in paradise. Soon after the diorama was put in storage, she got a call to show it to

MONUMENT, RUIN, AND REDRESS

FIGURE 4.6. *Bushman Diorama*, Iziko Museums, Cape Town. Photo by Pippa Skotnes.

Thabo Mbeki, who challenged her to think through the framing terms required for its reinstallation in the museum. "Well I said," Skotnes writes:

the museum would need to find a way to interrupt the narrative. And how would they do that, asked Mbeki. They might, I suggested, find a way to recurate the diorama, inserting into it something that would refer to the centuries of Khoisan resistance to Dutch settlement, something that might indicate that there was another more historical narrative intersecting with the one of the African Eden. Perhaps a rifle resting against the tree (mistaken at first by the viewer for bows or digging sticks), spent cartridges amongst the stone tools, I privately thought. What do you think might serve that purpose I asked President Mbeki. He thought for only a moment. How about a crumpled figure of a dead Boer, shot with a poisoned arrow?[20]

Shot with a poisoned arrow, that is definitely one way to change the narrative. Another would be to choose the Budapest model and relocate it to Saul Kersner's Lost City where it could preside for the tourist trade below the great elephant and around the corner from Stanley and Livingstone.

111

As of the time of writing this, in July 2010, the diorama remains without poisoned arrow, or other alteration, and in storage.

The museum is one thing, the history of science another. Critical to the castigation of the Bushman were (it is well known) the medical sciences of the nineteenth century, whose conceptual "innovations" were to articulate human profiling by assigning moral and cultural diseases on the basis of relevant body types.[21] Penny Siopis has made the medical castigation of the Khoisan body the subject of her painting of 1988, *Dora and the Other Woman*. The other woman is the tragic Saartjie Baartman, the "Hottentot" brought to Europe in the nineteenth century, stripped naked, and put on show before medical speculum in the form of cultural spectacle.[22] Medical control over Baartman's body caused her premature death. Such humiliation through the deployment of technologies of power would have its legacy in the apartheid state when it tested humans for their "colored status" by examining the hairs on their genitalia for signs of "kinkiness" or their noses for signs of those "grosser features of skin and bone." No wonder then that this painting was created as apartheid was crumbling in the late 1980s. Tragically, the culpability of medicine in the history of racial humiliation is part of what prepared Thabo Mbeki's wrongheaded antagonism against late-twentieth-century biomedical claims about the HIV virus (see the next chapter), his ranting against the biomedical establishment.

It was against this culture of the elite Eurocentric South African museum that the popular front ideal of bringing culture to the people on the streets took shape. Since popular culture already happened on street corner, in field, town square, on township walls, and in township centers, popular front thinking was about politicizing art where it was already happening for most people. As Steven Sack put it:

The only way in which art could regain its social purpose was by freeing itself of the museums, galleries and schools and moving into the streets.... The billboards, hoardings and neon-lights, controlled by government and big business, have in the past decade [he is writing in 1989] become an important arena for alternative artistic activity. This has often only been possible through artists and street activists working outside of the law and challenging the control of communications and visual media. Repetitive one-look images, images that sell products and insinuate themselves into the social customs and cultural values of people, have been defaced and replaced by graffiti, murals and

FIGURE 4.7. Penny Siopis, *Dora and the Other Woman*. Photo and rights courtesy of Penny Siopis.

innovative artworks that have attempted to offer an alternative visual culture, providing another view of reality.[23]

Following the work of Tom Lodge, Sack discusses the creation of various "People's Parks" in black townships, parks which dedicated themselves to an art not of individual makers but group expressions, instead, of popular spirit, designed from the bric-a-brac around in such townships, and about the United Democratic Front's ideal of local administrative government based in "popular democracy": "The images produced in the streets of these townships were of a diverse nature. In most cases the artists were untaught. There was extensive use of simple patterning; dots and stripes were painted onto rocks, tyres and tree stumps. When an occasional bench was found it, too, was decorated. Old motor-cars, or parts of cars, were painted and assembled into sculptures. Old signs were painted over and given new slogans. Whenever walls bounded onto public spaces they were painted with more ambitious images of animals or people."[24]

Post-apartheid South Africa freed popular front culture of its political correctness: its ideology that art must be a weapon in the struggle, foregrounding message over style, content over medium, comprehensibility over innovation, solidarity over diversity. This was in many ways due to an intervention by African National Congress freedom fighter Albie Sachs, whose influential pamphlet "preparing ourselves for freedom," written in preparation for post-apartheid state cultural policy in 1987, argued that art must no longer be thought a weapon in the struggle but rather a unique way of liberating the human imagination and foregrounding cultural diversity in the new South Africa.[25] Sachs's emphasis on the democratic/participatory power of cultural diversity and celebratory cross-pollination between traditions is in effect an image of heritage retrieved from the apartheid game of biopower and mobilized for democracy. Where the apartheid state actively cultivated separate and unequal heritages as part of the larger project of apartness, the Sachs image is of a vast toyi-toyi dance in which traditions are freed to become spontaneous at this precipitous, utopian moment of change. This spontaneous collision of traditions in a state of excited innovation is central to the theme of the Constitutional Court of South Africa, which Sachs shepherded when appointed to the Constitutional Court judge at the moment of its post-apartheid inauguration. In the building Sachs guided into being, post-apartheid themes of participation, diversity, and the free play of the imagination are paramount. And also memory: memory of past prisons, forms of imprisonment, injustice, control.

The closest thing to a national monument created in praise of political transition was the Constitutional Court. It is the clearest instance of the national narrative that guided the moment of transition, the narrative of redress, dignity, and diverse participation. Designed by OMM Architects and opened in 2005, the court combines the poetics of memory and redress, popular participation with the inauguration of a new constitutional regime for the country. Therefore it has a national narrative for which it seeks to become the national icon. This masterpiece in the use of African materials (slatted wood), deference to African space, the celebration of African forms of life is emphatically not designed as a mere reenactment of old African or colonial prototypes, not an act of nostalgia for the simple African hut, Zulu kraal, or the grand temple in a new, urban guise. Rather it is an experiment in Africanization through invention: the invention of new architectural forms through close attention to climate, population, circulation, and site. The steps of the courthouse zigzag because African people accustomed to walking long distances tend to perambulate from side to side when going up and down hills to keep their footing sure and save their energy. Its roof is partly made of sticks, in homage to the way African dwellings filter the strong sun through similarly simple uses of materials. This could be called architectural deference to simple forms of building, and, yes, these could be called a people's heritage or they could be described otherwise as a way of addressing problems in space and light relying on popular experiences, since the slatted forms allow for filtration of strong light into soft, produce airiness and climate control, and so on. Are these popular experiences a heritage or not? Graciously, the court seems content to have it either way. It is not actively seeking to reassign the word *heritage* to popular ways of doing things, but neither is it refraining from doing so.

Critical to this court is its desire to diffuse the relationship between heritage, monument, and national narrative, which was the colonial/apartheid prototype. The court's difficult yet profound aspiration is to stand as a national icon precisely by eschewing/diffusing this cultural logic. And to do so architecturally in a way that is in accord with the new Constitution's refusal of past legal hegemony.

An inaugural building must symbolize and speak to the function or "program" it has, and the function of this building is to be the physical place where justice is accessed by broad sectors of the population, where the precepts of the constitution are arbitrated for them. These ideals of access and of a justice speaking to and for the whole South African

FIGURE 4.8. OMM Architects, *Constitutional Court of South Africa*, 2005. Photographer unknown.

population are a decisive break with apartheid and colonial legal traditions. The break is similarly meant to extend to the legal epistemology of the old regime of constitutional interpretation. That regime of apartheid law was positivist, about sticking to the letter of the law, once that letter was made evident. The perfect instrument for shielding law from the morally repulsive system it was of, positivism removed interpretation from the fabric of human realities, turning it into an abstracted method. Positivism said: there is nothing the judge can do even if he dislikes specific legal statutes, the letter of the law is clear and the job of the judge is to grasp and apply it. In fact the letter of the law was less than always clear, and, when it was clear, it could be racially egregious. Moreover, *access* to the law was unequal along race and class lines (and also gender), enhancing the inequality of the legal instrument.

Beginning from a general concept of the dignity of the individual, the new Constitution of South Africa frames a panoply of rights which flow from that picture of dignity: civil and political rights, economic rights,

FIGURE 4.9. Lobby, Constitutional Court, OMM Architects. Photo courtesy of David Krut Publishing.

the right to housing, health care, and so on. A place is reserved for diversity through the mandate (impossible to maintain in practice) that education and media take place in all the eleven official languages of the country and through some allowance for what is called Customary Law, although custom is always trumped by individual rights when it comes into conflict with these. Article 39B prescribes a regime of legal interpretation which must take place in reference to the spirit of the constitution as a whole. This invitation to a regime of incessant reflection on the law as a whole, including its preamble, wherein rights are said to flow from a basic conception of the dignity of the human being, situates the Constitution within the changing and tenebrous world of culture and society, suggesting precedent should not be overriding but placed in relation to innovation when decisions are taken by judges. The walls, stairwells, ruins, art works, light, color, and dancing forms of the courthouse vibrate this vision of law and justice, which is about interpretation deferential to social diversity and circumstance and absolute access to the law on the part of every citizen. Everywhere public acknowledgment, imagination, and participation are encouraged in this user-friendly building. The letter of the statute gives way before the teeming flow of humanity. Thus does the law break with positivist heritage (although positivism remains in place more subtly than expected even in the new constitution).[26]

A constitution which breaks with positivist legal heritage is one requiring a house that breaks with its heritage symbols, the Palace of Justice or Inns of Court or whatever else. But the Constitutional Court building is more subtle than that. For it preserves legal heritage in another way, in the form of uneasy memory. Within the walls of the court are the ruins of the Old Fort Prison where many anti-apartheid activists were imprisoned without charges—including retired Constitutional Court judge Albie Sachs, who shepherded this architectural project. Indeed the lobby of the court is constructed around the former part of the prison where prisoners awaited trial (including Mahatma Gandhi). Thus in deference to apartheid, and before that the colonial heritage, a heritage of injustice stands within the walls of the new South African court as vanquished ruin, but also persistent historical memory. The thought is that judgment, justice require acknowledgment of this memory. The court openly retains the scar of its apartheid prison in the way Aldo Rossi spoke of fascist architecture in Italy as memory and heritage. Rossi also wishes to incorporate the wedding cake operatic monuments of Italian fascism into Italian modernist construction and cityscape, rendering the concept of heritage less exalted and more true to actual history.[27] By retaining old walls, the court transforms an old prison into a heritage. The gesture is heritage creating. It is also ruin creating, since the old prison, torn down, would not have become a ruin. This is the legacy of law, control, sovereignty, and biopower. Posed against these scarred walls, Sachs's filling of the court with an ebullient collision of art works can be thought of as a gesture of liberation-from. The counterpoint is between a permanent image of liberation and a permanent memory of control (prison). The didactic message is not only that judges should interpret the law in the light of a memory of injustice, but that those seeking access to the law should be similarly reminded.

The court and the art work in it are best, I think, construed as refusing to be tied down by master images of heritage. The constitution prescribes cross-pollination between human circumstance and legal judgment and in the name of a general picture of human dignity, which also means human diversity. This idealized concept of law is symbolized by the court's spontaneous, improvisational inclusion of all manner of diverse art and architectural forms and by its architectural resistance to profiling by reference to signature African buildings (the Zulu kraal, the West African mud city) or traditions (Ndebele painting). Heritage profiles do not rule, either in architecture or in interpretation. They are part of the conversation. The one heritage retained—in the form of ruined walls, is the Old Fort Prison. It is there as a haunting reminder. The acknowledgment of heritage is the acknowledgment of from whence one has come.

Albie Sachs has acquired for this court a diversity of amazing art objects from the southern African region, each livelier than the next. These are everywhere present throughout the building as if to solicit engagement, that is, participation from all present. The theme of the court is the openness of the law and the setting of justice in history and culture, which is an emblem of Article 39B of the Constitution (stating that all decisions of the court must be taken in light of the spirit of the Constitution as a whole). These art works spill across the space of the building like people.

The question is whether this court, with its iconic status, is a new kind of monument or old, and how heritage and monument align in its design and instinct. It is a prime example of state-generated construction and carries the aura of the new dispensation in every aspect. Can it be this and also demonumentalizing?

IV

For, if the court is a new kind of monument, it is written in a demonumentalizing script, celebrating authority based on open participation and constant innovation rather than hunkering down like a fortress of sovereignty and/or biopower. The South Africa of the 1990s was indeed such a demonumentalizing moment, a moment stressing redress and openness over proclamation and domination through stone. And, although inaugurated in 2005, the court followed suit on this moment. In fact, the period of the 1990s emphasized language (constitutions, testimony, words of remembrance) over granite.

South African intellectual and activist David Bunn described this turn as a "reluctance" regarding monuments:

We [in South Africa] have arrived at a transitional moment in the language of monuments. There are few grand plans for memorial buildings in post-Apartheid South Africa, and the dust of absurdity has begun to settle over some of the more venerable historical edifices. But for many, including the millions displaced from their homes under apartheid, and the relatives who died at the hands of the security police, there is a complete disjunction between personal suffering and public memory. Apartheid's worst torturers relied absolutely on the fact that it was possible to kill, maim and massacre without any record of their actions passing into the public domain.... When policemen like Gideon Niewoudt burnt the bodies of Siphiwe Mtimkulu and Topsy Madaka, wrapped the ash and bone fragments in rubbish bags and dumped them into the Fish River, they expected the waters to obliterate all traces of their victims.... Some months ago, the widows and children of the men murdered by Gideon Niewoudt finally learned, in confessions before the Truth and Reconciliation Commission, what became of those who were thought erased from the historical record. Some time after the hearing, a simple ceremony was held at the approximate site where the bone ash was thrown into the river. Those who had gathered to remember, tossed wreaths into the water and watched them carried away towards the sea.[28]

To appreciate this story of the widows of Mtimkulu and Madaka, one must understand that many southern African religions hold that the souls of the dead live in or near the bodies of the dead for a time, after which the souls gradually disperse. Many Africans expressed a desire simply to find the bodies of their loved ones when they gave testimony before the Truth and Reconciliation Commission. They wanted to be present to the souls of their dead loved ones, which they believed lingered near their remains. The ritual of casting wreaths into the river is one of making contact with the souls of the dead. It is also one of cleansing sorrow by enacting the gesture of relinquishment (mirroring the relinquishment of body which the souls will eventually undergo when they float away toward oblivion). Monuments in stone are utterly foreign to such gestures.

The 1990s favored script over monument, recitation over construction. The fifth volume of the Truth and Reconciliation Commission's 1998 report contains a complete list of victims of gross human rights violations whose names appeared in the commission's database as of August 30, 1998. Arranged in three columns, the list is nearly a hundred pages long. It is a factual compendium. For one crucial purpose of the commission was to gather evidence of atrocities in the name of the nation. It is also a memorial, not unlike the Vietnam memorial of Maya Lin in Washington, D.C. The Vietnam memorial is about the trauma of that war, not simply for the dead but for the veterans who came home to a country disgusted with them and slid into despondency and drug addiction. It is also a memorial for the nation, which has never been able to quite celebrate its narcissistic monumentality in the same way after Vietnam, in spite of the jingoism of the Iraq wars that followed. The reduction of the Vietnam Veterans Memorial to names and dates is right, for a name is nothing but a point of reference apart from a context, and here the context is trauma. By giving only names and dates, suffering remains powerful in its silence, its refusal to monumentalize according to utopian vision or nationalistic achievement. The list of the victims in the report is not cast in stone like the names in Maya Lin's memorial, but in the abstraction of the printed page. Nevertheless, when read as a memorial rather than a mere compilation of facts, and when read as a distillation of the powerful history of the commission, the list in the report takes on an aura akin to that of Lin's memorial. Those names are linked to the trauma of the past, are its living sign, its haunting absence. The book refuses monumentality.

The communal spirit in this litany of names is Tutu's spirit of reconciliation, eschewing excesses of power and their history of ruination. This is the essential spirit of the break with the past that is the inauguration of social transition in the South African moment of the 1990s.

There is something necessary about the refusal of monuments when the moment characterized by this kind of acknowledgment. Where the context is one of trauma, the appropriate form of acknowledgment is to say nothing, in particular to resist monumentalization. As in: there can be no poetry after Auschwitz (Adorno)—at least, not *immediately* after.

There is more to say than that about the general reluctance toward monuments in the early post-apartheid period. One would have to refer to a general tendency in the world to demonumentalize (from postcommunist Europe to America). One would have to refer to the fact that, by the end of the twentieth century monumentality has dramatically shifted to the skyscraper, mall, theme park where information circulates on computers in offices touching the sky. This shift breaks the link between monument and heritage, turning the monument into a neoliberal icon for the global marketplace and the deracinated subjects up in the air, circulating within it, achieving frequent flyer miles. It has shifted to the media where simulation of grandiloquent heritage is shaped into mega-entertainment (Las Vegas, Disneyworld, digital moviemaking). The neo-liberal monument is information-in-circulation, the medium of circulation, the signature skyscraper which serves as its corporate shell, signifying brand architect but also the very fact of the marketplace, which is the real monument. The lines between monument and circulation, space and time are therefore breaking down along with the link between monument and heritage. Put another way, monument and *event* are becoming merged. Plasticity of image has stolen power from eternal statues and buildings, privileging transient appearance over monumentality, circulation over the singularity. Even libraries, once the monument to the archive, are now becoming systems of virtual circulation and textual production. With these changes the terms of engagement around the monument are shifting, since there is no still point in the turning world (the monument thing) around which culture can dance, pray, ritualize, symbolize its past. We prefer the amber glow of the computer to the sunlit aura of the monument.

And so the Apartheid Museum located in Gold Reef City just to the south of Johannesburg is powerful like a prison. Built of concrete, it sorts those who enter into racial classifications, supplying them with relevant documents in an eerie opening hello. Discomfort is appropriately palpable. But this museum is also built of global circuitry, of the media palace in which the monumental nature of the anti-apartheid struggle is portrayed through the buzzing pixels of a web of floor to ceiling electrolight-projected images. The amber light of the computer-generated image is the gold standard of the twenty-first century, the neutral event-speak through which South African and other local realities may be profiled for an international set of users. We have seen that heritage language does this, turning local culture into the terms of a globally neutral language with easy comprehensibility, international profiling, and also marketability. It is the same for the currency of the new museum, which allows for direct recognition value from global tourists and consumers. Probably human rights language does the same within the international system of NGOs, human rights organizations and instruments, world courts, United Nations subcommittees and units, etc. Global profiling inevitably also means the neutralization of complexity, the denaturing of depth, a flattening of content. I think the apartheid museum is a monument to history, but also to neoliberalism.

Private industry has built this museum; not the South African state. As I noted in the introduction, by a bizarre act of Parliament any group that builds a new casino in the country must build an apartheid museum at the site. This passing of the monumentalizing work of heritage building onto private industry is the government's acknowledgment that it is too conflicted about the past to be able to mount a singular national heritage narrative or spatial form (monument, museum) in any monumentalizing way. The Department of Arts and Cultures can administer the Iziko Museums in the Cape province, but these are a diverse and fungible set of idiomatic museums without any singular narrative shape. No singular nationalizing vision of the recent past is at stake. The Truth and Reconciliation Commission seems to be the national/moral story that has gained global currency as the story of the South African nation, but this is perhaps because for forty years South Africa was global pariah in the eyes of the world, and the world loves the miraculous. This is not the story the African National Congress or the United Democratic Front would like to tell, and as soon as the story of the struggle begins to be told all unity of narration breaks down, with everyone vying for their angle on the narrative. This is a good thing, perhaps a great thing, because it means the past has become the occasion for acknowledging a multiplicity of stakeholders: which is democracy in action. Except that here democracy in action leads to stalemate: the absence of any state-driven narration of the past or even new history book for primary schools.

This stalemate in the production of heritage and monument on account of failure of state-driven consensus suggests the American model is more present than one thought. Privatize, privatize, privatize, then advertise, advertise, advertise. So the thinning of content in the buzz of the Apartheid Museum speak is perhaps a compromise formula for a conflicted, contentious nation.

It was partly in response to this fault line around the representation of the recent past that Thabo Mbeki launched the language of the African Renaissance in 1998 when he took up the state presidency. His vision of the African Renaissance short-circuits modern South African history, so difficult to recount, so fraught with controversy, by returning to an artificially constructed precolonial past, which becomes the material for official origin and myth. Mbeki's African Renaissance is filled with paeans to the great African monuments from the past at Timbuktu, Axum, in Zimbabwe, Aswan, praised in order to substantiate the claim that Africa's greatness resides in something both precolonial and monumental. I have written about this in my earlier book *Race and Reconciliation*.[29] Since monuments cannot be built by the South African state at this moment of distancing from the colonial/apartheid past, this moment of redress and transition, the monument morphs into another register: the script of language. In the 1990s what was monumental was the language of the African Renaissance, not the Freedom Park (which actively demonumentalizes). The monuments were artifacts of speech, Winston Churchill stuff, Frantz Fanon stuff. Mbeki's own discursive practice becomes the heritage-creating instrument. By celebrating a legacy of African monuments (and to exaggerated effect), Mbeki's words call these monuments back into existence, create them as monuments for the present. Hence Mbeki's top-heavy, somewhat stilted way of speaking (see the next chapter). The point of this postcolonial language is to overload words with significations of the monumental. In his words resides an Africa of the distant past where colonialism and apartheid do not yet figure, where black and indigenous Africa are the sources of virtue and value, where language itself becomes the new monument, and through it the future destiny of the continent may be inaugurated.

This monumentalization of language at a moment of transition compromised the aspiration of the African Renaissance to become the new national ideology, for it could not be expressed in architecture: monuments were eschewed. Transitional justice demanded the attitude and story of *demonumentalization as redress,* and demonumentalization is not sustainable as a national story. Indeed it compromised the African Renaissance by restricting its aspirations to words. Nothing could be built. The language of the African Renaissance was, we shall see, instead expressed in policy, and the state policy turned out to be nothing short of disastrous. But the aspiration to a new national story was not a peculiarity of Thabo Mbeki, it was a demand of the moment wherein transition turns into a more permanent vision of the state.

Thus was official culture in the 1990s *transitional*, a way of disempowering the concrete of the past and opening the future to participatory forms, a way of acknowledging controversy in the narration of the past, and, finally, a way of transposing monumentality to the register of official state language and keeping it there. Transitional justice is defined by mutual and contradictory aims which work in tandem but also against each other. It is the tension between these aims which defines the territory of destabilization, change, *transition*. Recent work on transitional justice argued that the kind of justice pertinent to a country's transition from dispensation of terror to democratic rule of law is distinctive (not the same as the kind of justice pertinent to stable democracies). Countries in transition have special needs. Among these are

1. the need to punish perpetrators from the past regime thereby strengthening the rule of law against forces of terror remaining in the society,
2. the need for the kind of social healing that comes from public punishment,
3. the need for the kind of social healing that comes not from punishment but instead from public images of reconciliation which allow citizens to reimagine themselves as at one with each other—this as a nation-building exercise,
4. the need for specific spectacles of transition, often in an international forum, which will build the moral capital of the new regime and garner support, and
5. the need to delicately appease those from the old regime, so that transition will not be derailed by a coup or other means,
6. the need for new, forward-looking ideologies like the African Renaissance,
7. the need to contain these so that they do not turn into the stuff of past authoritarian ideology,
8. the desire to set the terms of redress, openness, and participation as moral codes or regimes for the future,
9. the desire to do the opposite, to keep these terms datable, flexible, obsolescent.

These needs are not consistent: hence the *dilemma* of transition, the failure for transition to achieve unified national consciousness even if that consciousness is in some senses desired for nation building.[30]

There does remain the question whether the demonumentalizing stance central to transition, with its contradictory demands, was actually carried through in architectural practice or whether the buildings built at the time were far more monumental than the story told of them. And how one decides this question apart from a reading of the buildings, a sense of their aesthetics, a longer-term understanding of how they have settled into cultural practice and are now viewed. This question is therefore also historically datable: over time buildings have a way of turning into monuments or, alternately, turning from monument to ruin. I now want to return to the question of the Constitutional Court of South Africa and its theater of history. Is that court also a new kind of monument, or an old kind of monument, or something about which, perhaps, it is too simple either to say it is or is not a monument? Or is it a building instead changing the very terms of monumentality? Note that monument building has remained a globally active architectural endeavor—if in transformed/ neoliberal, branded form, through the signature building. Note also that the Constitutional Court is indeed a signature building, although perhaps not of the same kind as the neoliberal architect-profiled brand item. Compare it to Daniel Libeskind's Jewish Museum in Berlin, a museum uneasy with its status as museum, attaining visual coherence and meaning through its deconstructive reluctance, its refusal to monumentalize in the face of the ruined Jewish history of Europe (above all the Holocaust).

A monument to oppose monumentality perhaps, which aims for global iconic status through its technical virtuosity, thus playing to the market where it will be branded as a new architectural edifice in neoliberal times. The Jewish Museum absolutely resists the unity and dominating power of those older Berlin monuments whose resolutely closed and violent visions wrought trauma on their subjects (the Reichstag). Its snaking, compressed compositional form is almost an inscrutable sentential mark, a linguistic character repeated on its frozen, silvery zinc walls, an indecipherable script of a chapter from human life hardly comprehensible, a refusal of the resolute speech of the older monument.

I think the building's antimonumentalist stance is so taut with power as to erupt into a countermonument, which is reinforced in its scarified, unyielding walls and vivid virtuosity of design formula. And by countermonument I do not exactly mean what James Young means: a building posed to erase space so as to open up the consciousness of memory. It may have something of that, yes. But the building squarely, that is, topologically, aspires to be *monument* with the power to assert itself monumentally, in concrete and stone, even if one constituted in opposition to the pleasure of the beautiful, the grandeur of the sublime. The architecturally bold assertion is one hurled against monuments, as if nihilisti-

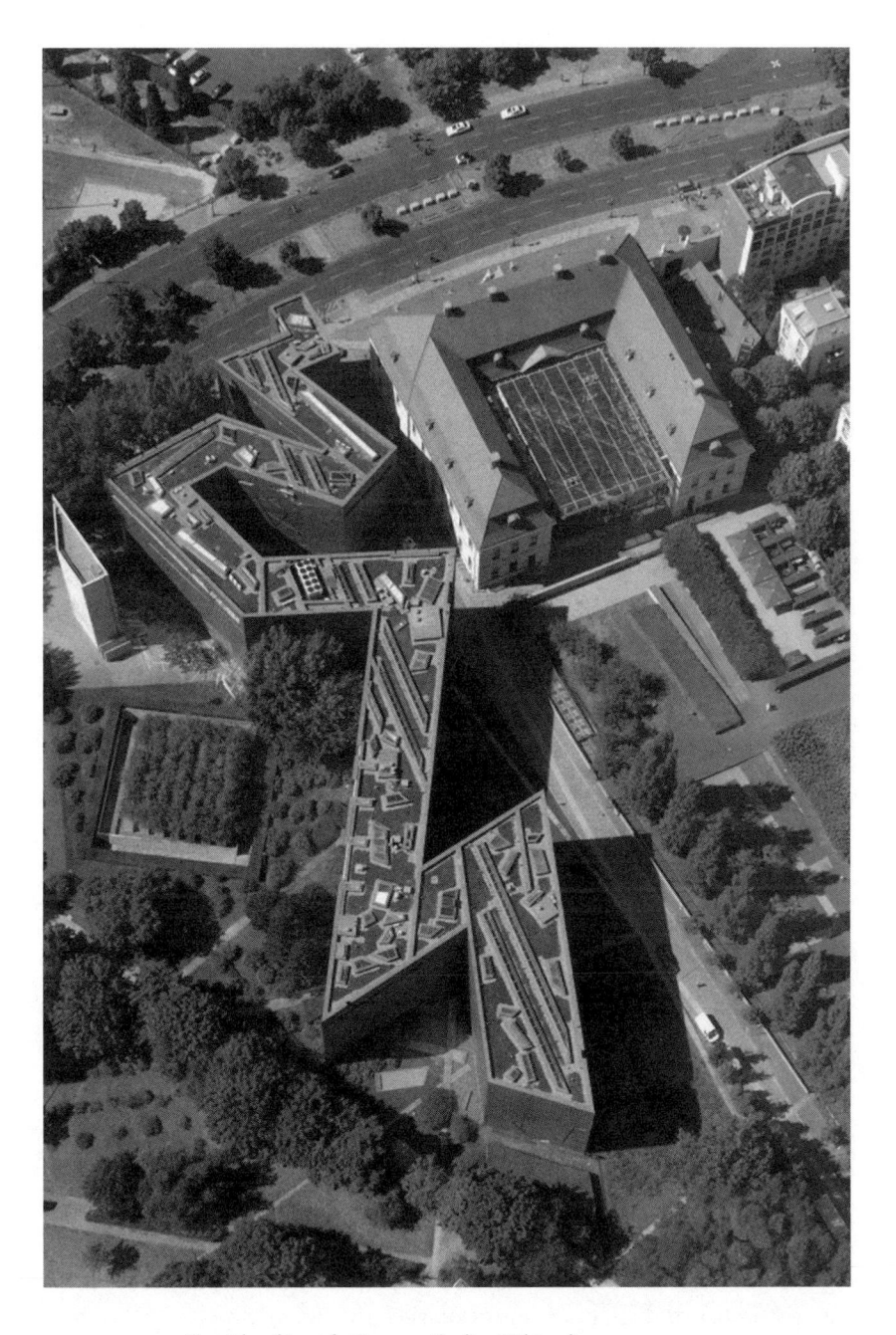

FIGURE 4.10. *Outside of Jewish Museum*, Berlin. Wikipedia.

FIGURE 4.11. *Spatial Void in the Jewish Museum.* Wikipedia.

cally, or as if to call attention to the nihilism deep in the monument game. Which this building is nevertheless completely buying into: this game of Frank Lloyd Wright grandiosity. The building is ambivalent, therefore, about its own exit strategy from this game.

Moreover, its monumentality is also that of a neoliberal brand item: the virtuoso *Libeskind building*, branding him, and using his celebrity to brand it. Perhaps the successor to the old monument with its identity politics is the neoliberal brand item which enters the marketplace with such astonishing bravura. In other words, perhaps the neoliberal successor to the old monument is not just the center of commerce (World Trade towers, Shanghai skyscraper), nor related circuits of technowizardry, but the virtuoso brand item. Neoliberalism has therefore morphed monumentality into a number of distinct arenas of market and circulation.

Do these define the Constitutional Court?

On the negative side: Although completed only in 2005, the Constitutional Court's decentralized part/whole structure does not have the fierce virtuosity of Libeskind's also decentralized building. It is not an implacable building posed against historical implacability. Rather the court has the quiet openness of the Freedom Park. It works against the old monumentalizing buildings of apartheid South Africa, which were designed to enforce unity by being closed circles or modernist bunkers in which each architectural part was subservient to the whole and spoke the message: we dissolve into you South Africa and through you to emerge initiated in the cenotaph, the Wagnerian ring of fire. The court is a beautiful, unruly set of semifragmented parts, parts which refuse such communalist subservience to a rigorously imposed design formula. Its use of materials and forms is more variegated than Libeskind's taut range of modernist materials. The court is moreover, more interactive than Libeskind's resolutely unyielding space. It opens to different kinds of circulation, from the art lover to the defendant. All are meant/made to feel at home in it. Libeskind's purpose (and he is right to do so) is rather to render the one who circulates through his building uncomfortable, to make him or her feel the alienation/anxiety of the Jew in Europe in its unyielding architectural disharmonies. Above all, the museumgoer must not be able to pass through this museum in disinterested/abstracted (mere) fascination. The building is meant to assault museological heritages of aesthetic contemplation, to threaten the museumgoer's sense of autonomy. To make the user that uncomfortable, the building has to exist as a closed bunker in its own right, a kind of black hole. That is at the core of its conception, a conception more about domination than user friendliness.

Libeskind's building is therefore more like a traditional monumental architectural form than the Constitutional Court is.

As to the matter of branding: because the Constitutional Court has neither architectural precedent nor sequel it resists becoming part of a branding formula (as yet). Its virtuosity is not raised into the circulatory power of a market brand. One is free to experience it as a singularity, an idiom, a celebration in and of civil society.

On the other side: the court is indeed an act of authority, of authorization, proclaiming the Constitution the law of the land, which is a kind of hegemony, finally, of law within civil society. And that is close to the spirit of the monument, where the buck stops in power. In the architectural bravura of its gesture, the court aims to become a national icon which proclaims that the Constitution is an overriding schema for the rule of law in civil society. Neither its architecture nor the Constitution the architecture embodies aims to be superseded. With both, the buck stops here. This, is after all, the Constitutional Court, the final arbiter of law. However, the *kind* of law celebrated in the texture of this building is improvisatory and fungible. It is a kind of law meant to constantly attune itself to the shifting contours of people's lives. The building is processive, incomplete, like the regime of judgment it aims to house. The court celebrates Article 39B, which prescribes that all judgments by the court must be taken in reference to the spirit of the Constitution as a whole. This is a regime of judgment that prescribes constant negotiation between law and the diverse swirl of cultural realities in order to produce a better culture. It asks us to step aside from the old formula of law as monumental, with her scales and palaces of justice. It activates a kind of law that is participatory, of the people and in deference to their changing circumstances. The ultimate power of the Constitution resolutely departs from the kind of old hegemonic power of law strictly, positivistically prescribed as the thing apart from the people that controls them. Every attempt is made to refuse the terms of biopower in the writing and architecture of this new law. The building cannot be called hegemonic in the way traditional buildings—or articles of law—have been.

This is why it is critical that the court is not designed to be a heritage building. It eschews self-profiling in terms of stereotypical images of the old African kraal, the European palace of justice, and other "heritage" architectural forms (these appear more readily in five-star game farm and urban mall architecture, which depend on heritage branding). The court shares with the Constitution an uneasy sense of the past, a past of Old Forts and their ruins. Its focus is on a future precisely *not* prescribed by the past but rather by templates of innovation. The Constitution is the platform for this building, this building for constitutional practice, as both shall evolve. The South African Constitution reserves an important place for linguistic diversity, cultural thriving, and even traditional law, but always overrides these where they conflict with deeper individual rights: civil and political, economic and health related, etc. Without deference to cultural diversity, law cannot stand in negotiation with people, cannot judge rightly. But neither can it defer to their moral and cultural heritages when they conflict with individual rights. And so the architectural design of the court invites rumination about monuments, heritage, and ruins, rather than asserting any "certainties." It invites heritages, but is also anxious about them, as law also does. It refuses the logical or grammatical connection between heritage (origin and destiny) and monument (the conduit for origin bespeaking destiny). As such, the building can neither reverberate monumentally nor profile heritage architectures. Perhaps one day it will become a monument, but that will be the day when law has become calcified, returned to stone, incapable of negotiation with social reality, and/or when the building turns into a brand item. Perhaps one day the new Constitution, and this building, will turn into old monuments, but this court is an inaugurating gesture, not a bunker against the past which selects origin and prescribes destiny. On that day the flexibility of the Constitution will become its undoing under a bad set of judges. Then the buck will really stop here, and the building will become a monument to the subversion of power.

In the new South Africa, the law has carried the burden of human rights excessively, and so this court, in idealizing a fabulous power of law as synonymous with "the people" and their dignity, is also making up a fable. The law cannot be the human rights instrument of first as well as last resort, carrying the ball in the absence of proper state policy and wide-scale change in class consciousness and practice. The court, in celebrating an excessive possibility for law, is utopian, which fits the moment of transition, but is also a fable.

V

At the moment of transition, a number of national narratives, from redress to transformation, linked democratic culture to the entrance of South Africa into the global marketplace. The African National Congress actively embraced neoliberalism, which anyway would have made its massive imprint of the society. Neoliberalism became fused with the idea of social development through a number of government acts and directives, above all GEAR, which would stimulate investment and through that alleviate joblessness and impoverishment. Demonumentalization was all well and good at the level of state directives and attitudes of redress, but, however morally profound, opened the field for the marketplace to build, build, build, monumentalize, monumentalize, monumentalize. And in a way that detached the monument from its former heritage role in articulating origin, identity, solidarity, instead turning the monument into an icon of neoliberal culture for its globally distributed producers and consumers. These subjects shared not heritage but hotels, frequent flyer miles, investment portfolios.

This is the second way in which a national narrative was contained or compromised: by the neoliberal turn. The market capitalized on heritage profiling in order to make new and inviting products suitable for locale. Game farms and malls are designed to profile heritage types, configuring the circular space of the kraal where cattle were prized into a salt-chlorinated swimming pool in the irregular shape of a waterhole, the tented camp where Stanley once met Livingstone into a Ralph Lauren interior. This celebration of an Africa somewhere in the mist and mountain between Kenya and Ceylon where the Club Med orange sun sets over five-star travelers in their private Jacuzzis, recovering from plastic surgery and other body work done on-site by world-class surgeons, allows for heritage profiling in the international style of a Mexico-Thai Relais hotel. Content revels in the specified heritage-speak of nostalgia magazines and old volumes of forgotten lore, while also being stylistically identical to what this same traveler may find on Phuket or Cancun. Even the heritage of pain management is neoliberal: in the apartheid museum, for which I read on August 2, 2002, the day I left South Africa after seven years at the University of Natal, Durban to return to the United States, an advertisement appeared in a prominent South African newspaper announcing: *The Apartheid Museum now does lunch.*[31] I wondered, sitting in the airport lounge, if I was back in America already, the answer being I could have been just about anywhere. The commodification of the past in South Africa began as early as 1996 with a television commercial widely broadcast during South Africa's bid to host the 2004 Olympic Games. That commercial featured a former prisoner from Robben Island recalling the importance of intramural games for prisoner morale during the terrible days of his imprisonment, while a camera lovingly lingers on the now empty site of the prison, the point being to sell the idea of having the games in Cape Town under the banner of South African liberation. The aura of that place of violent injustice becomes a national brand and plays two roles today: as memory of injustice and pit stop on the tourist map between winery and five-star hotel.

For a moment during the 2010 World Cup it looked as if the magnificent stadiums built across the country were new national monuments, but they have quickly turned fallow, become subdued in meaning.

Perhaps the new monuments are then the many five-star hotels that have been built for the World Cup? These, of course, break the link between the monument, identity politics, and power central to heritage, central to the Rhodes Memorial Monument, central to Soho the benefactor's monument. They market monumentality for a neoliberal subject without heritage interest (apart from the tourist brand) and with a lot of frequent flyer miles. Perhaps therefore the new state and society is a battleground in which distinctive kinds of monumentality pertaining to distinctive domains compete—or, at any rate, form a complex social pattern. Contemporary South African society is a battleground of monument versus monument, where the debate is between types of monumentality, each of which pertains to heritage in a distinctive way. On the one hand, the court, on the other, the hotel, with Robben Island the profound middle term between haunting remnant and advertising material.

Perhaps in neoliberal, globalized times the aspiration for a national narrative expressible in shared consciousness, and also in construction, architecture, city planning, and policy, is a thing past its sell-by date? Perhaps the national narrative is past its sell-by date also because diversity, built into the Constitution, in fact goes its own way, leads to a profusion of local heritages even when the aspiration to a national one is blocked? Perhaps there are many things working against the institution of a national narrative at this moment in the twenty-first century, including and especially the marketplace which moves in multiple directions, many contrary to the prospect of any singular narrative?

This is not to deny that there are unique issues pertinent to South Africa about national narration and heritage construction; these pertain to the difference between postsettler society narratives stressing redress from the violence of the colonial/apartheid settler project(s) and the African Renaissance with its decolonizing desire to recast heritage, and the future of Africa with it, by return to the distant precolonial past (the so-called magical time before the settler) and the first peoples who are thought to be its icon. It is to this quite different and equally live narrative cum state policy that I turn in the next chapter.

As for the connection between monument and ruin today, there are new roads leading from the airports to these centers of town, built and manicured for the remarkable occasion of corner kick and penalty goal, the Green Point Stadium: the FIFA World Cup. But, five kilometers away, things move more slowly if at all. There one finds shacks jerry-rigged precariously on sand, among the highest murder rates in the world, a people without running water or sewage in spite of government programs. Within the space of twenty kilometers monument disappears into ruination.

Chapter Five

Renaissance and Pandemic

I

Thabo Mbeki announces his project of an African Renaissance in 1996, two years before becoming state president. In the previous chapter I contextualized and motivated that heritage turn without discussing its shape or detail. Now is the time to do that.

The African Renaissance is a doctrine that preaches liberal growth through a return to, and reaffirmation of, the African past and related, shared African values. Mbeki declares South Africa at the helm of this historical surge, singing hymns of praise for the first generation of decolonizing heroes in whose shoes he would follow, monumentalizing Africa into a pan-African democratic alliance in pursuit of cultural reaffirmation across the continent and neoliberal gain. Mbeki is fierce in his criticism of economic inequality in South Africa, no Truth and Reconciliation Commission would fix that. But an African Renaissance of democratization, development, and the overcoming of racism would. This fierce critique of neocolonialism and racism in his country is balanced by the mythic language of new beginnings. Everything that Africa can become was already contained in the glories of its past, Mbeki preaches. It is a matter of return to these glories, affirmation of them, and creative use of them in paving the way for the new future: "So let me begin. I am an African."[1] He says this addressing the South African Parliament on the occasion of its adoption of the new Constitution in May 1996. And he goes on to incant: "I am formed of the migrants who left Europe to find a new home on our native land.... In my veins courses the blood of the Cape Malay slaves who came from the east.... I am the grandchild of the men and women that Hintsa and Sekhukune led.... My mind and my knowledge of myself is formed by the victories we earned from Isandhlwana to Khartoum."[2]

Incant is the right word; this is the poetry of political exultation. Mbeki's language is constitutive, befitting the moment at which a Constitution comes into being. In its scope and grandeur, Mbeki's speech recalls the writing in English of Winston Bulldog Churchill and John Kennedy.[3] It is an exile intellectual's attempt to reinsert himself into the mouth of river Africa, an exile's mythology of the river Jordan from which he was so long apart. Through a more direct lineage, it recalls the poetry of Léopold Senghor (written in French), with its praise of Africanness, and the writing of W. E. B. DuBois. Mbeki's is a language of authorization, of identification, of confirmation. His is a language which brings into being and confirms the being of a *people*, an African people, authorizing truth through heritage: "All of this I know and know to be true because I am an African! Because of that, I am also able to state this fundamental truth: that I am born of a people who are heroes and heroines. I am born of a people who would not tolerate oppression. I am of a nation that would not allow that."[4]

The place of Africa is to legitimate, prove, all that follows. *I think* (as an African), *therefore I am* (speaking the truth). *I am an African* is the Cartesian certainty from which all other truths follow. His personhood takes its dignity and power from the larger maternal and/or paternal ambience of Africa. And it is to Africa that this moment of constitutional celebration belongs in 1996 since Africa is its source, origin of its truth.

I have written about Mbeki's African Renaissance in an earlier book, *Race and Reconciliation*, using ample quotation from Mbeki's speeches, and will take the liberty of condensing some of that longer discussion here.[5] Mbeki's place of renaissance is an Africa which generously includes white settlers; Mbeki is reaching out to include the very populations whose politics enslaved his father, his Xhosa brothers and sisters. In many parts of his speeches his is an Africa that is admirable in principled diversity. The blood of the Cape Malay slave, Indian trader, Muslim cleric from Khartoum all course through his ample veins. Given that heritage functioned in the articulation of apartheid biopower, actively producing separated and profoundly unequal subjects divided by "race," this rescue of diversity into a shared project of African destiny is rehabilitating.

Mbeki's language also has, however, the tendency to gravitate toward an ideology of the indigenous, proclaiming (without quite saying it) that Africa is to be valued because of its unique and special Afro-indigeneity, because of that which the colonizer never touched during his long and brutal domination. This is the side of the language responding to the exclusion of African cultures from the apartheid, and before that colonial, origin of the nation. In response to this exclusion, the precolonial is fiercely proposed as the deepest and truest of origins, hence the deepest directive of future destiny, the future of country and continent.

It is this affirmation of the indigenous, which makes Mbeki's African Renaissance a language of decolonization (Fanon), a language of rehabilitation through assertion of essence. For what is being celebrated is a self felt to be long buried under colonialism and now again alive all over the continent, through Mbeki's very words, as if his words were an incantation calling it back to life.

Insofar as heritage is that instrument which aims to erase the settler from the truest origin of Africa, a clear and pristine distinction must be drawn between colonial/apartheid heritage and precolonial practices. Only then can the African Renaissance play a corrective role, returning origin and destiny to African values separated from, and truer than, anything the settler has offered. The category of the indigenous is called upon to carry a great deal of weight in this project because it is formulated to exclude the settler in the clearest possible way. Equally prominent, we have seen from the previous chapter, are the monuments datable to before the settler which confers upon them the authority of precolonial fact. Mbeki stresses the importance of monuments at Axum, in Senegal, and so on, referring to monuments which dwarf those of Cape to Cairo and Pretoria to Valhalla. In this war of monument versus monument, heritage is a battle he means to win (having already won the battle for democracy and state government). Against the repression of black African history so central to the practice of colonial/apartheid monument building, Mbeki mounts an arsenal of putative past monuments contained in his *words*. At this moment of South African transition where the state wishes now to claim the power of symbols but cannot build monumentally, discursive practice becomes the vehicle. His discursive practice is itself the heritage-creating instrument heavy with the rich weight of monuments signified within its terms (see the previous chapter). Hence the linguistic style: monumental, Shakespearean, words drenched in glory, seeking a hundred flowers of indigeneity, encompassing a Vatican of African unities, bespeaking the Medici, the great decolonizing leaders. Also important is Timbuktu, which Mbeki praises as a complete world of buildings, books, libraries, values, built independently of the colonizer, therefore purely "African" in its exemplary status as civilized. The message is: we have done it before, we can be great again.

And so Mbeki has two projects of rehabilitation. The first is a rehabilitation of diversity from the apartheid position of separated and unequal, allowing diverse peoples the status of equal and integrated heritages, all with entry into the destiny of the continent. The second is the rehabilitation of African cultures from their exclusion in the origin/destiny of the nation by apartheid logic by pinpointing pristine versions of precolonial values as the truest, deepest origin of country and continent.

There is more. For Mbeki's language of African Renaissance has a neoliberal agenda, proposing an African future of democratization and economic growth, of continent-wide empowerment, which will make Africa the kind of player in the world economic stage that Asia is. This is the 1990s, and Mbeki's prophecy of an Africa filled with efficient, productive, stable, globally trustworthy political democracies in which world capital will want to invest is a vision of entrance and enmeshment with the world's economic stage, not of distinction and differentiation from it. Here is the double meaning of the Comaroff's keyword: empowerment. Empowerment is rehabilitation through a return to specifically black decolonizing identity politics, a return to "ethnic" heritage writ large. And empowerment is the corporate, neoliberal adventure that these Africanist best practices will make possible. The retrieval of authentically Africanist culture is meant to be what drives Africa's entrance on the world stage, its neoliberal empowerment. But neoliberal gain is also meant to flow from his other image of Africa, the image of an Africa dynamic in its hybridized diversity. And these two images of Africa's destiny do not exactly mesh. His writing slides between them. Sometimes Mbeki writes as if there are in Africa ancient traditions of cooperation, work, community, justice, equality, indigenous knowledge, efficiency which should be the unique or primary values that undergird Africa's corporate adventure. Other times it is clear he believes African culture is ineluctably hybridized and diverse, a concatenation of San, Zulu, Indian trader, Muslim cleric, Catholic missionary, colonial immigrant, traditional and colonial forms of law, social organization, religion, and missionary zeal, and that this what makes it unique, vibrant, and capable of driving Africa's entrance onto the global stage. These ambiguities around African heritage abound. And they have to, since Mbeki's language is meant both to rehabilitate a specifically African identity (by posing heritage against the colonial/apartheid forms of it), while also acknowledging and legitimating contemporary African diversity.

Equally critical to Mbeki's purpose in reanimating the language of the African Renaissance is placing himself in the tradition of Léopold Senghor, first president of Senegal and poet of a singular African soul in the larger traditions of Negritude. The African Renaissance is itself an intellectual artifact of that history. By resuscitating the African Renaissance model, Mbeki stakes his place in its heritage, thus emphasizing that it *is* a heritage, part of Africa's resources and central to its project of decolonization. His speeches simultaneously *call into being* that heritage and define *his central place in it*. This is the only way he can begin to fill his predecessor Mandela's shoes: by speaking the language of Senghor, Mathew Arnold, and Winston Churchill, placing himself in the position of Kwame Nkrumah, Jomo Kenyatta, and Julius Nyerere, who he symbolically wished to claim as fathers, members of his clan, patrimony.

This is a national, a continental, a global narrative Mbeki wishes to declare and interpolate into South Africa. It is meant to guide the destiny of the nation.

And so Mbeki's rhetoric of renaissance is both late twentieth century, about global economy, and also mid nineteenth century, about mythologizing a singular heritage that is the origin and endpoint of all African culture. This is what makes it live action heritage.

II

I have said in the previous chapter that the words spoken by Mbeki are themselves the monumentalizing agency: this at a moment of transition when the country has also assumed a demonumentalizing stance, precluding Mbeki from building new monuments to this renaissance, the palazzi and churches and city squares of the Italian *rinascimento*. I have also said the renaissance is interpolated into South African nation building in the form of policy. How the African Renaissance is recruited to the purpose of

Mbeki's HIV/AIDS denialism is the story I wish to tell here. It involves the use and abuse of heritage.

Here is the context: by the years 1998–99 the country could no longer exist in denial of the fact that it had been wracked by HIV/AIDS. The province of Kwa-Zulu Natal in which I lived was by that time 39 percent HIV positive, indeed it was the AIDS epicenter. The rate of infection there was between 12 and 20 percent, depending on measurement. The first deaths were beginning to happen on a mass scale since the gestation period before HIV infection manifests as full-blown AIDS is shorter in Africa than for the American strains of the virus. The vast irony was that infection happened on a mass scale only at the end of, and as a result of the end of, apartheid. We go back to 1992 and this time, instead of following the CODESA talks between Nelson Mandela and F. W. De Klerk, we follow the trucking routes between a South Africa now, at the end of apartheid, opened to its neighbor states, and we follow the virus spread down from Mozambique, Zimbabwe, and Botswana into South Africa. We also watch as soldiers return to their South African homes from ANC training camps in neighboring states, bringing with them goods, love, ideas, and, sometimes, the disease.[6] Obsessed with the moment of transition—the writing of the interim Constitution of 1994, the inauguration of the first elections from the head-splitting violence which led up to them, the bloodletting and massive trauma of the Truth and Reconciliation Commission, the writing and completion of the final Constitution, the Mandela years, Rainbow Nation, moment of miraculous excitement, negotiation of new stance with business, economy, development—South Africa does not notice. It fails to notice that disease is spreading and spreading at an alarming rate. Those who are early to the pandemic (economist Alan Whiteside) are shouted down or ignored. Few are prepared; few wish to face a fire out of control, a conflagration of fatal intensity. An entire nation is taken by surprise and horror.

To see the origin of this "perfect storm" of disease, one must look further back in history, to the Land Act of 1913, which disestablished 70 percent of Africans from ownership of (their) lands and sent the men reeling into the cities as the cheap labor to mine, dig trenches, build roads, construct buildings for the then newly modern colony. One must revisit the single-sex hostel, the product of the mining company and its worker villages, codified as lifestyle by apartheid state pass laws preventing men from returning from these worker hostels to their families (in rural areas) more than once or twice a year, even if they had the wherewithal, which mostly they did not.[7] One must remember that male separateness, and the sexual license it engendered, became routine, prostitution a way of life. Traditional male values of sexual proclivity and multiple partnership (and wives) were already powerful, especially in Zulu culture. Apartheid grotesquely exaggerated polygamy by removing men from their wives and preventing them from visiting except very occasionally. And one must think about the free and enthusiastic lust of soldiers returning to South Africa after many years in exile. And one must turn to the way poverty vitalizes disease through close dwelling, unsanitary conditions, lack of running water, sewage, etc., which is even today a horrifying mark of many townships, in spite of what are now major efforts by the government at building housing and infrastructure.

And so by 1998–99 HIV/AIDS has spread out of control, especially and almost exclusively in poor/black South Africa. In short, the brunt of the disease is on the backs of black Africans. The male black body, always a "site" as the theorists like to call it, of degradation under colonialism, viewed as a body of brute force, illiterate stupidity, and sexual malfeasance, color coded in every way, this body is in 1999, at its very moment of liberation from the apartheid yoke, at its first celebratory moment of freedom, a body that finds itself contaminated and source of contamination. But this time the contamination is not symbolic, it is not a matter of some *representation* projected onto the black body. It is a medical issue, a matter of virus. At the moment when the male black body was meant to emerge from the traumas of colonial stereotyping, actual realities have, it seems, rebranded it again as illegitimate, lethal. And the agent of this diagnosis, which Mbeki sees as rebranding, is *science itself*. This State President Thabo Mbeki could not take.

In an address to the University of Fort Hare (traditionally the top black university, the university which trained the African National Congress elites), Mbeki spoke of the nation's medical schools as places where black South Africans were "reminded of their role as germ carriers." He went on to say: "Thus does it happen that others who consider themselves to be our leaders take to the streets carrying their placards, to demand that because we are germ carriers, and human beings of a lower order that cannot subject its . . . passions to reason, we must perforce adopt strange opinions, to save a depraved and diseased people from perishing from self-inflicted disease."[8]

Mbeki asserts in the same speech: "Convinced that we are but natural-born, promiscuous carriers of germs, unique in the world, they proclaim that our continent is doomed to an inevitable mortal end because of our unconquerable devotion to the sin of lust."[9]

In his remarks Mbeki voices a hatred of the history of colonial stereotypes and seeks to downgrade the diagnosis of HIV/AIDS to more of same. By reducing science to the ongoing cultural agency of stereotyping, the virus falls away into a mere (neocolonial) representation. And so there must be no *scientific fact of the matter* about black (and other) Africans who have and are sexually transmitting this disease; it is all a matter of whose stereotype you are going to believe. Mbeki is defending the freedom of the black body to resist the global consensus of medical science which is blind-sighting Africans at their very moment of renaissance: this is Mbeki's last-ditch attempt to keep his new society from reverting back to the misery of colonial Africa in chains which the West has made its history.

The fury is, according to Mark Gevisser, compounded by Mbeki's probable knowledge (or at least response to rumor) that AIDS may have first reached South Africa not through trucking routes but through black ANC comrades returning from exile.[10] That the returning liberator should have brought back disease along with his brave heart and AK-47 would be a major blight for the African National Congress, both with respect to its self-image and its voter constituencies.

If there is no virus, merely an ongoing process of stereotyping, then what about the symptoms, the illness, the pain and suffering, the deaths? Here Mbeki turns to his program for economic development. The African strain of HIV expresses itself in distinctive symptoms (different from HIV in America), and this aids Mbeki in his formulation of the disease as a cluster of development-related problems, problems of malnutrition, TB, impoverishment. There is no virus, there is global inequality, and it is this which keeps the black African ill. Of course there is truth in what Mbeki decides, since HIV is deeply related to cycles of impoverishment, and, moreover, the medical establishment at that time, failing to grasp the enormity of the public health issue, was instead preoccupied with vaccines and the like. Moreover, Mbeki's criticisms of global pharmaceutical companies, which offer Africa snake oils and poisons for profit, also has some truth. But not for the pregnant women who, if given antiretroviral drugs, will have 50 percent less chance of passing on the disease to their babies. When impoverishment is posed against viral illness in a way that allows Mbeki to refuse the roll out of life-prolonging drugs to desperately ill people, including pregnant women, his postcolonial desire to free the black African from ongoing stereotyping (as diseased) becomes a human rights disaster for the black African.

III

The key to the Mbeki story is the refusal of scientific consensus as truth: his profiling of science as nothing more or less than cultural policy when it comes to HIV and AIDS, his stereotyping of science as a marketing formula wherein Big Pharma makes its millions by ripping off Africa in a neocolonialist gesture. The implications are vast, because those postmodernists in the philosophy of science who believe that the results of science cannot be justified on the basis of some rigorous procedure or other and who also believe that science is finally a matter of social practice—nothing more and nothing less—open the door to a Mbeki who agrees, saying: "You yourselves argued that science is just social convention, well, I'm sick of depending on the social conventions of my former colonizers, the Euro-American community. I want an *African* consensus about scientific truth which reflects our needs." There is a lot to be said for the postmodernist position that scientific truth has no ultimate justification beyond social practice. Given that, how do you refute an Mbeki? I mean, in terms of epistemology? By forcing the consensus of scientists down his throat? By pointing out that even African scientists (the Medical Research Council, researchers at major universities) formed a consensus in agreement with global medical findings? But he has come up with other scientists and physicians (including his ministers of health) who do *not* agree with the consensus position, scientists at respected universities like Berkeley. Mbeki will say, "Live and let live. You have your scientists, I have mine. This is my continent, don't force Western values onto it any longer. I'm sick and tired of you." Of course, when most South African scientists are in disagreement with him, his claim to speak in the name of the continent is undercut, but let's leave that point hanging.

Mbeki's hubris reflects the desire of a postcolonial country to refuse global knowledge systems—those of science—in the name of articulating its own social project—for developmental justice, which is a claim of sovereignty by the state over its own affairs taken to the nth degree. New nations bred out of massive historical lacerations and long periods of injustice often claim new identities through radical rejection of global norms, disdaining global norms as colonial subjugation even while simultaneously instituting them. Partha Chaterjee has written about this with respect to an early modern India caught between 1. the setting up of institutional structures (government, courts of law) and ideals of modern economic development modeled on Western modernity, while 2. asserting radical difference from the "West" through a state-proclaimed Hindu religious national core.[11]

Frantz Fanon said it many years ago when he spoke of the dialectical swing between slavish identification and excessive rejection new nations often exhibit. The philosopher Achille Mbembe speaks of a "stark choice" between two forms of empowerment and the endless frustration of trying to keep them in balance:

> To secure emancipation and recognition . . . required the production of an apologetic discourse based on rediscovery of what was supposed to be the essence, the distinctive genius, of the black "race." It also required the actualization of the possibilities of this genius and its power to give itself a form of reason in history. . . . This struggle and naiveté had arisen out of adversity, the shadow of ancient—at times poetic, at times terrifying—dreams, of blind alleys, of the distress of existence deprived of power, peace, and rest. Their imagination was working on the memory of an Africa, a vast, petrified song, deemed past and misunderstood. But, as a result of the tension inherent in the twin project of emancipation and assimilation, discussion of the possibility of an African modernity was reduced to an endless interrogation of the possibility, for the African subject, of achieving a balance between his/her total identification with "traditional" (in philosophies of authenticity) African life, and his/her merging with, and subsequent loss in, modernity (in the discourse of alienation).[12]

We might think of Mbeki's position as this: to give in to the scientists is to yet again lose one's identity and power before the colonizer, this time the colonizer with his scientific papers on HIV and AIDS and his pharmaceutical price tags around medicines. That the neocolonial framework of choices between Afro-centrism and modernity was being played out around *science* was something unique to the Mbeki moment, while the game plan (the framework of choices) was not. Only because scientific truth is being reduced in the Mbeki cabinet to *cultural policy* can that cabinet's response to HIV/AIDS become a matter of *cultural politics*. This allows the field of choices to remain within the colonial framework outlined by Mbembe (alienated modernity versus Afro-centric refusal and celebration). Only through this folding of science into cultural politics can *heritage* take on the central role in the fight around HIV and AIDS that Mbeki gives it. Only through this weird twist of history can Mbeki's African Renaissance become part of the arsenal in his war with "Western" scientific diagnosis.

But the African Renaissance is not a discourse that stands in opposition to Western science: for Mbeki was actively recruiting his own "dissident" scientists (all three or four of them from U.S. universities). The African Renaissance was both an attempt to oppose Afro-centrism to European modernity understood as colonizing, and it was an attempt to embrace global modernity on Afro-centric terms. By returning to indigenous Africanist values, one would find, it was believed and prophesied, the best route to empowering the African continent with economic development and democracy. And not only that, a return to Afro-centric roots would revitalize long subdued moral and cultural lessons and build a new society based in deep self-recognition. It should be pointed out that a focus on indigenous knowledge or practice has had wide resonance in the new South Africa and has stimulated a variety of archival projects, linguistic studies, projects about indigenous peoples, about rock art, culture and social organization as well as traditional forms of health practice. Intellectuals have of course been fascinated with the African past since Africa was "discovered" by Europe. What is new is the idea that the African past, now thought of as precolonial, should become a *learning* terrain, a place from which new ideas, morals, and stories can be extracted of importance for today's world. This fascination with the precolonial past as potential exemplar for the twenty-first century, and not simply place of remembrance, mourning, and memorialization, has currency in art, scholarship, and culture in the new South Africa. It is a heritage fascination not restricted to state ideology. The African Renaissance is, taken as a state policy, ideological to the core. But parts of it respond to wider postcolonial heritage constructions that seek to idealize and learn from the past in this way. Such heritage constructions are cultural drivers for the emergent postcolony in India (see chapter 2) and elsewhere. This is important, because it shows that Thabo Mbeki, however over the top, spins his web from ideas widely held within and outside South Africa at the moment of decolonization: ideas motivated by a desire to find and construct an exemplary past through which the society can achieve (idealized) self-recognition and take example. This is a general heritage formation.

The pride of place given in the African Renaissance to indigenous people and their practices was (and is) also part of a larger neoliberal project of research and acknowledgment at the service of significant capital gains. The category of the indigenous came to occupy a national research priority.[13] This research priority included research into indigenous plant life (looking for materials to invent vaccines and disease inhibiting agents), but also research into indigenous knowledge practices that could serve as prototypical alternatives to "Western biomedical practice."

The very *naming* is important for the African Renaissance: the research category is ideological. In a special government directive to the National Research Foundation in the year of its formation (2000) the government established what it called the new research funding category of "Indigenous Knowledge Systems." This categorical name already had currency at the World Bank and in intellectual property law. It was, in the first instance, a response to the fact that biomedical researchers were in the business of studying—then ripping off—traditional peoples by watching how they use medicinal plants, isolating active medicinal ingredients in the laboratory and patenting them with no financial gain or scientific recognition for those peoples. To prevent this, such peoples were first dignified as scientists themselves, and so dignified then taken as worthy *part owners* of whatever could be patented so that money could flow back to them. All well and good, and South Africa wished to capitalize on its many traditional medicines while also dignifying formerly downtrodden peoples (the Khoi, the San) as knowledge makers themselves.

The neoliberal Mbeki strongly believed in this project, one deeply associated with new and "first" nations. In their book *Ethnicity INC,* John and Jean Comaroff draw a distinction between two ways ethnic groups enter the marketplace. Relying on examples of first nation peoples in North America, their contrast is between "those First Peoples that began their corporate life by virtue of being shareholders in commercial enterprise enabled by their sovereign legal status, and . . . those that began their corporate life by virtue of the rendering into intellectual property of their vernacular signs, knowledge or practices."[14]

Mbeki's neoliberalist project of indigeneity was both. The African Renaissance asserted the collective sovereignty of "Africa" to claim corporate control over resources—gold, diamonds, bauxite, platinum, sugar, tea, coffee, and oil—and also medicinal plant life by virtue of land/national claims as well as indigenous practices. Nationalization of the mines (the claiming of state control over landed resource development) did not happen in South Africa, indeed it was a big sticking point of the Kempton Park negotiations that led to the interim Constitution of South Africa in 1994 that Mandela was willing to relinquish that African National Congress demand, and it almost led to the breakdown of negotiations. But it was high time indigenous knowledge be given its due; it was high time dispossessed indigenous peoples should gain payola in a joint venture with the South African government and industry from their special knowledge of earth and culture. Indigenous Knowledge Systems were in the National Research Council's agenda about claiming indigenous plant cultivation and use, as well as myths and rituals, as intellectual property worthy of capitalization in the marketplace.So now we come to the point where the African Renaissance is recruited to the arsenal of weapons Mbeki hurls at global medical diagnosis. It is where Afro-centric refusal of putatively colonizing medical claims and pharmaceutical price tags grafts onto the heritage claim that indigenous peoples represent the identity and dignity of Africans writ large and the corporate claim that their knowledge practices are what should prove paramount for the new Africa. Mbeki announces that the cure for HIV/AIDS must come from an *African* solution, meaning from the soil, values, creativity of Africa. And so Mbeki invokes *heritage* in addition to development as the terms for a cure for AIDS. South Africa's problem can only be solved by authentic African indigenous knowledge. I would bet that had a drug been extracted from an indigenous South African plant capable of doing what antiretroviral drugs do Mbeki would have heaped praise on it, since that would have been Africa curing itself. Just look how he adulated Virodene when two scientists from Pretoria announced this industrial waste product would cure AIDS. Suddenly he was tacitly ready to acknowledge HIV as a virus, AIDS as its effect, so long as it was South Africa at the helm of the solution rather than international Pharma.

And so the research category of Indigenous Knowledge Systems became at that time hitched to AIDS denialism. Traditional knowers were dignified as scientists (with their knowledge "systems"). And were presumed, *avant la lettre,* to be the *only authentic antidote* to Western science and its particular hegemonies. "Just wait," the research and policy message implied (without being clearly stated but rather everywhere hinted), "and you will find among these indigenous people a science capable of addressing this most African of diseases." By dignifying indigenous peoples as scientists before the fact, and African plants as ready and waiting to be used as African cures, the underlying myth of the African Renaissance linked soil to solution.

However, indigenous peoples and their knowledge heritages did not manage to produce an authentically African solution to the AIDS problem. So tacitly membership in the category of indigenous peoples got expanded to include scientists from Pretoria, medical researchers of all kinds, and scientists to enter its subtly expanding ranks. This was a chief point of the research category: to blur the distinction between genuinely indigenous (first nation) peoples and scientists wherever they might be working in South Africa, so long as they were working on something South African (soil, plants, whatever). You didn't have to be indigenous to work on Indigenous Knowledge Systems, all you had to do was work from South African soil toward South African solution. In doing this you qualified for membership, became indigenous. In short, membership in an indigenous community was subtly replaced by participation in the cause of indigeneity: the indigenous became a matter of how authentic you were.

If you participated in the African Renaissance you became a true African. If you fought it you were inauthentic and working against your own indigeneity. A personal example of mine speaks to this. In June of 2000, at the moment of the Durban World AIDS Conference, I wrote a piece with two coauthors, Jerry Coovadia, chief researcher for the Nevirapine antiretroviral trials and chief organizer of that AIDS conference, and Ahmed Bawa, theoretical physicist, university deputy vice chancellor and a major player in formulating educational policy for the new South Africa.[15] The piece was highly critical of the state's HIV policy and was published in the *Sunday Independent*.[16] The minister of health, Manto Tshabalala-Msimang, answered us in the same paper, with a voice widely assumed to have come from Mbeki. In her scathing response, the minister accused Coovadia and Bawa of betraying their own South African indigeneity by writing this article against the state president. That was the word she used: *indigeneity.* Her fury made us think we'd hit the government where it really lives. What we attacked in our article was the African Renaissance, insofar as it stressed indigeneity over international canons for the evaluation of science. To the government any attack on indigeneity was a betrayal of it and of oneself. Naturally, being an American white guy, I didn't count in this. But Coovadia had been a leader in the United Deocratic Front and Bawa had suffered in apartheid's jails and later been active in the African National Congress, so these people really did count for the new regime. But apparently their rights of indigeneity were being earned through their struggle credentials and also through their color, since neither is anything remotely close to the descendent of an indigenous person. Both are fourth-generation Muslim immigrants from the Indian subcontinent whose families came to southern Africa as traders. Struggle and color had earned them indigenous status, and now disloyalty meant losing it. You don't criticize the state if you are a member of the African National Congress, the minister was saying. If you do, you are no longer entitled to the name: indigenous. This is pure political correctness, betraying, I think, the Soviet training of the ANC, an abuse of heritage at a moment of decolonization.

The final act of this drama was staged in 2002 when Mbeki's minister of health declared that the best way to combat AIDS was to eat authentically African foods: beetroot, lemon, potato, and garlic: Heritage in the form of the food that is indigenous to African soil, and to African people, cures. One can only add that none of these foods, with the exception of certain kinds of beet, are indigenous to Africa at all.

And so the indigenous became a heritage hurled against the West, a "better than thou" mythic mix of soil and soul where South Africa was to seek solution. Such politicization of lineage is an old South African tradition. Being of English descent, an English settler, bearer of "Englishness" was a moral determinant justifying rule. For the radical Afrikaner, lineage was biblical, and the land of the Old Testament was the Transvaal with its ox wagon, Bible, and musket. "White people" were called "European," meaning of European descent and (therefore) character. Lineage was a program of exclusion. By a sad irony, Mbeki's ideology of indigeneity derives from the same racialist discourses of the nineteenth century that produced these former ideologies of white racism and rule: but in reversed form. The Mbeki government was adhering to the strictest traditions of South African as well as European colonial heritage by politicizing the indigenous as that specific biogenetic and cultural type from which Africa derives its content and character (to the downplaying of all others).

Today the politics of heritage are so controversial in South Africa that the state finds itself in a bind as to how to write history books, build museums to the political past, or even remake formerly European and colonial museums across the country (see the previous chapter). Thabo Mbeki's decade shows this stalemate around heritage, this ongoing controversy at the national level, is preferable to any project of lineage as renaissance. It is better to exist in openly acknowledged stalemate around the past than create closed fortresses of cauterized myth disguised as truth. It is better to stake heritage as an issue than issue heritage as a stake.

Perhaps it is a good thing that South Africa cannot achieve a singular, binding narrative/ideology, a single set of self-mirroring images and ideals, shared aspirations and stories. Perhaps it is a difficulty, the sign of political blockage and ongoing strife between groups of citizens. Certainly it is the sign of a country complex enough to be emerging from a settler society, emerging with an emphasis on transitional justice: redress, reconciliation, reparation in the light of that settler/colonial past. While also the sign of a country seeking empowerment alternately: through narratives that glorify the pristine/precolonial, the time before the settler, and the indigenous person who dwelled there then. Perhaps then South African peoples have emerged from their long history of inequality and strife with demands for power and myth too different to be held together by any single narrative.

In this chapter and the previous one I've addressed two narratives, both inadequate to the task of taking up the thread of this nation. The narrative of redress is in essence transitional: about transitional justice, the moment of *emergence-from*, the moment of reparation, restoration, reconciliation. Its constitutional vision (of a broad range of human rights adumbrated in the name of human dignity) sets a legal and moral template for the future, but, apart from the legal/moral template, this narrative lacks long-term vision. It is (to repeat) in essence transitional. This may be a good, but it has obsolescence built into it, for the story fades in power as the new state takes on a more stable or different (no longer immediately "transitional") form. This narrative of transitional justice therein has nothing to say about economy, little about development, less about ongoing strife and argument. The narrative of an African Renaissance is by contrast destined to collapse because of its failure to address the problems and possibilities of a twenty-first century society: health, globalization, even democratization. Its images of the past and adulation of first peoples represent a fine antidote to colonial castigation but don't go far enough beyond building postcolonial self-esteem. Nor do the two narratives together happily combine: they differ on too many fundamentals (including heritage) for that. Both pretty much hit the wall before neoliberalism, which does not narrate but rather "speaks" in the currency of designer monumentality, heritage profiling for a global business/consumer culture, and corporate empowerment.

The result: a diversity of forms of heritage thinking and making (which is good), a failure of narrative center (which is less good but potentially livable), a set of heritage constructions representative of deeply divided experiences of a shared past, equally divided images of the way forward. A twenty-first-century condition, surely.

Chapter Six

Tocqueville on the Bridge to Nowhere

I

America is the first postcolonial nation, the one Ralph Waldo Emerson sacralized in a paean at the completion of the Battle Monument, April 19, 1836. Every New England schoolchild has (until recently) been taught to recite this poem:

> By the rude bridge that arched the flood,
> Their flag to April's breeze unfurled,
> Here once the embattled farmers stood,
> And fired the shot heard round the world.
>
> The foe long since in silence slept;
> Alike the conqueror silent sleeps;
> And Time the ruined bridge has swept
> Down the dark stream which seaward creeps.
>
> On this green bank, by this soft stream,
> We set to-day a votive stone;
> That memory may their deed redeem,
> When, like our sires, our sons are gone.
>
> Spirit, that made those heroes dare,
> To die, and leave their children free,

> Bid Time and Nature gently spare
> The shaft we raise to them and thee.

My brothers and I recited these verses like little tin soldiers as the Stars and Stripes were hoisted to the tip of the school flagpole. On Thanksgivings we gathered together to ask the Lord's blessing who hastened and chastened his will to make known. Each morning we assembled in the auditorium to recite the Lord's Prayer. This ritual of recitation confirmed story as fact, fact as myth. And so we grew up on a heritage of liberty and justice for all.

Emerson's poem, written fifty years into the American experiment, commemorates the revolutionary deed that begat it. The experimental nature of the American project runs deep in Emerson's thinking: it is a calling. Fifty years into the American independence, he believes this calling remains promissory. This he makes clear in an address to the graduating class of Harvard Divinity School in 1837. There are as yet no American scholars, Emerson proclaims, no thinkers or writers adequate to the newness land, settling, and sociability demand of culture, no thinkers who have as yet brought the American soul into being by discovering or inventing it. America wants epistemologies rethought, certainties unmade, risks in representation pronounced as resolutely as shots fired. These are yet to be. The alternative to discovery and invention is for Emerson rank imitation, the failure to become oneself, mere repetition of the European past, a parody of personhood, what scholars will later on call *Eurocentrism*. If America cannot inhabit the condition of experiment, Americans will remain pale shades of the continent, mere heirs to neocolonial dependency.

America's anxious waffling between the poles of Eurocentrism and (Emersonian) exceptionalism places America within the ambit of the postcolonial, which has the tendency to exhibit, Frantz Fanon told us, similar dialectical swings between imitation of and differentiation from the colonizer. Eurocentrism is the celebration of ongoing dependency on the (former) colonizer, whose values are taken to be the only ones conferring truth and distinction for a settler in search of superiority. Exceptionalism is, by contrast, faith in the settler's own unique destiny, which steers him toward his or her own drummer. The drummer is so unique that no European or other model will suffice for its playing. America can take no advice in matters of truth or policy, whether about what to wear or the kind of health care system to develop and maintain. That another has already done it means it cannot be for us. This resolve turns independence into an extreme worthy of its counterpart: dependency. Settler societies celebrate such an extreme in their myths of confrontation with the new, as in their clearing of the land and establishment of order and dominion. Their heritage making is hardly one of idealizing some precolonial past (contra India and to an extent South Africa), rather a violent and unsettling going it alone in the world of the untamed and wilderness. America's origin resides (Emerson tells us) in this its unsettled state, in its process of becoming through reckoning with its own extreme newness (difference). To claim dominion, whether over land or over one's own soul, demands a resolute will, courage, bravery, endurance, but also curiosity, practicality, openness to thought, imagination, genius: And so the panoply of icons: on the one hand, the iconic George Washington, on the other, Benjamin Franklin.

The vitality of the settler project resides in a double charting of immensities: immensity of battle and of wilderness and immensity of an as yet unarticulated soul or identity. The goal is settlement, colonization, the establishment of institutions articulating dominion (towns, states, provinces, finally suburbs), but the goal is also to find and invent identity, to make the soul live. This is how national character is minted. America, South Africa, and Israel belong in the same book of heritage, in spite of vast differences in people, society, and historical circumstance. The values they celebrate and gradually turn into heritage are those pertaining to survival, exploration, community, and conquest: values of ingenuity, thrift, bravery, inventiveness, resolve, the ability to withstand hardship, the will to stick together in adversity, trust in providence, pragmatism, a sense of adventure, practical imagination (the list is not exhaustive). Such societies also value *experiment*, which comes to form a heritage template. For the origin of the society and its destiny reside in dominion over peoples and place, exploration and cultivation of place, the raising up of a society which can reflect and embody its adventurous spirits, its settlers. These self-made men and women find their origin in themselves and their acts, find their destiny in their claim on place and self. Theirs is an origin staked on an endless process of *becoming*. This is Emerson's promissory note.

Over time the event of settling, endlessly repeated, becomes a bible in America, as elsewhere (in South Africa). The act of settling in all its bravery, valor, dignity, drama, and myth, with its cast of resolute pilgrims, renegade explorers, immigrant dreamers (and rootless nut jobs), justifies the reward. Plot and characters become magnified through repetition (in oral telling, school recitation, written book, and then, many years later, movie and media). Recitation turns event into bible, bible into a heritage exalted by "biblical roots" in ox wagon, wagon train, faith and will to battle. Dominion over tree, valley, mountain, stream, peoples therein is justified in virtue of this vast event, expanded through the retelling. We did it and so we are entitled to it. This is our inheritance (our heritable past, our heritage). None other may share that right because they were not central to our Great Trek into the Northwest territories, our exploration of the Mason-Dixon line, our claiming of Louisiana and defense of Texas, our wagon trains and "Indian" wars, not to mention our spiritual purifications (heritage values) that are a result of the process.

The claim that destiny is dominion over land and peoples, a destiny carved out against all odds and apart from the colonizer, brands settler societies with three faults. They are fiercely exceptionalist: refusing all received paths. Exploration is all. They are zenophobic, in a permanent state of mistrust of any and all powerful outsiders, having been established out of historical wrongs done to their group, having broken away from the colonial center through all manner of difficulty. Moreover they fear those whom they conquer, displace, obliterate, contain on their long march to dominion, the Palestinian people they remove from their homes, the Zulus whose land they take, the Lakota Sioux they put on the reservation. Zenophobia and exceptionalism lead directly to the third settler fault: communalism. Only by dint of community and character does the settler survive in the wilderness, vanquish on the field of battle. Community, character, and Bible are all the settler has to go on (that and superior weapons). Mistrusting all others, believing others incapable of understanding their aims and predicaments, the settler raises communalism into a principle of knowledge. Only those who are part of the community can adequately understand the unique character of their social dynamics, their social truths, and their relation to land and native peoples. *If you are one of us then you know we are right; if you are not then we don't trust you. You can only know us by living among us and becoming one of us.* This was the eleventh commandment of the National Party in South Africa and is the eleventh commandment of the right wing in Israel.

About America I shall say more, later. About South Africa I've already written. Very briefly (and inadequately) about Israel: the long scar of Judaic dispossession and then horrifying near annihilation led to the ratification of the state of Israel by the United Nations. This was largely an act of reparation. The urgency of the Jew's return was a long-recited dream, an oft-recited commandment. *If I forget thee oh Jerusalem may my right hand be cut off.* For two thousand years in the Diaspora the Jew recalled a heritage of ruins: the dispersal of the twelve tribes, the fall of the Second Temple under the Romans. Jews were never secure in Europe, seldom treated as proper citizens, always anxious, liable to threat. The entire history of the ghetto, from Venice to Krakow, the pogroms of Eastern Europe, the difficulty of even breaking into the middle class and remaining there forged a deep spirit of remembrance for the Holy Land of the distant past. Then the camps, the horror of near annihilation, this ongoing story that began with Lord Kitchener and his Boer War concentration "facilities." And, in the end, 1947: nowhere to go, nowhere to remain.

Right of return was authorized by the United Nations as reparation for the Holocaust, but the recitation of return had become part of the furniture of certain modern Jewish communities. Zionism is a modern doctrine that claimed nationality and in most instances right of return to the Holy Land on the basis of a heritage formulation in terms of lost, that is, endlessly remembered origin. If one way heritage arises in the nineteenth century is through the sense that modernity has gone wrong, leaving one in a state of degradation, nowhere was this sense more potent than in certain Jewish quarters of Europe, where persons tired of the endless struggle to attain and/or maintain European citizenship and rights turned the heritage of remembrance into a thesis about right of return. The Jewish people could only rest easy, live in peace, prosper politically and spiritually in the Holy Land, and this because of their unique alchemy of language, race, heritage, and land. Lost origin became through the heritage formula future destiny (by a similar alchemy of language, race, heritage, and land certain African Americans formulated the doctrine that they belonged back in Africa where he or she would no longer suffer the humiliation of slavery, the indignity of racism).

Had history been different they might have gotten along with local populations and found a more equitable way of settling in the context of those already settled, even if certain parts of Zionist doctrine extended unique right of return to Jews, it being their homeland uniquely. Local populations were not consulted or fiercely disagreed with this mandate and with the United States ratification, which in 1947 led to immediate war. At that point Palestinians were expelled from their homes and Israel became a state founded on its own history of dispossessing others, a situation that has haunted it ever since and finally and sadly led to the brutality of Israel's current occupation policies.

I am not in this book interested in pursuing a highly overpoliticized theory that Israel is an apartheid state. I do not believe this. For one thing there is no equivalent in Israel of that basic apartheid architectural instrument, the constructed Bantustan, or homeland, which became a way of disenfranchising South Africans of color from citizenship and rights by claiming they in fact were not South African, but belonged in their own dingy outposts (nations), except as controlled labor. What I do believe and am interested in here is that an irony of a quite different kind took shape in Israel, which is that the United Nations mandate in 1947 institutionalized the right of Israel to become a *settler society*, with the kind of heritage that pertains to that postcolonial type. The right to a Jewish state marked a historical adventure of charting, occupying, and building a new life in the new land.

The settler component to this Israeli heritage was similar to that accreted over time in settler America and also in South Africa. It celebrated values of toughness, thrift, ingenuity, bravery, identification with the land; it praised communalism (against the threat of the world), the planting of trees, the building of institutions (hospitals, universities, courts of law, museums of archeology to celebrate the ancient Judaic world). It forged society as a new social experiment (the kibbutz) and was in its own way *Emersonian*. Only later did the religious fundamentalist tip the balance toward the far right, although this (given the examples of America and South Africa) might have been expected (even if unpredictable). This is because of the settler origin in religious principle and puritan(ical) practice, which is then secularized as a nationalism, and because the event of settling so quickly has the tendency to turn, through recitation (especially in adversity), into its own kind of bible (a newer than New Testament). Over time, and like all other settler societies, Israel became, through its endless cycle of attack and counterattack, increasingly communalist, zenophobic, and wedded to exceptionalism. Many of the attacks on Israel were very real, and quite disastrous, unlike South Africa where during the apartheid period much of the attack was invented by the state to ensure its violent domination had a rationale. But the cycle of attack, dispossession, occupation, increasing zenophobia pertains to Israel in its own way, as it does to the history of America (and in its own way South Africa).

There is a particularly interesting commonality between Israel and America (less so to South Africa), which leads me to the center of this chapter. This has to do with the need to continue the experimental act of settling beyond its date of completion. The issue can be posed as a question. What happens to a settler society when the act of settling completes itself? How does it react? One might think the society waves the flag in a grand hurrah and settles back to live comfortably within its newly achieved dominion, enjoys the fruits of its new Zinfandel vineyards and its gleaming aerobic gyms. No doubt the settled society will remain anxious because liable to all manner of real and more often imagined threats (from illegal immigrant, terrorist et al.), threats that activate old settler resolve/aggression in the manner of a Texas Alamo and in fact serve to reunify the populace at moments of internal difficulty. But one might expect otherwise, contentment. This is not however what happens. For a settler society has grown up on its commitment to the experiment and on those cultural and moral bonds which have been spiritualized through that trial and tribulation, It has come to depend for its well-being upon ongoing confrontation with the new, the wilderness of place, the evolution of its people in accord with new territories conquered, on its commitment if not commandment to endure and prevail. The enormity of the act of settling is a social driver and heritage instrument, and there can be massive deflation at the moment when the event comes to an end (when the land is settled). A settler society can never quite cease to lay claim to new territory, real or imaginary, which it associates with its spiritual growth, moral capital, ongoing youth, and abundant futurity. America the first postcolonial nation and the oldest modern democracy, with a constitution in many ways past its sell-by date, must still perceive itself as young and in the lead. It has to ceaselessly botox itself into a wrinkle-free state, apply every youth-preserving formula known to pharmaceuticals so that it may regard itself in the mirror and consider itself still in infancy. This need to keep the experiment in settling permanently alive, and with it the Emersonian project of endless self-discovery and becoming, leads to a basic anxiety in settler society and heritage. The goal of the society has been to complete the process of settling, thereby establishing dominion, and yet as soon as this happens, the society runs out of steam, loses touch with its sense of its origin and destiny, shrinks in spirit. Settler societies (America above all) celebrate the *perpetual* call to experiment. Even if star wars cannot colonize space, or America Iraq, or Israel new parts of the West Bank, the heritage template demands continuation of the *consciousness of process* even when that process is complete or incapable of continuation. This is highly paradoxical. You have to keep the act of settling alive in some altered form even after the actual history of settling is complete or inactive. And in keeping the consciousness of settling alive you keep the aspiration for a historically completed process alive, even when it has already expired, reached its end point or finale. The spiritual aspiration of being young and in the middle of a vast experiment must remain compelling even when the work has already been done.

And so the settler society is constantly in search of a new script, a new domain, a new medium where the experience/consciousness, if not actual act of settling, can recur. One way in which the *process* of settling may be kept intact is by morphing it into new kinds of settling, by new kinds of people, more recent to the land, for example the great process of immigration to the United States that only bursts into full activity at the turn of the twentieth century (although it is very active throughout the nineteenth century). The immigrant becomes a new settler, right off the steerage into the wilds of the Lower East Side of New York or the deep freeze of upper Wisconsin. With the immigrant a new set of corresponding myths become possible, myths, that is, about *becoming*. And so the Walt Whitman overture to the great tracts of land and the great experiment is reborn in the minds of first-generation immigrants who compose bounteous symphonies and ballets about the canyons, cowboys, and great valleys they have never seen. This spirit is what sustained my grandmother through her traipsing, sewing, and swelling of bone during her own settler years in Salem, Massachusetts. *Give me your tired your poor / your huddled masses yearning to breathe free* (words by Emma Lazarus, from her sonnet "The New Colossus," engraved on the Statue of Liberty). My grandmother dreamed her children would be the inheritors of an America whose heritage was precisely the welcoming template for their becoming this. In the American experiment they too could arrive, becoming part of the great chain of big shots, happy to recite the national anthem at baseball games, eat popcorn and peanuts, and stake their forty acres and a mule in a designer's designing and a Green Acres farm. The movies were a part of it all: Mary Pickford, Greta Garbo, Gloria Swanson demonstrated to my grandmother an

America that was simple, innocent, staked against corruption and big banks, abundant with virtue, and cast this America in a halo. Through the films she and my forebears could recognize an America hovering above their lives, a beacon from the movies toward an ideal world. They fell in love with this world projected six feet above the ground, where the wall of the cinema theater ends and the screen rises like a white, open land to be filled with liquid light.

A second, related way the society keeps the aspiration to settle, and the related sense of experiment alive, is by finding ways for it to recur in the realm of culture, making culture the marker of society's fantasy of endless becoming. And so the movies came into being in 1891 through the invention of the Edison box, just at the moment when the settling of the American West was complete. By 1901 the first movie was released, *The Great Train Robbery*, a Western as it happens, live action with guns and ambush and the stealing of valuables. So the Western arose just at the moment when the West was "won," allowing the history of its winning to have a second life as story or myth in which lawlessness (the moment before statehood), native threat and damn fast six-shooting could live a second, more imaginative life than they ever did in the actual settling of the West the century before. Larger than life, larger than the Ponderosa or Monument Valley, film became the living monument to the act of settling, the wagon trains, Indian wars, planting of fields, six-gun battles between good and evil. Through film the fantasy that the settler process was happening all over again found its popular voice and vehicle. On the silver screen an American public too young to have actually settled the Wild West on the wagon trains could experience this story live and (as if) for the first time. On film it could only get better. Without this transposition from a history of wagon trains and "Indian wars" (now complete) to a culture (capable of endlessly repeating it on the silver screen), the American soul, Frederick Jackson Turner would have said, could only atrophy. Turner, the most celebrated American historian of the turn of the century, believed the promise of open land and the drama of its settling to be fundamental to American national integrity and bemoaned its end point, formulating a famous thesis that American dignity and value resided in that open land, which, once settled, could only lead to a decline in spirit and values, a diminished, less noble America. It was the vast expanse of land, envisioned as destiny, that generated high-mindedness and national spirit. It was the aspiration to *future* sovereignty over land that impelled everything great in America. Hence the need to recapitulate that moment before the land was actually colonized and tamed in order to keep the grandeur of American spiritual life alive, hence the import of the Western as a genre of myth.

The myth underlying the Western (and all the great Hollywood genres have their underlying myths) is this: settling is an act whose violence is redeemed by its mission of extending sovereignty and American settler values to what was otherwise bereft of them. Settler values embodied in settler characters suited for the big screen, like the big Ponderosa, that is, an exalted generation of actor personages including Gary Cooper walking nervous because alone to meet his enemies at high noon, John Wayne swooping the fleeing Debbie into his arms because he has bettered his own nature, Jimmy Stewart keeping his knees from buckling as he faces the crazed Liberty Valance because he holds the law high. These images replayed endlessly on-screen helped keep American heritage and destiny alive, America young in accord with the demand for an endless state of innovative big-styled becoming. These replays of American sovereignty over land and native peoples represented an unending public aspiration which could be grafted onto such things as the American participation in two world wars and a cold one thereafter.

And so the political and spiritual demands for an ongoing recurrence of the settler story gave rise to a specific genre of movies, also to immigrant ideals and other live action remaking of heritage terms.

This leads to the main theme of this chapter: A third way the consciousness or imagination of settling may be kept alive after the completion of the historical act is by formulating heritage as a driver of politics. Heritage then morphs through new media to profile candidates and parties, turning person into persona, message into star spangled sound bite. Grafted onto politics heritage serves to communalize the relevant part of the society. It energizes constituencies with the thought that something remains unsettled in the land, demanding the renegade, the scout, the good townsperson to take up arms—with zeal. And zeal is very close to aggression, if not zenophobia. At stake is the taking or defending of land, the issue of dominion. There is an enemy among the "us," some false or degraded spirit who requires exorcism, some recalcitrant piece of the country over whom the people must fight. Heritage can, in the extreme case, turn the candidate into a leader of a crusade (whether about health care, taxes, or "big government"). There is an enemy among the "us" who is denoted as apostate without anyone having to say so purely through the recruitment of heritage instruments. Heritage performs the ideological function of turning opposition into enemy, and enemy into a threat to the very character of the land. By speaking positively one can speak negatively. Heritage in such cases becomes a vehicle for the double-speak so prevalent in politics today. This it has shared with members of the apartheid state in South Africa, members of the Knesset in Israel, and others (America is not unique but one of a kind).

The goal of settler heritage transposed to politics will be to win by a landslide by elevating politics into a spiritual and aesthetic quest whose stakes are (subliminally) the land. That settler land that demands proper occupancy is called the White House.

II

The present state of American politics is indicative of exactly this third form of heritage rewriting. In American politics heritage, constructed from original settler experiences and values, allows tea parties to cast their politics in the frame of myth. The original tea party was a political statement against taxation without representation by Boston rebels who boarded ships and tossed tea into the ocean. The Tea Party today plays to the media, tossing taxation off the port side (to the right) and with whatever goes under the slogan of "big government" (health care, etc.). This is the gesture of settlers still profiling themselves in a theater of settler independence, of townspeople who choose community and communalism over rule by the outsider (meaning Washington). And so a piece of American history long recalled as heritage becomes the vehicle through which the disaffected, annoyed, independent, and just plain gaga may declare their self-sovereignty against whatever power appears to be preventing it (the Obama presidency).

The vehicle through which heritage is grafted onto contemporary politics is a media-driven one. The Tea Party plays to the likes of Fox TV, which provides it ample and sympathetic live action coverage. Without TV the Tea Party's whole way of commanding in-your-face attention would lose its power of sound bite. By the rude bridge that arched the flood, its candidates aim to stand on their various bridges and act rudely while the flag unfurls. Rudeness is a national virtue when harnessed to refusal, when harnessed to America's colonial heritage. Above these candidates stands Sarah Palin, on a bridge so high up in the stratosphere that it can only be a bridge to nowhere. She has recently been their mother lode. Less than two years after her defeat as celebrity vice presidential candidate she has become a political eminence (of a kind) capable of blessing and shepherding her flock in their tea-totaling activities. Only in a celebrity society could a person catapult from political obscurity to political *grandamerie* in two years' time. Usually it takes forty years in the Senate (Edward Kennedy, Tip O'Neal) to achieve this status of *éminence grise*. She has become a gray eminence while remaining brunette and young.

Against big government we have the heritage of the little people, of the wilderness, the rural area, the community, church, Sarah Palin the small town girl turned governor of a state, then champion of a movement, and with all the heritage values associated (courage, true grit, community spirit, strength against adversity). When this heritage is enlarged by the media, it carries a big stick. Naturally, Alaska is the perfect place for such heritage stories to be set, since Alaska is the last place in America that is still largely wilderness, and considered such in the public imagination, where America can be imagined from the perspective of the not yet settled or, rather, settled within endless wilderness, hence in some modified form: the experiment. You can see moose there and Russia from there. Alaska is where the rough and tumble are meant to go to work on the pipeline, Sarah Palin's husband Todd, for example, champion of the dogsled races through forest and across tundra as if majordomo explorer and scoutmaster. The movies feature significantly in this American popular imagination of Alaska, a movie legacy of wilderness and town, fiddler and preacher, homespun virtue and moral prophecy. Alaska, that last open landscape cum state of mind where you say no to big government, regulation, the welfare state, and yes to communal small town and wilderness spirit. With Palin, Alaska is the last untamed wilderness where the American soul may be found in pristine form and where the project of taking dominion (of settling) may still take shape. And so Alaska becomes a point of reference for American politics, a wide open space where the project of taking dominion can appear to be still alive. Thus it turns into a point of reference for the battle over Washington D.C.

The activation of heritage is by itself insufficient to motivate American politics. Given the centrality of the media in framing American persons and positions, star power or some other media-friendly celebrity form is required of candidates, hence the need in 2008 for John McCain (who totally lacked any form of it) to bring Sarah Palin on board as his running mate. She ran her own game of course (to his astonishment and malaise), eclipsing him (with positive and negative results) in just about every way, turning his candidacy into the straight man who plays opposite the TV star, while Obama became Lincoln the statuesque, the larger than life, with his deep portent of moral rationality and his let-freedom-ring speeches. This elective affinity on both sides was less their choices and more the amalgam of person, camera, media engineering, and public demand/delight. Both candidates became personae, a recipe for somewhat incoherent politics with a lot of pizzazz.

In order to get a grasp on how the media becomes the instrument for restaging heritage in American politics (the 2008 election being my example), there is one further concept I believe must be outlined first, signified by a phrase I've just used: the *density* of the media. By this I mean its capacity for selective projection, this media form onto this person, that onto another. There is a distinctive way in which persons constantly in the media eye become occasions for all manner of projection: for dense layers of projection. The public grafts aesthetic features from all manner of media onto its celebrities, stars, media personae, giving them visual and narrative density. The public's projective stance is partly caused by media programming (subliminal, sometimes manipulative), the kind of TV commercial designed to get you to see the new car as a meter added to your manhood, the linen bath towel as a lover purring to envelop you, the American financial adviser as your nearest and dearest friend who has dedicated the past twenty years to personally shepherding your money so that you can retire to Hawaii in the bungalow next to his, sharing pink martinis with his wife and children as azure sun sets over wine dark sea. These advertisements could only manipulate and persuade because the (American) public takes delight in passive suggestion, enjoys having its unconscious fired up, seeking voyeuristic pleasure without moving a muscle. But those media audiences are also active in what they bring to the media that barrages them daily. Part of the aesthetic pleasure in watching has to do with calling forth (subliminally or deliberately) everything that has already been watched and painting the present program with the palette of the past. This is a general point about aesthetic experience: the way a particular experience is deepened by audience recall. Marcel Proust made a racket out of it. In this case the ballpark of audience recall is a supersized one, including radio, newsprint, magazine, film, television, text message, blog, Internet chat session, and more. Drawing on selective media experiences from this ballpark, Americans become masters colorizing as they watch.

And not just Americans: The point was brought home to me while I was watching the Lady Diana funeral live on BBC sitting at my TV in Durban, South Africa, where I lived and worked in the 1990s. The Diana funeral was the second most watched television program in South African history, after the Diana wedding. Glued to my set, I was struck by how easily the BBC commentators elided Lady Diana and Grace Kelly.[1] Two princesses, each known through the mirror of the other, the one a film star turned princess of an ersatz European kingdom (Monaco) run on fast cars and gambling, the other a royal, with a classical beauty and screen presence perfectly suited to film star, which is the lens through which the public saw her. This is the point: the way the public transposed the aura of film star onto Diana's crown, although she'd acted in no film, and also turned her into TV soap opera queen, although she herself had appeared on television but once. Yes, her mug shot was there every day in tabloid and TV news program, yes, she lived the life of disposed queen then hunted celebrity, but it was the public's share to have grafted these media formats from film and TV onto her persona. The star icon cannot be what she is apart from this active projection of aesthetic and religious qualities onto her head. The aesthetics of film and television need to be closely studied to figure out how this spreading of qualities from point of origin through public imagination to a persona like Diana happens. She demands a new kind of aesthetic approach, since she is the joint creation of film and television, tabloid and star system, star system and consumer culture. And she is the joint creation of media persuasion and public projection. Earlier aesthetic philosophy concentrated on individual media: film, television, painting, whatever. But public life, fantasy, pleasure, today, where the media is engaged, is about synergy between media, not individual medium. To write the aesthetic story of the star icon in terms of a specific way film, television, tabloid, newsprint, consumer society conspire is what I tried to do in my book *The Star as Icon*.[2]

This approach is however particularly needed in order to understand American politics. The media are now a central, intrusive, constituent part of the American political landscape and have been since the fatherly fireside chats of President Roosevelt, indeed so long as there were newspapers to cartoon and caricature politicians. The media formulate canons for debate, in many ways control the flow of information, and turn presidents into, well—here is what a recent blog in the *Economist* said about it: "The occupant of the White House must be "a combination of scoutmaster, Delphic oracle, hero of the silver screen and father of the multitudes."[3] I would add, he or she must also be talk show host, TV commentator, and late night television comic.

This is the key idea behind media density: the media are often lumped together as a single thing, but this is wrong. There is a complex of distinctive media types (cinema, TV, blog) which only together construct a Diana or a president, and these must be prized apart so that their synergy is understood and appreciated. This is the density of the media: that images from film, TV, radio conspire to make up the persona (of the person) who lives, like Diana, mostly on-screen for most of us. It is because these figures live mostly if not entirely for most of us through the media that we so naturally project our accreted media experiences onto them, turning them into the multiply produced persona they then become for us. Once placing them in this role, we take pleasure in, project fantasy onto, and make undo demands upon these figures, since they are now elevated far above and beyond into a kind of wizardry.

Moreover, the media generate density in distinct ways. This candidate becomes referred to certain genres of TV (serial, talk show, reality TV), this to blog and movie, this to celebrity, this one becomes constructed and perceived as a star. The ways candidates and parties are variously configured is a matter of what their message is, how they appear before camera, how they are constructed by their scriptwriters and profilers, how they talk. Just as Diana was treated as film star although never having acted in any movie, so Obama (I will say momentarily) becomes Lincoln although never having occupied the slot in any historical drama or movie. He has star quality; a matter of message, physiognomy, race, media construction, profiling, the seriousness and intelligence of his language. Some candidates or situations or parties are not particularly media friendly, remaining media colorless, just as certain people do not photograph well or fail to project through the screen take. The most famous example was Nixon during the Kennedy/Nixon presidential debates in 1960, when the poor man fell into five o'clock shadow. In what follows I will rehearse the 2008 presidential election and try to show how Sarah Palin and Barack Obama are media constructed in highly opposing ways, ways that require an understanding of the differential effects of film and television. Each "oversignifies," becoming a media semilegend or, at the least, celebrity. But what they become and through which media references varies dramatically.

Therefore two elements (and the list is not exclusive) are critical to the story of American politics today. First a story of how heritage is grafted through media formats into the persona and message of the candidate and how this grafting of heritage motivates ebullience, communalism, and/or aggression if not zenophobia, zeal if not crusade. Second a story about how the synergy of media in any particular case differs from that of another and what the political effects are of this difference in candidate excess or oversignification. To understand the aestheticization of politics today, the role of seduction, subliminal association, pleasure, ideality, and adoration in political practice is to understand how multiple kinds of media interact with heritage to oversignify a candidate, turning him/her into a levitated persona (celebrity, star, TV dream girl, big-time wrestler, crime drama hero in some dense combination.

This oversignification turning candidate or party into persona courtesy of heritage, new media, profiling, marketing, and political message making levitates politics into something close to illegible. But it is deeply, if subliminally, felt. Parts of the American public float between cool judgers of political message and hot-blooded devotees, as if to a cult.If I have a theoretical source for these essayistic remarks, it would be in the Frankfurt School, which was, earlier on, much concerned with the role of mass culture, media, and seduction in American ideology formation. Their analysis is in many ways a model for how aesthetics, media, mass culture, and politics form a system. However, the Frankfurt School's picture of mass culture tends to be too uniform, its theories too intrusive, and its vision of American mind and fantasy too one dimensional. One will never understand the aesthetic dimension to American politics without appreciating the pleasure a public takes in bringing television, film, Internet to particular media experiences here involving politics.Nor the way that public scrambles meaning as a result. One must be a willing child of television, film, video to grasp the aesthetics of these media while also being astonished and appalled at American political life and process. The brilliant refugee thinker Theodor W. Adorno was too contemptuous of America during the dispiriting decade he lived in Los Angeles to understand the magic in the Edison box and TV console.[4] Better to speak of the analysis of ideology in terms of pleasure taken in the experience of imaginary wholeness so aptly applied to American popular culture by Slavoj Žižek and adapted from Lacan.[5] Or of Jean Baudrillard and his concept of "hyperreality,"[6] that Disneyland of mind and meaning in which real life and its simulacrum merge to the point where no one can (or wants to) prize them apart. The scrambling that results is indeed dazzling, indeed disturbing, and is sometimes disastrous for the conduct of democracy.

I think the American public is ambivalent about such a current political culture. It is sickened by the commercialization of politics and by the eclipse of genuine public debate that results from the formatting of politics over the American TV. And it loves it, craves it, because information can reduce to mythic slogan, belief to image, turning America again simple, wondrous, a president from a person into a Wizard of Oz, activating old heritage myths about character and its role in the emplotment of (American) destiny. This has everything to do with how that public desires and eschews the extreme makeover of politics into film and television, as if politics were a reality TV show and Obama, McCain, and Palin the contestants who have to exit the island with the tropical plants, mixed drinks, and poisonous snakes to "win." Caught between ground and levitation, the American public exists in a state of manic excitement, obsessive expectation and perpetual disappointment. Moreover their candidates, now raised up to utopian film stars, can never deliver on their promise of happiness in the way film actors can by the end of those Hollywood films which are so deeply now part of the American unconscious as to structure how many Americans think about political outcomes. This veering between real life and hyperreality may be even more confusing than mere hyperreality itself. Disneyland is stable and finally comprehensible; American political perceptions and processes are neither.

This extends to the way American heritage is constituted and brought into the political process. The heritage relied upon is as much a construction of the media as coming from other parts of "reality." *The American Heritage Dictionary* is in part a dictionary of movies and television and, more recently, Internet and blog.

Obama was staged as Lincoln before, during, and after his inauguration, taller than his public, monumental, in communion with that oversized, larger-than-life Lincoln Memorial in Washington. There are three Lincolns in American history: the actual one, steering the nation through its darkest of times, writing the Gettysburg Address on the train, the one etched into the monument, larger than Lincoln himself, who was already larger than life, sculpted from marble, his immortal words made immortal by being scripted into that stone, then the Lincoln of the cinema, Henry Fonda, Raymond Massey, the Lincoln dark and dulcet, silver in the silver screen, glowing through the aesthetics of the medium. *American heritage is all three: the man, the monument, the movie.*

American heritage is the blending together of these three registers. They merge with Obama's screen presence to create the Obama persona. The Lincoln persona casts him as emancipator, but also lightens him, whitens him (Lincoln was dark of spirit but light of skin). This lightening of him by kismet with the former president sets him apart from the stereotypes some Americans would project onto a candidate who is African American. It helps him rise to the position of national emancipator that he becomes (closer to) white in a society which is not free of racism. Paradoxically his being from Africa also contributes to freeing him from stereotypes directed at African Americans. Africa sets him apart in an obscure, hazy origin somewhere in the ancient land of ancient tribes. The distant lens of an African background (never articulated, even though his father was in fact a major Kenyan economist and critic of policy), combined with an unusual childhood in Hawaii and Indonesia, a beautiful, judicious-speaking voice, and star physiognomy seems to make him arise from mysterious sources, as if he were born a figment of the cinema, Raymond Massey or Henry Fonda who famously strides on screen from darkness to the light. And so a particular fantasy is activated in the American political constituency. Obama is (somewhat) deracialized (according to stereotypical American formulas) and instead becomes a star, standing outside of time. On the down side, his distant obscure past causes politicians with rugs on the top of their heads to demand copies of his American birth certificate, which he is able to produce.

By being cast as Lincoln, Obama stands outside of time while acting within it. It is as if his work has already been done and is simply being replayed as a movie. He will succeed in sculpting a new and fair America because he is Raymond Massey and has already won the Civil War! Cinema takes physical reality and places it in an eternally replayed past: where the happy ending has already been achieved. The public takes cinematic pleasure in its visual recitation after the fact. Obama the real

FIGURE 6.1. *Presidential Inauguration—"We Are One: Opening Inaugural Celebration."* U.S. president-elect Barack Obama speaks at the opening inaugural celebration at the Lincoln Memorial in Washington, January 18, 2009. Copyright © Jim Young/Reuters, reproduced courtesy of Corbis entertainment.

person is the candidate who needs to solve the issues of the day. Obama the star persona is the Lincoln who has already solved them and stands as a monument cast in stone to his own achievement.

That Obama is, in virtue of his star quality (elongated height and limbs, shattering intelligence, commanding, high moral voice), cast as Lincoln seems to me enough to argue in boldface that the American heritage dictionary is alive and well and part of American politics. In constructing Obama as Lincoln, a particular version of American heritage is invoked, come down through the ages as the origin of emancipation. This heritage is a product of the density of the media in which event, monument, and movie blend together in a complex perception, often implicit/subliminal. Heritage is therefore partly a *subliminal* construction.

Obama was elected president in 2008 because of the U.S. banking collapse, the need for health care reform, the war in Iraq; he was elected because he changed the rules of the game, bringing community organizing to party politics. He was elected to do a difficult job. Who knows if he would have been electable without the star quality that allowed him to cast his language in terms of destiny? The double perception of him as person and persona produced a convulsion of expectations in the American public around his agency as president. The American public expected wizardry, because it had cast him as the Wizard of Oz, the man, monument, and movie. He was then set up to disappoint.

We may now come to Obama versus Palin: Obama is a figure with the screen presence of a film star (like Diana). Palin is not, she is the quintessential TV actor, from sitcom, talk show, reality TV. Both are objects of dense media projection (from many quarters), but the essential difference remains. This difference is paired with a difference in the kind of heritage each preaches. Obama's is Lincolnesque: about return to origins and redirection to destiny, about discovering again who we are and yes we can. Palin's is about the long conservative arch of small-town values, accreted over time, time tested, as American as apple pie, America as an ongoing church gathering of friends. Palin's performance of small-town heritage is pure TV, relying on television aesthetics of intimacy, regularity, guys and gals like us hurling one-liners in sitcoms, spilling their guts, teary-eyed on talk shows, beaming as they emerge the winner on reality TV. TV is about intimacy between program, character, and audience, as if we are all ordinary Joes at the picnic together and Jerry Springer is our salubrious uncle.

This is the Palin heritage, that of the small town. Obama's image was instead cinematic, about the distance between star and rapt audience, the compelling aura of star presence on screen, the hypnotic effect of things and persons mysteriously present from far away (on screen). In this election the gravitational field of the candidates split between cinema and TV. It doesn't always break down like that. This time it did.

The previous chapter was about the use/abuse of heritage considered as the return to origin and destiny: in Africa. This chapter is about origin as dominion, origin as experiment, origin as destiny, as sovereignty. But it is also about accretion of heritage values over time, conserved and conservative, deified and exalted. These small-town American values, found in places like Wasilla, Alaska, Grover's Corners, New Hampshire and Bedford Falls, New York, are half fact, half storybook, half movie, half TV, meaning a 200 percent/proof cocktail in which heritage morphs into a mélange of family values, family movies, and family TV. But it is not just about heritage in this way because of the deeper origin of this subliminally accessed heritage in settler ideas of manifest destiny, sovereignty over land and people, tough-minded independence from big government believed to be the stuff of colonizer (British ruler) writ large as Washington government.

American games played out in politics around heritage turn heritage into a newly morphed set of myths around origin, destiny, and values courtesy of the density of the media: film, television et al.

III

Here is the Republican National Convention in Minneapolis–Saint Paul, Minnesota, on September 2–3, 2008. I take you back to that moment in a close-up of Sarah Palin walking to the podium from stage door left. "The governor of Alaska and the next vice president of the United States," blares the announcer as the crowd cheers. She is wearing a simple beige top, black skirt, and pumps when she walks onto the podium. The outfit is dwarfed by the American flag behind, like a vast cinema screen. Her trademark chestnut hair droops down one side of her forehead and is tied at the back with a barrette where it cascades down to her shoulders. She is elegantly ordinary, everybody's idea of an American soccer mom, but also of a pretty, petite working woman, perhaps a real estate salesperson or accountant, perhaps also beauty queen of your local town. As she appears, there is wild applause, no doubt dictated by signs that say "applause please" in the way other television audiences are directed to laugh at the punch lines of sitcom jokes. Perhaps some of the sound is canned. But a lot is genuine: after all, this is a political convention.

She acknowledges the crowd.

I accept, I accept I accept, she says. I am ready to serve with a man "who has come through much harder missions . . . and met graver challenges,"[7] meaning John McCain and his five years as a prisoner in "Hotel Hanoi." "It was just a year ago when all the experts in Washington counted out our nominee because he refused to hedge his commitment to the security of the country he loves. "With their usual certitude," she goes on, "they told us that all was lost—there was no hope for this candidate who said that he would rather lose an election than see his country lose a war." Immediately, she comes out against the experts, which has been a theme of John McCain's campaign, drawing him to Palin: we need to get away from the Washington insiders and make a fresh start, free of cant, corruption, and lobbying. As far away as possible, he looks to Alaska, home of the grizzly bear, the elk, the moose and . . . the pit bull. "What is the difference between a soccer mom and a pit bull?" she asks in her gelatinous, homespun smirk of a voice and answers, "Lipstick," to uproarious applause. Signs are raised over heads proclaiming "Soccer Moms 4 U."

At the moment of this convention, John McCain is losing ground to the Democratic presidential candidate Obama (who will win by a landslide). And so she says, "The pundits who are predicting Democratic victory" are wrong because John McCain has "character." This election is and should be about personal virtue. He's got "determination, resolve and sheer guts," and "the voters know better," meaning they know that.

It is well known that the role of an American vice presidential candidate is to be the presidential candidate's pit bull. She is attacking Democrats by branding them Washington insiders, for a consummate insider (McCain, long-time senator), so he can be magically transformed into an outsider able to sweep all the effete corruption aside. He's got the guts: anyone who can take five years in Hotel Hanoi will find clearing out Washington a piece of cake. She is channeling the energy (read: aggression) of soccer moms to do battle against big government. Their homes and families are being marshaled as a fortress against government policy, calling on settler and town values against big government. Specifically, her combat

FIGURE 6.2. *Vice presidential nominee Alaska Gov. Sarah Palin acknowledges the crowd at the 2008 Republican National Convention in St. Paul, Minnesota, September 3, 2008.* Copyright © Jim Young/Reuters, reproduced courtesy of Corbis entertainment.

mission is to get out the women's vote for McCain. We gals are men too, and our screaming on the school athletics field is just as decisive as the whooping of men charging up San Juan Hill in mortal combat, routing the enemy, Teddy Roosevelt's men.

By turning the debate from the political issues to "character," she and her scriptwriters seek to rewrite politics as pulp fiction, which, Quentin Tarantino has shown, mostly means movies. Character calls up men with stamina, integrity, true grit, the ability to get the job done. Floating on the silver screen in the public imagination should be ranchers, farmers, Indian scouts. Some will think Gary Cooper, others Harrison Ford. It doesn't matter: the point is to levitate politics through the halo of the movies in which her audience projects their top guns onto McCain.

The turn from issue to character is also a Palin flight from losing ground. She has at this point had two disastrous television interviews which have convinced many she knows nil about the political issues, indeed is so ill informed she may not be able to find Asia on the map—this in spite of being able to see Russia from her backyard. She needs to inspire trust in the swing voter who is proving so crucial to this election. Making the outsider the person with character is a strategy of turning her incompetence into a virtue. Because she is the diva from the wide open spaces, she is gifted intuitive knowledge of simple and homespun truths, the truths ordinary people know in virtue of being upstanding, churchgoing, friendly, and helpful members of their communities. Like them, she is a hard worker and a girl of common sense. She knows where and when the rip-offs take place, and by whom, and it ain't Joe the Plumber. Joe the Plumber, McCain's own stalwart, a man without a last name, but we're all on a first name basis, members of the same family. This is communalism pure and simple. By speaking positively about "character," one thereby speaks negatively about those who lack it, and are out of sync with traditional American values. Character, like family, is a weapon through being a bond. It is critical therefore that Palin introduce her family, which has happened almost at the outset of her acceptance speech. Her family makes her someone others can trust and confirms that she comes from good stock. The ritual of introducing family in this convention hall turns that hall into a family gathering like a wedding or anniversary where at a certain point this person and that are thanked. The convention ballroom becomes informal, a place where friends and family reunite, meet new friendly people, eat peach cobbler, drink elderberry wine, and barbecue pork, the whole time singing songs around the old campfire while venting spleen about the government. Yep, regular folk! And we, the TV audience, are by proxy also there, intimate with this group, willingly part. Who comes first: the nephew about to be deployed as a soldier to Iraq, and on the magic date of September 11, as if he personally will take revenge for the collapse of the twin towers. Then we meet and greet her children, followed by her faithful husband Todd, who holds Bristol's baby whom he occasionally passes to one of the granddaughters. Mr. He-Man of the oil fields and dogsled competitions is also a good mother. In this gender bend within clearly defined limits, Todd frees Sarah the wife to become just man enough to lead the nation (because he is woman enough to mother this child for a few minutes). All the while she remains for him his slinky girl. "I was just your average soccer mom," she says, "signed up for the PTA" at which point the audience erupts volcanically. "We grow good people," she adds. Last but not least we meet her hardworking parents, as ordinary as can be. Then the camera pans around the audience, to ensure everyone is included, including the home TV-watching audience.

If things are working according to plan, the audience should be subliminally associating to TV programs. This acceptance speech *is* a TV program and the camera angles and one-line introductions are pure TV, the realm of the talk show and even more the happy serial. The scriptwriters bank on audience gravitation to prime time TV shows like *The Brady Bunch, The Waltons; Leave It to Beaver,* and *My Three Sons* for the over-fifty crowd. The kind of TV show subliminally called for is the one revolving around family, friends, neighbors in tiny and always resolvable dramas of small town or suburban life with comic elements squishy as Velveeta cheese. Government and global affairs are excluded from these network shows. Nothing very bad ever happens to anyone. Density of association brings pleasure, because these programs engage TV audiences in a repetitive zone of life where characters are defined within setups and limits sharper than their own, offering a comfort zone of life run parallel to their own where no one will divorce, lose a job, move to Australia, or die. The television aesthetic of these programs is one of intimacy and regularity. For me it was a child's pleasure knowing I could rush in from a winter's sledding, take off my parka, wolf down a bowl of Campbell's soup, a different one for each day of the week, and expect Lucy to drive Desi Arnaz batty over the fire in the kitchen, Samantha to make magic work domestically, and Beaver to trample his hypertensive neighbor's rose garden just when the boss was over for an alfresco dinner. This is the America of Andy Warhol, whose desire in life was to eat the same soup and sandwich at Oscar's every day of his life. There is no more abundant nor passive security than mother's milk turned into a consumable item, which is what soup with Fred MacMurray in *My Three Sons* (watched by two brothers and I) was. Only an American reader can instinctively appreciate the TV aesthetic which Palin's performance is meant to solicit.

If the family gathering is a TV program, it is also a church. Heritage arose as a church, whose authority was that of religious truth, bespoken in the exalted eloquence of Joseph Conrad's Kurtz reeling it off to Marlow and the natives, ringing terror. All Europe contributed to Kurtz's meaning, Conrad tells us. Who contributes to Palin's? Here is Palin reeling it off to convention audience and beyond, shielded from rain by the soccer mom's umbrella (who is meanwhile eating freedom fries, watching

FIGURE 6.3. *Vice president nominee Sarah Palin addresses the third session of the 2008 Republican National Convention in the Xcel Energy Center in St. Paul, Minnesota.* Copyright © David Howells, reproduced courtesy of Corbis entertainment.

her child score a goal, and speaking on her cell phone directly to God). Palin is her pope. Kurtz's heritage is that of European civilization. Palin's is the heritage of small towns, rugged individuals, settlers, and communities. Both are heritages with a capital *H*, lineages and origins bespeaking special, superior authority. Before it was converted into a form of life with a lineage worthy of being shoved down other peoples' throats, Palin's American heritage was the stuff of egalitarianism and communitarianism of which Tocqueville waxed so perspicuous and enthusiastic in the pages of his *Democracy in America*. Surely the best book ever written on American civil and political life, composed by a genius training the fascinated telescope of a foreigner on America, *Democracy in America* is the work of one who, having lived through the emergence of popular/radical democracy in France, now wants to understand another version, the American one, possibly he thinks, better. He travels to America early enough in American history to capture the country when its habits were young: his book appears in the 1830s when the American democracy had been in existence for the same fifty years as when Emerson penned his poem and his essay. Tocqueville did not think of himself as describing a heritage, rather something new—a new way of living with a particular kind of communitarian and egalitarian spirit. I would like to say all Tocqueville contributed to the making of Palin, whose twist on this communitarian/egalitarian legacy is that of fundamentalism writing civil and political habits with a capital *H*. I would also like to say that in fact Tocqueville was describing the way a form of life, the small town, emerged from settler society and put a specific twist on those settler values which were slowly becoming American heritage.

In his book the great foreigner harped upon the central connection between civil and political associations for the conduct of American democracy, the formation of American character, and the process of electing American officials. "In my view," Tocqueville states, "nothing deserves to attract our attention more than the[se] intellectual and moral associations of America."[8]

Americans of all ages, conditions, and dispositions constantly unite together. Not only do they have commercial and industrial associations to which all belong but also a thousand other kinds, religious, moral, serious, futile, very general and very specialized, large and small. Americans group together to hold fetes, found seminaries, build inns, construct churches, distribute books, dispatch missionaries to the antipodes. They establish hospitals, prisons, schools by the same method. Finally, if they wish to highlight a truth or develop an opinion by the encouragement of a great example, they form an association. Where you see in France the government and in England a noble lord at the head of a great new initiative, in the United States you can count on finding an association.[9]

Why do Americans form associations? Tocqueville says Americans form them because loneliness of the prairie, displacement, as well as individualism weakens, invites freedom, but also the relative powerlessness with respect to government that comes from standing alone. Americans love to glorify this capacity of theirs to stand alone in a wild landscape of prairie or desert, granting it mythic proportions, the Palin/McCain power of outsiders to shake up Washington and restore it to ordinary people's values. Since McCain is the consummate Washington insider, he needs a Palin to legitimate outsider status. And he also needs someone to counteract his old, dilapidated looks; old does not play well in America without the proverbial face-lift. She is his face-lift, his Nanook of the North in a skirt, adding cover girl sex to his candidacy.

Tocqueville is more sanguine about American individualism. He sees the American bent for associations and clubs, alumni societies and groups of all kinds as a cure for the loneliness of its individualism and a corrective to its essential powerlessness. One man alone finally can't do much when bucking an entire system, even if the weight of Hollywood films tilts toward the opposite. Tocqueville is much impressed by the up-from-the-bottom quality of American democracy, by the ability of these associations, civil and political, to charge their elected officials with weight in Washington politics and keep these officials honest. From the town hall and church club to the Senate Chamber, America is thereby a model of democratic representation.

Of crucial importance, Tocqueville notes, is this blurring of civil and political institutions. American politics happens where American communities bond together: at church, in the town hall, at home; a political candidate even today campaigns at the local diner, the bowling alley, the hall of the Veterans of Foreign Wars. American communalism takes the form of carrying over group associations into political parties, values formed in civil society into voting practices. Such Americans trust their own neighbors; character counts politically. And they distrust those outside their towns, above all "big government," in the way the eighteenth-century settler looked skeptically at politicians living half a world away from his ranch or outpost and even more skeptically at the claims of government to assume legislative authority over local town life in the name of constitutional right: "In the eyes of [American] democracy, the government is not a blessing but a necessary evil. Some powers must be granted to civil servants for, without such power, what use would they be? But the external appearance of power is not vital for the conduct of affairs and is unnecessarily offensive to the public."[10]

Tocqueville was struck by how decentralized the structure of American political society was, coming as he did from a French monarchical history of centralized government and authority. When you have a political culture that exists in highly decentralized form, spread out across the vast American territories and where in those days it was very hard to circulate information between the states, then government is far away and the family and town the almost total reality of life. People will consider themselves mostly in allegiance to those. Such places are in the United States today called Alaska. And we may hear Sarah Palin echoing the Tocqueville observation while, in her capacity as governor, pardoning a turkey at Thanksgiving: "There are so many good Americans who are just desiring of their government to kind of get out of the way and allow them to grow and progress, and allow our businesses to grow and progress. So, great appreciation for those who share that value."[11]

The early history of the American nation was a series of conflicts between the will to central government and the desire for independence of the various states. Moreover, the eighteenth-century formulation of liberty which stamped American political heritage is John Locke's vision of the social contract, that the role of government is there to ensure individual liberty and little more, and by ensuring liberty is largely meant doing as little as possible apart from guaranteeing the rights to life, to bear arms, and to property. The government may demand military service in the name of protecting individuals from tyranny; it may demand minimal taxation so it can do its job. Should the government wish to tax its citizens beyond the minimum, it should be voted out of office as illegitimate.

It is important to note that the imaginary America Palin is performing has two strands, and these in fact sit uneasily together. On the other hand, there is the America of rugged individualism, of scout and explorer, rancher and wilderness guide. On the other, there is the America of the small town.

Rugged individualism is occupied by the John Wayne who is too big and idiomatic for the town. The town depends on him, but can no more abide him than he the town. Town values are communalist, town activities shared. Individualism hunkers down in its own world, the world of the man still settling the country, if only for the movies or on a TV program. Sarah Palin is an individualist from Alaska, her husband the oil rigger and dogsled racer even more so. But she is also mayor of a small town and speaks communalist language. However, when as governor of Alaska she was forced to cut the state budget, how did she do it? By holing herself up with husband Todd, whose abilities as an oil worker and dogsled racer apparently gave him special outsider knowledge of states and budgets, consulting no one else. That is the thinking of the rugged individualist, not the small-town citizen. It is because Sarah Palin is both rugged individualist and small-town girl that she can appear to reconcile their opposition in a gesture of hand holding to the Americans constituted against big democratic governance. The way she unites both is by performing both, and also through that combination of cornball, good looks, aggression, and kitsch which excites their shared dislikes and religious "fundamentals."

There is something odd about the dislike of expert culture than drives homespun American politics. For America is the most expert-driven culture in the world, with Americans relying on professionals to help them with their taxes, diagnose their diseases, solve their marital problems, counsel them on how their children can manage their play dates, work out their traumas, explain to them what foods to eat, which cars, TV sets, and all other products to buy, how to dress, wear their hair, plant gardens, lose weight. America is a country filled with art advisers, landscape architects, celebrity makers, agents, managers, and financial advisers, where all you need do is hang out a shingle and you're a massage consultant or marriage therapist. Obsessed with finding the best doctor, psychiatrist, accountant, garden consultant, or college adviser, when they turn to politics these very Americans will turn to a belief that equality means distrust of anyone who claims to know more than they do about any issue, as if solving the economic or health care crisis were a matter for the soccer mom and her individualized Internet research. This leveling of the playing field in the name of individual rights and self-respect is in fact pure self-assertion, which to the player would instead be called entrepreneurship.

To suit this propensity to think of equality as the refusal of expert knowledge or elitism, the upper classes and pundits must appear as Joe the

Plumber to gain legitimacy. This is part of what made George Bush so attractive to many Americans. A personally nice guy who, like Clinton, greets everyone with friendly respect, Bush is the uniquely talentless legacy child, bred to the bone, student at Andover and Yale, top-drawer schools, who learns to talk like Todd, an oil worker on the Texas oil field with whom you'd be happy to share a beer and barbecue. Bush carries the weight of money, but with sleight of hand disguises it. This performance comes naturally to him. But consider the illusion in it, given his true class interests which are not those of the oil field worker in the country music bar. By talking the talk and walking the walk, Bush convinces America that his own personal assets (class, trust fund, business interests) are theirs, as if shared on the small-town dance floor. Because he is one of us, his interests are ours; we can trust him; he is sharing the wealth. I am reminded of a joke. What is the definition of a Republican: someone who believes that everyone in the bar just got rich because Bill Gates walked in.

IV

The political heritage of the little guy, the small-town friend, the guy with character, is also the creation of Hollywood, a lineage of the silver screen and this is part of the subliminal background for the Alaskan outsider and her quest. And so hello Frank Capra—filmmaker from the 1930s, champion of the little guy, poet of the outsider to Washington, the guy with character who can stand up to the men with bellies, three-piece suits, gold watches, and cigars, power brokers who conduct their brokerage in back rooms at the expense of the little people. With Sarah Palin we are in the world of Capra's *Meet John Doe, Mr. Deeds Goes to Town,* and the like, the presence of Gary Cooper's twitch, height, and lanky baseball demeanor, the physiognomy of impertinent beauty without a manicure, always the sign of backwoods or small-town individuality—stubborn vision, good sense. The camera loves this guy because of his beauty and his individual traits: Gary Cooper's awkwardness and stutter, for example, which, with the help of Robert Riskin's screenplays and Capra's genius, become signs of his vulnerability (liability to fail) but also his ability to think. It sets him apart so he can be great in the way outsiders with spunk can be great. He is part of the subliminal ambience wherein small-town heritage is silently active in the American public's imagination.

In *Meet John Doe,* Gary Cooper is John Doe, a down-and-out baseball pitcher, riding boxcars with his friend. He is "adopted" by a newspaper so it can write copy about a "man of the people." Halfway through the film, John Doe breaks rank with his paper to invent, almost spontaneously, "John Doe Clubs," clubs where the little people can band together to empower themselves with political voice. They take off all across America. It is as if the screenwriter of this movie stole his story about these clubs (read: civil/political associations) from Tocqueville where it was being kept under lock and key by some Hollywood agent.

In that film the John Doe Clubs are taken over by an unscrupulous politician who will manipulate them for his own benefit and the benefit of big corporate interests. This politician is always played by Edward Arnold, whose image is one of corpulent, cigar-chomping corrupt brutality. He is a fascist. And he virtually crushes John Doe, who finds himself disgraced and in despair, and we find him at the top of the Empire State Building about to jump. In the end the little people save him, not to mention the girl, who is played as usual by the streetwise fast-talking Jean Arthur, and who has throughout this and other films been the one who has manipulated this small-town guy with a big physique and bigger spirit before falling head over heels for him. In the end the John Doe Clubs survive because the people want them to and the girl loves him enough to risk all for him.

Thus also does Mr. Smith go to Washington. Jefferson Smith is junior senator from Idaho, appointed by the senior senator and his political honcho friend Taylor, played by the ever corruptible Claude Rains and the ever corpulent cigar-chomping Edward Arnold, because he is believed naive enough to serve as a target. Jeff's father had been a noble senator, champion of lost causes, whom the senior senator Rains had once admired, before falling into the usual corrupt insider practices Rains calls a "man's" world. Jeff's is a boy's world; he is noble outsider, in britches, funny accent, unkempt, communing with the Lincoln of the Gettysburg Address, and, like that monument, taller than the others. Tall is always a code in Hollywood for standing above, walking tall, being as uncorrupt as the flagpole, bigger in spirit than other men. Cinema makes everyone look taller than they are, which is why it suits America. It is larger than life, and Jeff, that is, Jimmy Stewart, is even taller than that.

Jeff's ideal is to turn the Willow Creek Dam in his state into a boy's camp, where youth can learn the beauty of nature and the rightness of basic American virtues. But this dam is where the senior senator and his corporate buddy want to divert funding for a project of their own benefit. So when Jeff refuses to sit silent and rises to speak against their project on the Senate floor he is framed and disgraced. After a Senate inquiry in which he is tongue-tied, lost, unable to speak up for himself, we find him alone, bags packed, at the Lincoln Memorial, ready to leave for home, a lost man. He breaks down and weeps. At that moment Saunders (Jean Arthur) shows up, the good lady Washington insider who has before made sport of him and now wishes to assist him. Naturally, she has fallen in love. She convinces him to fight, in the name of Lincoln and of all those good boys in need of their camp. The camera gives us a close-up on the Gettysburg Address, eternalized in this monument's stone. "Now we are engaged in a great civil war" the text says. Here emancipation means a camp for American youth. Lincoln was equally homespun, equally outsider to Washington, so the myth goes, learning to read by candlelight in his simple home in Illinois. Jeff is his avatar. It is the young who will keep America honest.

In a great and dramatic day of filibuster, Jeff refuses to cede the floor and remains standing and talking for hours so that his message can "reach the people of his state," bypassing this corrupt group of senators. But the corrupt politician Taylor controls the media of their state and the message does not reach the people. Moreover, many are manipulated by Taylor, paid off probably, to demonstrate against Jeff. Saunders, the girl, tries to commandeer the little boys of his state to get Jeff's message to the people, but they are beaten up by Taylor's thugs. This is called fascism, the steering of mass crowds into propaganda and a violent crushing of opposition, even by children. It is a chilling moment in the film, this image of public corruptibility and manipulation. Eventually fifty thousand telegrams from the people of his state are wheeled into the Senate, all condemning Jeff. The girl expects Jeff to give up in despair, but he's now grown into a man's world, this Senate world, while keeping his boy's wisdom, and he knows they are all manufactured by the Taylor political machine. Exhausted, Jeff stumbles away from the letters, rises, and, standing tall, confronts Rains directly, saying once you too stood for what my father believed, once you too said the lost causes were the ones worth fighting for. Jeff then collapses. Rains, overcome with guilt for his botched life and loss of ideals, rushes out of the Chamber and tries to shoot himself. He then returns to the Senate and confesses. Jeff has won. "Yippee, he did it!" Saunders yells from the wings above. They will be married.

Jefferson Smith is the outsider who arrives to sweep things clean in the name of the ordinary people of his state. He is Palin before the fact, or so the Republican convention might wish us to believe, anyway. I am not arguing for an explicit, intended connection between Capra's Mr. Smith and Palin's staging, although this just might be there. I am arguing that it is such Hollywood myths, reconvening deeper and more popular images of political heritage (Lincoln), that are activated in viewers around the Republican event. Cinema has pride of place in the creation of these myths.

But the association of Palin with Jefferson Smith is in fact out of sync with Capra's films. This is because Capra and Riskin depart significantly in their conception of the American crowd. *Mr. Smith Goes to Washington* reveals just how fickle, how volatile the crowd can be. The voice of the people and its civil/political associations (the John Doe Clubs) are in Capra's films easy prey to corporate greed and manipulation. Capra's films are made in the 1930s and 1940s, when the specter of fascism is a genuinely imaginable American possibility, the crowd as virulent in its rages against immigrant outsiders, communist agitators, Jews, African Americans, and anyone else it doesn't happen to like as it can be contagiously effervescent. The crowd can kill, and in Jeff's case almost does, because it can be manipulated by big interests, not to mention (and this does go beyond the film) spontaneously violent. It is the voice of the people as well as *their* corruptibility that is at stake in this film. In the film, youth wins out, including Jeff's naïveté and outsider status, which is associated with being a man and a boy, in favor of democracy and boy's camps, at the same time. Beware, we might add, the soccer mom even now in the twenty-first century.

Frank Capra was himself a bigot. Beware therefore the immigrant Italian or Jew who excessively idealizes small-town America, beware even my own father with his gifting of heritage to the college girls he adored. There was something right about my grandmother's distrust of his catering to the "goyim." Such idealization as his can conceal self-hatred, a despising of the America that is dirty, immigrant ridden, filled with your tired, your poor, your huddled masses yearning to breathe free, meaning your own grimy origins. Those are the real ones, and to turn to myth spinning as an exit visa from immigrant reality into the America of the branded item, the film among the fruited plain, can turn one contemptuous, arrogant, fill one with loathing. Where there is a perfect world imagined to be ordinary

America, the imperfect (meaning actual world) appears all the worse by comparison. Capra was rabidly on the right, his small American town an ideal posed against what he (and J. Edgar Hoover and a lot of other Edward Arnold types) believed was disruptive immigrant anarchy. My father began in the Franklin Roosevelt camp but gradually swung to bitter dislike of newer immigrant groups wanting in. They were his own past staring him in the mirror and he didn't like it. America licenses that kind of contempt, success being its own moral justification. Such attitudes are dangerously close to self-hating.

And how could the Republican convention admit that its own audience is liable to persuasion by the very persons who distrust if not despise them when the point of that convention is to inflate the ideality? Conflate the ideality and thereby hide the fact that the men of the people are in fact men of interests which (like Edward Arnold's) oppose the people. Palin's candidacy is put forward by McCain to help make him a man of the people, not merely because he needs a celebrity figure like everyone else does. Palin's family gathering (to which all are invited) conceals the fact that McCain is a corporate giant, parading in the voice of the people, a voice he feels in his soul, yes, but one that also allows him to swan around with his nearly ten houses (to which the public are *not* invited) and cater to a bevy of corporate lobbyists. In the words of David Halbfinger writing for the *New York Times* (reprinted in the *Seattle Times*), "When he is in Washington, he lives in a luxury high-rise condominium in Arlington, Va., owned by his wife, Cindy Hensley McCain. Cindy McCain also owns their condos in Phoenix, San Diego and Coronado, Calif., and their vacation compound near Sedona, Ariz. The beer business she inherited from her father—Hensley & Co.—is the source of the McCain family fortune."[12]

He represents those lobbyists, seven of whom were stewards of his campaign, that corporate power, and such hidden powers eclipse the people, cut the link between the little guy and his voice in representative democracy. Again Halbfinger:

The booming Hensley business financed John McCain's entry into politics: after marrying Cindy, he retired from the Navy in 1981 and planned a run for Congress the next year. To that end, he took a public-relations job at Hensley and began introducing himself to voters. His father-in-law's wealth—

Cindy McCain was given $639,000 by a Hensley affiliate in 1982—also enabled John McCain to lend his campaign $167,000.

Today, Hensley & Co. is a major donor to Arizona politicians and above all has fought increases in the state excise tax, now about 1.5 cents a beer. The tax has risen only three times since the repeal of Prohibition, last in 1984, and remains 16 percent below the national median.[13]

McCain really does need Palin to symbolize his closeness to the values Tocqueville is applauding, the little people he is praising. She is his Gary Cooper, his Jimmy Stewart, his girl Friday, the ultra-individualist, former believer in Alaskan separatism, as happy to live among bears and coyote as humans, good with a rifle, able to catch salmon with her own bare hands. She is his revolutionary war scout. Americans love this sort of riot of images which they can bring to the imagination of politics.

V

Palin herself is the quintessential TV figure. Obama may carry the star quality of Lincoln, the auratic sense of height, distance, awe. Palin is Fox TV talk show intimate, successful *American Idol* candidate whose progress we follow from ordinary college girl to future vice president as if she were a contestant on that singing program making it through the semifinals to the finals and on to a career of fame and recording contracts. She is our intimate. As such, she seems to be part of our own homes, our daily life. Television has from the beginning been a domestic medium, enlivening the living room with its fare of live comedy, daily news, and serialized lives lived in parallel to the American family's own. Lynn Spigel has written about this in *Make Room for TV*.[14] My own childhood was lived drinking milk and eating cookies watching a parade of comics, zany housewives who could produce dinner with a twitch of their noses, sitcoms set in German prisoner of war camps, horses that could talk, castaways on desert islands arguing over who has rights to the open air bathroom. TV was in America the domestic instrument for families eating preprocessed TV dinners on trays at home.

The Republican convention creates the illusion of this domestic situation by seducing the viewer into the belief that it is taking place within each and every home like all other TV does. Its audience can then fall into the fantasy that they are all Palin intimates, vicarious associates. At the end of the day we are *there* with Palin in the convention hall, as if in a TV studio, as she makes her journey to the White House. Or alternately the event is felt to be happening in our own living rooms where she has journeyed to be with *us*. Through this sense of spatial contiguity and participatory intimacy comes the illusion that our candidate represents us politically. The Oval Office is inside our own living rooms, with Bush speaking directly to us from the distance of across the living room table, or we are in the Oval Office with him? By being there, we are included in the representative process of democracy. Being a guest on a TV program means the talk show host represents your interests.

I would like to call this magical thinking. It is a kind of magical thinking that is very much occasioned by the myth of the heritage bond, now transposed to television.

Americans are of two minds about magical thinking. For Sarah Palin did not make it all the way through the *American Idol* program to the White House in 2008. Her convention speech, with its intention of gathering the Republican clans into a single church picnic, fell apart: there is finally no way such diverse voter groups can all sit comfortably at the same table, in spite of the George Bush/Karl Rove aim of marketing to all constituencies. The liberal wing of that Republican Party voted for Obama, especially after the collapse of Wall Street one month later, in October 2008. At the end of the day, few believed the myth of Palin as outsider capable of curing the ills of Washington. She simply proved too uninformed and off-key with remarks like being able to see Russia from her house. She's resigned from her governorship in order to find a more lucrative way of paying back the half-million-dollar legal fees she incurred defending herself against multiple ethics charges and is playing celebrity candidate for all the cash value it's worth, the advance contract on the memoir, the lecture circuit, and, most recently, she's offered herself and Todd as dinner companions for twenty-five thousand dollars a pop. Twenty-five grand is the magic number, the same amount Andy Warhol wanted to paint your portrait. This is Andy's universe. At the moment she is grandam of Tea Party politics. Whether her crystal ball contains a vice presidency, membership in Congress, or even stewardship of the land, or merely permanent position as Republican guest on Jon Stewart's comedy hour, one cannot, at this moment of writing, glimpse.

Watching TV and its Internet replay during the 2008 election, what America also saw was Sarah Palin played by her *Saturday Night Live* double: Tina Fey. Fey held a mirror held to Palin of such comic accuracy that Palin could not live it down, even if at the start it looked like the Fey parody might enhance the celebrity value of her candidacy. However, Fey's comic mirror finally brought the message home in a way the American public likes to have it brought home: in the form of high-quality entertainment that trampled Palin. Most people watched it on YouTube, where it had a tremendous second life for people of all ages, as word spread that this was the real imitation.

Many young people get their news and information from blogs, Internet Web sites and late night comedy TV. For them it is the media which carries the power to counteract the media. And this is the real message of the density of the media image. That the media is diverse, oppositional, anarchic: once one becomes a media persona, all hell may break loose pertinent to one's media image. Total anarchy rules out there; no one can predict what the effects of multiple media weighing in on your image will be. You may end up looking like a star or a tramp or a has-been. This would be true for Barack Obama and JFK as well as Sarah Palin: it is a general condition of the media. There is no way to control image; everybody is scrambling.

People in America do also vote for their political representatives (Obama in November 2008) on the basis of genuine issues: health care, taxation, employment, banking, and regulation. But that is only *half* the story, the other half being a story about self-reliance, church, political process, bedtime, Internet surf and turf, and Hollywood—about a particular version of settler heritage filtered through media, myth, and illusions of consumer choice. This is Palin's version, and it is here to stay.

Epilogue

The settler claim of experiment (through which dominion will be established over land and peoples) along with the settler values of the small town and rural area slowly become a heritage. This heritage is alive and well and central to American politics. In other regions of the postcolony, a glorious, unified past (located somewhere between Pretoria, Timbuktu, the poetry of Léopold Senghor, and the rhetoric of England) is on the job being constructed and set forth as the route to twenty-first-century Africa. Both versions of heritage turn a motley/diverse group of locals into that new thing: "indigenous/native peoples." In the one version of heritage the native falls under settler dominion, outside of settler values, and must be conquered and/or relocated. In the other version the native is idealized, turned into a scientist *avant la lettre,* not to mention venture capitalist extraordinaire.

Heritage has been a piston of energy in the postcolony, serving to fabricate nations, resurrect forgotten and abused peoples, place new societies on the geopolitical map, generate income, and bring about acknowledgment. But it has also done more than its share of damage. Then by what means shall the claims of heritage, the legacies and instruments of heritage, be reformulated, if not renounced?

Renunciation is a fantasy. No decision/gesture could unravel a practice as deep in the texture of modern life as heritage: decisions (and the acts that follow) do not carry such power (not in the imaginable future anyway). This is just as well. Were heritage practice capable of being junked, too much of importance would disappear with it.

Rather the question is how to live within, while also against, the practice of heritage. This is a question of how to *revalue* heritage (to use language of Friedrich Nietzsche), deconstruct it, take the sting out of it, find ways to deploy it differently, etc. . . . It is a question which exists in boldface not only for art, museums, and universities (whose critical installations, exhibition practices, and culture wars have already engaged it) but also for contemporary life as a whole. There is no single answer to this question of how to revalue heritage, no single experiment adequate to the task.

Notes

1. THE HERITAGE OF HERITAGE

1. Frantz Fanon, "On National Culture," in Patrick Williams and Ian Chrisman, eds., *Colonial and Postcolonial Theory: A Reader* (New York: Columbia University Press, 1994), p. 37.
2. John Comaroff and Jean Comaroff, *Ethnicity INC* (Chicago: University of Chicago Press, 2009), p. 10. The Comaroffs acknowledge the importance of earlier work by Barbara Kirschenblatt-Gimblett in what they say.
3. Nick Shepherd, private conversation.
4. Comaroff and Comaroff, *Ethnicity INC*, p. 15.
5. This remark should be complicated by work about the subverting effect of colonial subject on missionary.
   John Comaroff and Jean Comaroff, *Of Revelation and Revolution: Christianity, Colonialism and Consciousness in South Africa* (Chicago: University of Chicago Press, 1991).
6. Alexandre Kojève, *Introduction to the Reading of Hegel: Lectures on the Phenomenology of Spirit* (New York: Basic Books, 1969).
7. Benedict Anderson, *Imagined Communities* (London: Verso, 1991).
8. Achille Mbembe, *On the Postcolony* (Berkeley: University of Chicago Press), p. 102.
9. Homi Bhabha, *The Location of Culture* (London: Routledge, 1984), pp. 85–92.
10. Daniel Herwitz, *Key Concepts in Aesthetics* (London: Continuum, 2008).
11. Richard Wollheim, *On Art and the Mind: Essays and Lectures* (London: Allan Lane, 1973), pp. 177–201.
12. Matthew Arnold, *Culture and Anarchy* (Oxford: Oxford University Press, 1996), p. 5.

13. This project of tracing languages back to cultural origins had a certain amount of shenanigans, because 1. the origin of Europe was meant to be in the Greek, the Hebrew, and the Roman, but Hebrew is of a distinct linguistic tree (the Semitic) from European languages (Indo-European), while 2. Sanskrit, a genuine linguistic ancestor of European languages, was to the colonial imagination scion of an inferior culture (the Indian sub-continent).

14. Arnold, *Culture and Anarchy*, pp. 119–20.

15. Fanon, "On National Culture," p. 37.

16. Mahmood Mamdani, *Citizen and Subject* (Princeton: Princeton University Press, 1996).

17. Ibid.

18. John Comaroff and Jean Comaroff, *Of Revelation and Revolution: Christianity, Colonialism, and Consciousness in South Africa*.

19. Friedrich Nietzsche, *Untimely Meditations* (Cambridge: Cambridge University Press, 1997), p. 62.

20. Ibid.

21. Ibid.

2. RECOVERING AND INVENTING THE PAST

1. Edward Said states: "Rather than listing all the figures of speech associated with the Orient—its strangeness, its differences, its exotic sensuousness, and so forth we can generalize about them as they were handed down through the Renaissance. They are all declarative and self-evident; the tense they employ is timeless eternal; they convey an impression of repetition and strength; they are always symmetrical to, and yet diametrically inferior to, a European equivalent, which is sometimes specified, sometimes not." Edward Said, *Orientalism* (New York: Vintage, 1979), p. 72.

2. Quoted in Pratapaditya Pal and Vidya Dehejia, *From Merchants to Emperors: British Artists and India, 1757–1930* (Ithaca: Cornell University Press, 1986), p. 39.

3. Bernard Cohn, *Colonialism and its Forms of Knowledge: The British in India* (Princeton: Princeton University Press, 1996), p. 78.

4. Ibid., p. 5.

5. Ibid., p. 29.

6. Christopher Miller, *Blank Darkness: Africanist Discourse in French* (Chicago: University of Chicago Press, 1985), p. 44.

7. Georg Wilhelm Friedrich Hegel, *The Philosophy of History* (New York: Dover, 1956), p. 91.

8. Pratapitya Pal and Vidya Dehejia, *From Merchants to Emperors: British Artists and India 1757–1930*, p. 186.

2. RECOVERING AND INVENTING THE PAST

9. When India was instead held up to the scrutiny of nineteenth-century progressivists as a living monument to everything in the European past that the great nineteenth century was overcoming –poverty, disease, intolerance—the focus changed. Again, the West has been inconsistent about the values of the past.

10. Quoted in Yashodhara Dalmia, "From Jamshetjee Jeejeebhoy to the Progressive Painters," in Sujata Patel and Alice Thorner, eds., *Bombay, Mosaic of Modern Culture* (Bombay: Oxford University Press, 1995), p. 182.

11. Ibid.

12. Ibid., p. 183.

13. Partha Mitter, *Much Maligned Monsters: A History of European Reactions to Indian Art* (Oxford: Oxford University Press, 1977).

14. Partha Mitter, *Art and Nationalism in Colonial India, 1850–1922* (Cambridge: Cambridge University Press, 1994).

15. Homi Bhabha, "Foreword, Remembering Fanon," in Frantz Fanon, *Black Skin, White Masks* (London: Pluto, 1986), pp. vii–xxvi.

16. Homi Bhabha, "Foreword, Remembering Fanon," pp. vii–xxvi.

17. Partha Chatterjee, *The Nation and Its Fragments* (Princeton: Princeton University Press, 1993), p. 8. Tapati Guha-Thakura, *The Making of a New "Indian" Art: Artists, Aesthetics, and Nationalism in Bengal, 1980–1920* (Cambridge: Cambridge University Press, 1992); and Mitter, *Art and Nationalism in Colonial India.*

18. For the classic texts of Subaltern Studies, see Ranajit Guha and Gayatri Spivak, eds., *Selected Subaltern Studies* (Oxford: Oxford University Press, 1988).

19. Gayatri Spivak, "Can the Subaltern Speak?" in Patricia Williams and Leonard Chrisman, eds., *Colonial Discourse and Postcolonial Theory* (New York: Columbia University Press, 1994), pp. 66–111.

20. Maqbool Fida Husain, *Passage Into Human Space* (private printing), pp. iv–v.

21. Francis Souza in *Exhibition Catalogue of the Progressive Artists*, Bombay, July 7, 1948. Quoted in Dalmia, "From Jamshetjee Jeejeebhoy to the Progressive Painters," p. 191.

22. Francis Souza in *Exhibition Catalogue of the Progressive Artists*, Bombay, July 7, 1948. Quoted in Dalmia, "From Jamshetjee Jeejeebhoy to the Progressive Painters," p. 191.

23. Husain, *Passage Into Human Space*, pp. iv–v.

24. Daniel Herwitz, *The Star as Icon* (New York: Columbia University Press), pp. 35–36.

25. Maqbool Fida Husain and Daniel Herwitz, *Husain* (Bombay: Tata, 1988).

26. Thomas Blom Hansen, *Reflections on Salman Rushdie's Bombay*, in *Midnight's Diaspora: Critical Encounters with Salman Rushdie*, ed. Daniel Herwitz and Ashutosh Varshney (Ann Arbor: University of Michigan Press, 2008), pp. 91–111.

3. SUSTAINING HERITAGE OFF THE ROAD TO KRUGER PARK

1. Steven Sack, *The Neglected Tradition* (Johanneburg: Johannesburg Art Gallery, 1988).
2. Ibid., p. 12.
3. Sue Williamson, *Resistance Art in South Africa* (Cape Town: David Philip, 1989), p. 9.
4. Ibid.
5. Ibid.
6. Peter Rich, "The New Jerusalem," in Ricky Burnett, ed., *Jekisemi Hlungwani Yagani: An Exhibition Catalogue* (Johannesburg: BMW, 1989), p. 27.
7. Ibid.
8. Ibid.
9. Ibid.
10. Patricia Hobbs and Elizabeth Rankin, *Printmaking, Transforming South Africa* (Johannesburg: David Philip, 1997); Elizabeth Rankin, *Images of Metal* (Johannesburg: University of Witwatersrand Press, 1994); Patricia Hobbs and Elizabeth Rankin, *Rorke's Drift: Empowering Prints* (Cape Town: Double Story, 2003).
11. Anitra Nettleton, "The Crocodile Does Not Leave the Pool: Venda Court Arts," in Anitra Nettleton and W. D. Hammond-Tooke; *African Art in Southern Africa: From Tradition to Township* (Johannesburg: Ad Donker, 1989), pp. 67–89.
12. Ibid., pp. 73–74.
13. Ibid., p. 75.
14. For a discussion of the dialectic through which missionary Christianity and traditional belief systems interacted in the missionary community of the Twana, see the work of the Comaroffs. John Comaroff and Jean Comaroff, *Of Revelation and Revolution*, vol. 1: *Christianity, Colonialism, and Consciousness in South Africa* (Chicago: University of Chicago Press, 1991). And John Comaroff and Jean Comaroff, *Of Revelation and Revolution*, vol. 2: *The Dialectics of Modernity on a South African Frontier* (Chicago: University of Chicago Press, 1997).
15. Rayda Becker, "Visions and the Viewer," in Burnett, *Jecksemi Hlungwani Yagani*, p. 20. I am grateful to Rayda Becker for help in understanding the South African art history of the late 1980s and also Vha-Venda and Isi-Tsonga sculpture.
16. Colin Richards, "That Authentic African Look Fades Into Glib Cliche," *Weekly Mail,* August 28–September 3, 1987.
17. Charles Baudelaire, *The Painter of Modern Life and Other Essays* (London: Phaidon, 1970).

18. Achille Mbembe, *On the Postcolony* (Berkeley: University of California Press, 2001), chapters 3 and 4.
19. Ludwig Wittgenstein, *Philosophical Investigations* (New York: Macmillan, 1968), #122.
20. This was related to me by Stephen Toulmin, Wittgenstein's student and my beloved teacher and friend.
21. Ludwig Wittgenstein, *Philosophical Investigations*, #66, #67.
22. Baudelaire, *The Painter of Modern Life and Other Essays*.
23. Dilip Gaonkar, D. A. Wachtel, L. Ou-fanLee, and R. McCarthy, eds., *Alternative Modernities* (Durham: Duke University Press, 2001).
24. Charles Taylor, "Two Theories of Modernity," ibid., pp. 172–96.
25. Dilip Gaonkar, "On Alternative Modernities," ibid., p. 23.
26. Emmanuel Wallerstein, *The Capitalist World-Economy* (Cambridge: Cambridge University Press, 1979). It is worth remarking that Wallerstein's first published book was about Africa: Emmanuel Wallerstein, *Africa: The Politics of Independence* (New York: Vintage, 1961).
27. The implications concern a longstanding debate in aesthetic philosophy about how an art market/artworld plays a defining role in turning an artifact, event, even idea into a work of art. On the one side of the debate, Arthur Danto has argued that an interpretation or "theory" held by the art world at a particular time is the essential and sole defining agent. On the other side of the debate, George Dickie has argued the art world is a sociological agent (he mistakenly calls it an institution) and that this agent performs the act of establishing or enfranchising something as art on whatever basis, perhaps by fiat. In fact both philosophers are half right. Entrance into the category of contemporary art is a process involving interpretive "theorization," aiming for recognition but also profiling for circulation by the market. Profiling is also, in its own way, an interpretation, and recognition a kind of branding. There is no escaping the dialectic between recognition and consumer branding. And yet these two ways of supplying an object, event, or idea with the status of contemporary art are not identical. They can and do conflict. One can recognize an object to be art by interpreting it, even if it fails to circulate in or even be profiled for circulation by the market. Conversely, one can exclaim, "That is not art!" about some artifact that has entered the art market and is circulating in the galleries and which one considers appalling. But one is at best half right. For the fact that the object is profiled within the system also confirms its status as contemporary art. There is no one way something becomes art today. The category of contemporary art is *itself* a sliding signifier, slipping between recognitional interpretation and sociological profiling/inclusion/circulation. "Art" is an overlapping set of games played in and around objects, events, ideas, within and in criticism of markets at differing registers.

The loci of the debate in aesthetic philosophy may be found in Arthur Danto, *The Transfiguration of the Commonplace* (Cambridge: Harvard University Press,

1981); and in George Dickie, *Art and the Aesthetic: An Institutional Analysis* (Cornell: Cornell University Press, 1974).

28. Note that any market (be it an art market, a currency market, or a pork belly market) values its commodities through a combination of interpretation, theory, trust, profiling, inclusion, circulation, and consumption. Any market has multiply interacting aspects or parts. Markets are speculative, and the word *speculation* is instructive. Speculation is a matter of holding beliefs, interpretations, and theories about where the market is going. But it is also an act of plunging in and investing (staking capital, circulating art, purchasing currency).

29. See, for example, Jane Duncan, "'They Say Venda Is Winning but We Cannot See How': Artists from the North-eastern Transvaal and the Struggle for Nationhood," *African Studies* 55, no. 2 (1996): 21–42.

4. MONUMENT, RUIN, AND REDRESS IN SOUTH AFRICAN HERITAGE

1. Steven Robins, "'Long Live Zachie, Long Live': AIDS Activism, Science, and Citizenship After Apartheid," *Journal of Southern African Studies* 30, no. 3 (2007): 651–72, p. 664.
2. Ibid.
3. Leslie Witz, *Apartheid's Festival: Contesting South Africa's Apartheid Pasts* (Bloomington: Indiana University Press, 2003).
4. Sue Williamson, *Resistance Art in South Africa* (Cape Town: David Philip, 1989), p. 20.
5. Jennifer Law, "Penny Siopis: The Storyteller," in Frank Herreman and Mark D'Amato, eds., *Liberated Voices: Contemporary Art in South Africa* (New York: Prestel, 1999), p. 97.
6. Nick Shepherd, *Heritage*, in Nick Shepherd and Steven Robins, ed., *New South African Keywords* (Athens: Ohio University Press, 2008), pp. 121–22.
7. Annie Coombes, *History After Apartheid: Visual Culture and Public Memory in a Democratic South Africa* (Durham: Duke University Press, 2003), chapter 1.
8. See its Web site: http://www.freedompark.co.za/cms/index.php.
9. Ibid.
10. James E. Young, *At Memory's Edge: After-Images of the Holocaust in Contemporary Art and Architecture* (New Haven: Yale University Press, 2002), p. 118.
11. Ciraj Rassool, "Community Museums, Memory Politics, and Social Transformation: Histories, Possibilities, Limits," in Ivan Karp, Gustavo Buntinx, Ciraj Rassool, Corinne Kratz, Lynn Szwaja, Tomas Ybarra-Frausto, Barbara Kirshenblatt-Gimblett, eds., *Museum Frictions: Public Cultures/Global Transformations* (Durham: Duke University Press, 2006), pp. 286–321. See also M. Jeppe and C. Soudien, *The Struggle for District Six: Past and Present* (Cape Town: Buchu,

1990). And C. McEachern, "Mapping the Memories: Politics, Place, and Identity in the District Six Museum, Cape Town," in Steven Watson, *Museums and Their Communities* (London: Routledge, 2007), pp. 457–78.

12. Coombes, *History After Apartheid*, p. 126.

13. Shepherd, *New South African Keywords*, p. 121.

14. *The Neglected Tradition*, exhibition curated by Steven Sack at the Johannesburg Art Gallery; the exhibition was published as Steven Sack, *The Neglected Tradition* (Johanneburg: Johannesburg Art Gallery, 1988).

15. Ibid., p. 12.

16. See Pippa Skotnes, "'Civilized off the face of the earth': Museum Display and the Silencing of the /Xam, *Poetics Today* 22, no. 2 (2001): 299–321. Also Pippa Skotnes, "The Politics of Bushman Representations," in P. Landau and D. Kaspin, eds., *Images and Empires: Visualities in Colonial and Post-colonial Africa* (Berkeley: University of California Press, 2002), pp. 253–74. See also Leslie Witz, "Transforming Museums on Post-apartheid Tourist Routes," in Ivan Karp et al., *Museum Frictions*, pp. 108–34.

17. The catalogue was published as a book: Pippa Skotnes, ed., *Miscast: Negotiating the Presence of the Bushman* (Cape Town: University of Cape Town Press, 1996).

18. Ibid., p. 20.

19. We were lucky to have one such installation of her *Book of Iterations* at the Institute for the Humanities, University of Michigan, where I have been director. The date of this was December, January 2009–10, part of a larger project on heritage courtesy of the Andrew W. Mellon Foundation.

20. Pippa Skotnes, "Fugitive Archive: A Response to the 'Bushman Diorama,'" unpublished paper presented to the University of Michigan Museums in the Academy Lecture Series, *Making Meaning*, Ann Arbor, December 2009, p. 4.

21. Arnold Davidson, *The Emergence of Sexuality: Historical Epistemology and the Formation of Concepts* (Chicago: University of Chicago Press, 2004).

22. For a discussion of the Baartman case, see Sander Gilman, *Difference and Pathology: Stereotypes of Sexuality, Race, and Madness* (Ithaca: Cornell University Press, 1985), pp. 76–108.

23. Steven Sack, "'Garden of Eden or Political Landscape?' Street Art in Mamelodi and other Townships," in Anitra Nettleton and W. D. Hammond-Tooke, eds., *African Art in Southern Africa: From Tradition to Township* (Johannesburg: Ad Donker, 1989), pp. 191–92.

24. Ibid., p. 205. See also Tom Lodge, "The United Democratic Front: Leadership and Ideology," unpublished MS, African Studies Institute, University of Witwatersrand, 1987.

25. Albie Sachs, "Afterword: The Taste of an Avocado Pear," in Ingrid De Kok and Karen Press, eds., *Spring Is Rebellious: Arguments About Cultural Freedom by Albie Sachs and Respondents* (Cape Town: Buchu, 1990).

26. See, for example, Patrick Lenta, "Deconstituting Transition: Law and Justice in Post-apartheid South Africa," Master's thesis, University of Natal.

27. Aldo Rossi, *The Architecture of the City* (Cambridge: MIT Press, 1984).

28. David Bunn, "Whited Sepulchres: On the Reluctance of Monuments," in Hilton Judin, H. Vladislavic, and Ivan Vladislavic, eds., *blank—architecture, apartheid and after* (Rotterdam: Netherlands Architectural Institute, 1998), section B3, 4C, 9–10.

29. Daniel Herwitz, *Race and Reconciliation: Essays from the New South Africa* (Minneapolis: University of Minnesota Press, 2003).

30. A qualification is in order. So that the reader does not get the impression that South African politics (about monuments or any other thing) are without variation across region, I should also note that these remarks do not entirely pertain to the province of Kwa-Zulu Natal, where the Zulu kingdom was busy reconstituting the face of the province with monument, street name, and shopping center in homage to king, clan, memory. In response to Zulu nationalist monumentalization, the African National Congress Provincial Government has become equally embattled around the cultural icon. City manager of Durban Mike Sutcliffe responded by changing the names of Durban streets from old colonial appellations (King George V Avenue) to struggle icons (Ruth First Boulevard). So far so good, since this change of street name is a classic form of public redress, but Sutcliffe went the limit, changing *every* street name. Since he quickly ran out of names with iconic recognition value (Nelson Mandela Street), most of the street names used are unrecognizable. To prevent drivers from getting lost, he then preserved the old names with an *X* crossing them out, and the new name under, as if colonialism was being crossed out of history. Most important, Sutcliffe's crossing out of names extended to old *Zulu* street names (M. Buthelezi), making his politically correct gesture a clear provocation against anti-African National Congress Zulu nationalism (the Inkatha Party), not to mention a gesture of near Stalinist monumentality. The embattled province pits monument versus government over issues of heritage and ethnicity.

31. *Johannesburg Star*, August 2, 2002.

5. RENAISSANCE AND PANDEMIC

1. Thabo Mbeki, *Africa: The Time Has Come* (Cape Town: Tafelberg, 1998), p. 31.

2. Ibid., p. 32.

3. Johan Jacobs has pointed out that these acts of "mimicry" can be understood as the dependent position of a non-native speaker of English on the idioms of the "great English writers" Mbeki has read.

4. Mbeki, *Africa*.

5. Daniel Herwitz, *Race and Reconciliation* (Minneapolis: University of Minnesota Press, 2003).

6. Mark Gevisser, *Thabo Mbeki: The Dream Deferred* (Johannesburg: Jonathan Ball, 2007).

7. Shula Marks, "An Epidemic Waiting to Happen? The Spread of HIV/AIDS in South. Africa in Social and Historical Perspective," *African Studies* 61, no. 1 (2002): 13–26.

8. Ahmed Bawa, "Science, Power and Policy Intersecting at the HIV/AIDS Pandemic," in *South Africa: The Second Decade*, special issue of *Social Research* 72, no. 3: 612–13.

9. Ibid., p. 613.

10. Gevisser, *Thabo Mbeki*.

11. Partha Chatterjee, *Nationalist Thought and the Colonial World* (Minneapolis: University of Minnesota Press, 1998).

12. Achille Mbembe, *On the Postcolony* (Berkeley: University of California Press, 2001), p. 12.

13. For a good overview of the construction of the category of indigeneity in recent South Africa and globally, see Kai Horsthemke and Lesley Green, "Indigenous Knowledge," in Nick Shepherd and Steven Robins, eds., *New South African Keywords* (Athens Ohio: Ohio University Press, 2008), pp. 129–42.

14. John Comaroff and Jean Comaroff, *Ethnicity, INC* (Chicago: University of Chicago Press, 2009), p. 84.

15. Ahmed Bawa was then deputy vice chancellor, academic, of the University of Natal, South Africa. Jerry Coovadia was professor of pediatrics at the University of Natal Medical School.

16. Ahmed Bawa, Daniel Herwitz, and Hoosen Coovadia, "Leave Science to the Scientists, Mr. Mbeki," *Sunday Independent*, June 25, 2000, p. 8.

6. DE TOCQUEVILLE ON THE BRIDGE TO NOWHERE

1. *BBC World News*, live coverage of Princess Diana Funeral, September 6, 1997.

2. Daniel Herwitz, *The Star as Icon* (New York: Columbia University Press, 2008).

3. Lexington Columnist, "The Obama Cult," *Economist*, July 25, 2009, p. 32.

4. Theodor Adorno, *The Culture Industry: Selected Essays in Mass Culture* (London: Routledge, 1991).

5. Slavoj Žižek, *The Sublime Object of Ideology* (London: Verso, 2009).

6. Jean Baudrillard, "Simulacra and Simulations," in *Selected Writings* (Stanford: Stanford University Press, 1988). Also Jean Baudrillard, *America* (London: Verso, 1988).

7. All quotes from the Sarah Palin acceptance speech at the September 2008 Republican convention in Minneapolis–Saint Paul are taken from http://portal.gopconvention2008.com.

8. Alexis de Tocqueville, *Democracy in America and Two Essays on America* (New York: Penguin, 2003), p. 600.

9. Ibid., p. 596.

10. Ibid., p. 237.

11. Sarah Palin, quoted in T. Purdum, "It Came from Wasila," *Vanity Fair* 31 (2009): 142.

12. David Halbfinger, "McCain's Wealth Is Hard to Track," *Seattle Times Online* (2008).

13. Ibid.

14. Lynn Spigel, *Make Room for TV: Television and the Family Ideal in Postwar America* (Chicago: University of Chicago Press, 1992).

Index

Abstract expressionism, 67
Abstract grammars, 12
Abstraction, 43
Accretion, 16, 18
Achievement, xii
Acknowledgment, 107; cultural, 58
Activism, 89
Acultural theory, 72
Adorno, Theodor W., 167
Aesthetics, 7, 15, 90, 93; philosophy, 165, 197n27; of vulgarity, 64
Africa, 31, 34, 138; alternative modernities and, 73; art of, 58–79; identity and, 139; resources of, 147; values of, 135; *see also* South Africa
African Americans, 169, 200n30
Africanization, 115
African National Congress (ANC), 83–84, 89–90, 141–42; indigeneity and, 149; Mandela and, 147; neoliberalism and, 131
African Renaissance, 81, 123–24, 133, 135–51; Afro-centrism and, 80; as doctrine, 135; HIV-AIDS and, 140–49; Mbeki and, 22, 80, 100; narrative of, 150
Afro-centrism, 80, 100, 144–45, 147
Age of space, 48
AIDS, *see* HIV/AIDS
Alaska, 163
Alienation, 35

Alternative modernities, 71, 73, 78
Amakhosi (chiefs), 20
Ambivalence, 38, 43
America, 25, 152–53; African Americans, 169, 200n30; association and, 179; democracy, 178–80; early history of, 180; individualism and, 179–81; Israel and, 158; John Doe Clubs and, 183; media and, 164–65, 167; movies and, 159–61; Obama and, 169; origin of, 154; Palin and, 163, 172–82; politics of, 162; popular culture, 168; ratification of, 157; small towns and, 22, 171–72, 185–86; television and, 187–89
American dream, 1
American Girl dolls, xv
The American Heritage Dictionary, xvi, 168
American Heritage Magazine, xvi
American model, 103, 123
Amnesty, qualified, 84–85
ANC; *see* African National Congress
Anderson, Benedict, 9, 13
Anglo Boer War, 97
Anti-apartheid, 7, 89, 106, 108–9, 122
Antimonumentalism, 126
Apartheid, 84, 94–95, 101, 105; anti-apartheid, 7, 89, 106, 108–9, 122; biopower and, 104, 114, 136; cultures of, 81; end of, 83–84, 103;

INDEX

Apartheid (cont.)
  Israel and, 157; live action heritage and, 100; modernity and, 64, 66; monument, 103–4; polygamy and, 141; regulation, 64; rescripting story of, 3; transitional art and, 63
Apartheid Museum, 122–24
Appadurai, Arjun, 89
Ara, K. H., 39
Architecture, monumental, 101
Arnold, Edward, 183, 186
Arnold, Matthew, 17–18, 19, 139
Art: abstraction, 43; aesthetic philosophy and, 197n27; African, 58–79; avant-garde movements, 66; Chinese, 68; color in, 52; contemporary, 76, 78; dynamic statue, 49; expressionism, 39, 43, 44, 52, 67, 69; global markets of, 75; India and, 26–57; innovation in, 43; Islamic, 40; market for, 54; multiplicity of, 70; peri-urban, 63; rural, 77; spirituality and, 60; surrealism, 43; township, 63; transitional, 62–63; Vha-Venda and Va-Tsonga, 59, 61–66, 68–70, 73, 75–76; as weapon, 114; *see also* Modern art; Painting; Sculpture
Arthur, Jean, 183, 184
Article 39B, of South African Constitution, 85–86, 117–18, 130
Artifacts, 16, 17; African Renaissance as, 139; choice of, 43; Indian art and, 44; of "indigenous" culture, 2; origin and, 40; of speech, 123; of transition, 80; *see also* Museums
Art Nouveau, 33
Assimilation, 30
Association, 179; density of, 176
Authority, xvi, 129; of past, 13; political, 20
Avant-garde art movements, 66

Baartman, Saartjie, 112
Baker, Herbert, 106
Bakre, Sadanand, 39
Bantustans, 99, 100, 157
Battle Monument, 152
Baudelaire, Charles, 63, 71

Baudrillard, Jean, 168
Bawa, Ahmed, 148, 149, 201n15
Becker, Rayda, 196n15
Becoming, 154, 159
Benzien, Jeffrey, 85
Berenson, Bernard, 17
Berger, John, 54
Berlin model, 103
Beuys, Josef, 7, 69
Bezuidenhout, Evita, 61
Bhabha, Homi, 12, 34
Bible, 154–55
Big government, 162, 180
Bildung, 17
Biopower, 100, 104, 114, 119, 130, 136
Bleek, Wilhelm, 109
Blogging, 105
Body types, 112
Boer War, 94–95, 97, 156
Book of Iterations (P. Skotnes), 110
Books of iteration, 109
Botha, P. W. "Old Crocodile," 83
The Brady Bunch (TV series), 176
Branding, 1–2, 75–76, 86–87, 105, 128–29
Braque, Georges, 39
Britishness, 15
Brooks Brothers, xiv
Brunelleschi, Filippo, 28
Budapest model, 103, 111
Bunn, David, 119
Burke, Edmund, 15
Burnett, Ricky, 59, 61, 68, 77
Bush, George W., 182, 188
Bushmen, 110, 112
Bushmen Diorama, 111
Buzzwords, 6

Cage (Husain), 48
Cage V (Husain), 49
Canonization, of culture, 53
Cape Town, 7, 59, 82, 86, 91–92, 107
Capitalism, 14
Capra, Frank, xiii, 182, 185
Carving, sculptural, 59
Catholicism, 61
Celebrity, 56, 76, 163
Chaplin, Charlie, 94
Character, 175

INDEX

Chaterjee, Partha, 144
Chavda, Bal, 39
Chilean Truth and Reconciliation Commission, 84–85
China, 34, 87; art of, 68
Chinnery, George, 26
Chola bronzes, 40, 44, 52
Christianity, 61, 62
Christies, auction of, 54
Churchill, Winston, 124, 136, 139
Cinema, 169; *see also* Movies
Citizenship, 56
City Lights (film), 94
Civil institutions, 179
Civilization, 14
Classicism, 19
Clinton, Bill, 182
CODESA, *see* Convention for a Democratic South Africa
Cohn, Bernard, 30
Collecting statues, xv
Colonial elites, 8–10
Colonialism, 14, 20, 26, 40, 42; ideology of, 16; neocolonialism, 135; precolonialism, 10, 81; subjection, 45
Colonial photographers, 32
Color, 52
Comaroff, Jean, 5, 21, 138, 146
Comaroff, John, 5, 21, 138, 146
Commercialization, 3
Commodity, 79, 198*n*28
Communalism, 155, 162, 179
Connections, 69
Connoisseurship, 17
Conrad, Joseph, 177
Consciousness: double, 24; national, 40, 92; of process, 159
Constitution, of South Africa, 85–86, 88, 104, 116–19, 130–31
Constitutional Court, 88, 114–15, 117, 126, 129–30
Constructivism, 67
Contemporary art, 76, 78
Contemporary heritage invention, 13
Content, thinning of, 6
Contradictions, 47
Convention for a Democratic South Africa (CODESA), 84, 140
Coombes, Annie, 104, 108

Cooper, Gary, 161, 175, 183, 187
Coovadia, Jerry, 148, 149, 201*n*15
Crocket, Davy, 2
"The Crocodile Does Not Leave the Pool: Venda Court Arts" (Nettleton), 61
Cultural acknowledgment, 58
Cultural diversity, 130
Cultural policy, 145
Cultural theory, 72
Cultural trust, 16
Customary Law, 117
Customary rights, 85

Damon, Matt, 91
Daniell, Thomas, 26
Daniell, William, 26
Danto, Arthur, 197*n*27
Dark Continent, 70
de Brosses, Charles, 31
Decolonization, 2, 22
Dehejia, Vidya, 32
De Klerk, F. W., 84, 140
Democracy, 24, 105; in action, 123; American, 178–80; multiparty, 89; participatory, 106; popular, 114; representative, 186; transition to, 84, 104
Democracy in America (Tocqueville), 178
Democratization, 138
Demonumentalization, 93–94, 119, 121, 122, 124, 125, 126, 131; as redress, 108, 124; Web and, 105
Denialism, of AIDS, 88, 89, 140, 147
Department of Arts and Cultures, 123
Destiny, 14–15, 20, 95, 98, 155, 159
Devaluation, 4, 20, 81
Dialectic, 196*n*14
Diana (Lady); *see* Spencer, Diana
Dickie, George, 197*n*27
Diffusion, 45–46, 71; global, 67
Dignity, 85, 86, 107, 116
Diogenes, 73
Dirk-Uys, Peter, 61
Dissent, 89
District Six Museum, 107–8
Diversity, 136, 151; cultural, 130; of linguistics, 85; rehabilitation of, 138

205

INDEX

Dominion, 155
Dora and the Other Woman (Siopis), 112, *113*
Double alienation, 35
Double consciousness, 24
Double-edged sword, 6–7
Doubleness, 12
Downgrading, 20
D'Oyly, Charles, 26
DuBois, W. E. B., 136
Durban World AIDS Conference, 148
Dynamic statue, 49

Eastwood, Clint, 91
Edison box, 160, 167
Egyptians, 16; painting, 63
Eighteenth century, 13
Elites and elitism, 34, 42, 181; colonial, 8–10
Emerson, Ralph Waldo, 152–53
Emersonianism, 157
Empowerment, 6, 138, 144
Encrypted heritage, 36
Epistemology, 143
Ethnicity INC (Comaroff and Comaroff), 5, 146
Eurocentrism, 71, 98, 153
Europe: Jewish history of, 126; languages and, 194n13; lineage and, 149; modernity and, 71–72, 145; Renaissance, 28, 61–62, 66; self-mirroring, 30; *see also specific countries*
European Union, 93
Exceptionalism, 153, 155
Exoticism, 29
Experiment, 154, 159, 160, 190
Expert culture, 181
Exploitation, 16
Exploration, 155
Expressionism, 39, 43, 44, 52, 69; abstract, 67
Fanon, Frantz, 4, 20, 34, 144, 153
Fascism, 118, 184, 185
Fergussun, James, 30
Fey, Tina, 189
FIFA World Cup, 82, 133
Film, *see* Movies
Fluxus, 69

Fonda, Henry, 169
Ford, Harrison, 175
Foreign investment, 92
Foucault, Michel, 48, 100
Fox TV, 162, 187
Fragmentation, 38
France, 45
Frankfurt School, 167
Franklin, Benjamin, 154
Freedom Park Monument, 104–5, 106, 124
Freeman, Morgan, 91
French model, 103
French Revolution, 15
Fugard, Athol, 61

Gabor, Eva, xiv
Gade, Hari, 39
Gandhi, Indira, 53
Gandhi, Mahatma, 21, 43, 118
Ganga Jamna or *Mahabarata* (Husain), 47
Gaonkar, Dilip, 72, 73
Garbo, Greta, 159
GEAR, *see* Growth, Employment, and Redistribution Act
Genealogy, 12, 66
The Gentleman's Game (Ndou), 64
George V (king), 94
Germany, 45, 97
Gettysburg Address, 184
Gevisser, Mark, 142
Gini coefficient, 87
Global art markets, 75
Global diffusion, 67
Globalization, 74; of modern art, 46, 68
Global knowledge systems, 143
Gold Reef City, 3
Grammar, abstract, 12
The Great Train Robbery (film), 160
Great Trek, 23, 95, 99, 155
Greeks, 16, 19
Green Point Stadium, 91, *91*, 133
Growth, Employment, and Redistribution Act (GEAR), 87, 90, 131
Guatemala, 25
Guernica (Picasso), 57

INDEX

Guevara, Che, 105
Gupta, 47

Haiti, 45–46
Halbfinger, David, 186
Hanson, Thomas Blom, 57
Harvard Divinity School, 152
Hebbar, 39
Hebraicism, 19
Hegel, G. W. F., 9, 31
Hegemony, 14, 16, 115
Hellenism, 19
Herwitz, Daniel, 124, 136, 165
Hinduism, 43, 46, 56
Historicity, 20, 28
History After Apartheid (Combes), 104
HIV/AIDS, 80, 87–89, 140–49
Hlungwani, Jackson, 59–62, 73, 75, 77
Hodges, William, 26, 29
Hollywood, *see* Movies
Holocaust, 156; memorials, 106–7
Hoover, J. Edgar, 186
Housing crisis, 88
Human capital, 5
Human rights: language of, 5, 68; violations of, 85
Hume, David, 15
Husain, Maqbool Fida, 38–40, 44, 46–53, 55–57
Hybridity, 38

Identity, xv, 10, 29; African, 139; imitative, 32; national, 15; politics, 3, 6, 94, 97, 98, 128; resurgence of, 5
Ideology: of colonialism, 16; of indigeneity, 137, 149
Imagination, 18
Impoverishment, 142–43
Improvisation, 11
Indian art, 26–57; artifacts and, 44; assimilation and, 30; colonial representations, 29; diffusion and, 45–46; as drama, 26; folk traditions, 36; Husain and, 46–53, 55–57; innovation and, 43; landscape painting, 27–28; markets and, 54; museumizing and, 26, 36, 38; photography, 32; Progressive Artists'

Group, 39–40; subaltern and, 37–38; transformation and, 45
Indianness, 35, 36, 38
Indian wars, 160
Indigeneity, 137, 146, 148–49, 201*n*13
Indigenous Knowledge Systems, 146, 147
Indirect rule, 20–21
Individualism, 179; rugged, 180–81
Inequality, 74
Inferiority, 4
Inkatha Party, 84
Integrity, 29
Intellectual property, 5
Internationalized profile, 6
International Monetary Fund, 90
Internet; *see* Web
Iraq, 159
Islamic art, 40
Israel, 154–58
Iziko Museums, 123

J. J. (Jamshetjee Jeejeebhoy) School of Art, 32
Jacobs, Johan, 200*n*3
Jewish Museum, 126–28, *127*, *128*
Job Seeker, 64, *65*
Joe the Plumber, 175
Johannesburg Art Gallery, 2, 59, 109
John Doe Clubs, 183, 185
Juxtapositions, 47

Kandinsky, Wassily, 63
Kelly, Grace, 165
Kempton Park, 147
Kennedy, Edward, 163
Kennedy, John, 136
Kentridge, William, 67, 94
Kenyatta, Jomo, 139
Kersner, Saul, 111
Khoisan languages, 109
Kibbutz, 157
Kiefer, Anselm, 69
King William's Town, 97
Kirschenblatt-Gimblett, Barbara, 193*n*2
Kitchener (Lord), 95, 156
Klee, Paul, 39

INDEX

Knowledge: global systems, 143; Indigenous Knowledge Systems, 146, 147; transmission of, 18
Kojève, Alexander, 9, 33
Kruger, Barbara, 67
Kruger Park, 58
Kumar, Ram, 38, 39
Kumhar (Potter) (Husain), 37
Kwa-Zulu Natal, 87, 140, 200*n*30

Lacan, 168
Lam, Wifredo, 45–46
Land Act of 1913, 140
Language, 18, 120, 123; games, 71; of human rights, 5, 68; Khoisan, 109; of Mbeki, 137–39; monuments to, 97; of redress, 104; tracing, 194*n*13
Latin America, 25
Lauren, Ralph, xiv–xv
Law, 8, 100; access to, 116; customary, 117; idealized concept of, 119
Law, Jennifer, 101
Lazarus, Emma, 159
Leave It to Beaver (TV series), 176
Le Corbusier, 97
Leipzig monument, 97
Libeskind, Daniel, 126, 129
Libeskind building, 128
Lin, Maya, 120
Lincoln, Abraham, 168–69, 171
Lincoln Memorial, 168
Lineage, 14, 149, 150
Linguistics, 19, 137; diversity of, 85; philology, 18
Literacy, 8
Live action gesture, 22, 78
Live action heritage, 11, 12, 25, 98, 100
Lloyd, Lucy, 109
Lobbyists, 186
Locke, John, 180
Lodge, Tom, 113
Lorrain, Claude, 27, 28, 31
Luddites, 79

McCain, Cindy Hensley, 186–87
McCain, John, 164, 168, 173, 175, 179, 186
Mabasa, Noria, 77
Madaka, Topsy, 120

Magical thinking, 188
Mahabharata, 46
Make Room for TV (Spigel), 187
Male separateness, 141
Mamdani, Mahmood, 21
Mandela, Nelson, 8, 75–76, 84, 86, 104–5, 140
Manet, Eduard, 72–73
Manuel, Trevor, 87
Manufacturing, 87
"The map of life" (Hlungwani), 60
Markets, 198*n*28
Market economy, 16
Mass culture, 167
Massey, Raymond, 169
Matisse, Henri, 40, 44
Maya (Husain), 48
Maya or *Tribal Girl* (Husain), 50
Mbeki, Thabo, 110–12, 123–24, 135; African Renaissance and, 22, 80, 100; HIV/AIDS and, 88–89, 141–45, 149; language of, 137–39; speech of, 136, 139
Mbembe, Achille, 11, 64, 144
Media, 86, 165; density of, 164, 166, 172; image, 189; synergy of, 167; Tea Party and, 162
Medical Research Council, 88, 143
Medicine, 112
Meet John Doe (film), 182, 183
Melding, 44–46
Melodrama, 37
Mexico, 25
Midnight's Children (Rushdie), 11
Miller, Christopher, 30
Mimicry, 5, 12, 39, 200*n*3
Mines, nationalization of, 147
Miniature painting, 52
Minnelli, Vincent, xiii
Miscast (Skotnes, P.), 109
Mitter, Partha, 33
Modern art, 37, 39, 41–42, 63; globalization of, 46, 68; innovation and, 44; as language game, 71; markets and, 54; primitivism and, 63; Vha-Venda and Va-Tsonga art and, 69–70, 73–74
Modernism and modernity, 8, 13, 21, 28, 39, 41, 45; alternative, 71, 73,

78; privileging, 73; source, 44; South African, 64; terms of, 72; theories of, 72
Moerdyk, Gerard, 95, 96, 97
Monument (film), 94
Monuments, 93–134; antimonumentalism, 126; of apartheid, 103–4; demonumentalization, 93–94, 105, 108, 119, 120, 121, 124–26, 131; to language, 97; refusal of, 121; ruination of, 102; *see also specific monuments*
Monumental architecture, 101
Monumentalizing, 139
Moral capital, 87, 93
Morality, 9
Moretti, Giovanni, 17
Mourning, 94
Movies, 159–61, 182
Mr. Deeds Goes to Town (film), 182
Mr. Smith Goes to Washington (film), 183–85
Mtimkulu, Siphiwe, 120
Murray and Roberts Construction, 91
Museums, 2, 8, 16, 17, 42; *see also specific museums*
Museumizing, 28, 38
Museum of Modern Art, 54
Muslims, 56, 149
Mysticism, religious, 62
Myth, Westerns and, 161
My Three Sons (TV series), 176, 177

Narayan, R. K., 53
Narrative: of African Renaissance, 150; national, 82–83, 132
National consciousness, 40, 92
National identity, 15
National imagination, 10
Nationalism, 5, 14, 26, 36, 41, 157
Nationalist Party, 23
Nationalization, of mines, 147
National narrative, 82–83, 132
National Party, 61, 83, 84, 95, 97, 155
National Research Foundation, 146–47
National unity, 9
Nation-states, 14, 16

Naturalization, 110
Nature morte, 39
Ndou, Goldwin, 78
Ndou, Owen, 64, 77–78
Negritude, 100, 139
Neocolonialism, 135
Neoliberalism, 128, 131–33, 151
Neoliberal marketplaces, 87
Nettleson, Anitra, 61
"The New Colossus" (Lazarus), 159
New Jerusalem, 59–60
New Testament, 61
Newtown Gallery, 61
New York Times, 186
Nietzsche, Friedrich, 6, 18–19, 22–24, 191
Niewoudt, Gideon, 120
Nineteenth century, 13
Nixon, Richard, 166
Nkrumah, Kwame, 139
Nostalgia, 38, 40
Nyerere, Julius, 139

Obama, Barack, 170, 171, 187; image of, 172; as Lincoln, 22, 164, 166, 168–69
The Old Farmer's Almanac, xvi
Old Fort Prison, 118, 119
Old Testament, 61
Olympiad (Reifenstal), 101
OMM Architects, 115, *116*
O'Neal, Tip, 163
"On the Study of Indian Architecture" (Fergussun), 30
Origin, 18, 95, 159, 172; American, 154; artifacts and, 40
Orozco, José Clemente, 45

Painting, 41; Egyptian, 63; landscape, 27–28; miniature, 52; of subaltern, 38; *see also specific paintings*
Pakistan, 43
Pal, Pratap, 32
Palace of Justice, 118
Palestinians, 157
Palin, Sarah, 163–64, 166, 168, 171–81, 185–86; Fey and, 189; as TV figure, 187–88
Pan Africanist Congress, 84

INDEX

Parody, 64
Participatory democracy, 106
Participatory redress, 107
Paternalism, 79
Patience on a Monument—a History Painting (Siopis), 101, 102
Patrimony, 41
"People's Parks," 113
Performance, 3
Peri-urban art, 63
Peronist party, 90
Persona, 167
Philology, linguistic, 18
Philosophical Investigations (Wittgenstein), 70
Photographers, colonial, 32
Picasso, Pablo, 39, 43, 54–55, 57, 63, 76
Pickford, Mary, 159
Pienaar, Francois, 91
Place, pride of, 146
Political authority, 20
Political correctness, 114, 200n30
Political history, 3
Political institutions, 179
Polygamy, 141
Popular culture, 109, 112, 168
Popular democracy, 114
Popular front politics, 108
Popular participation, 109
Positivism, 116
Postcolonial social formations, xvi
Practice, 8, 11, 13, 17, 191
Precolonialism, 10, 81
Presence Africaine, 100
Preservation, 23
Presidential Inauguration—"We Are One: Opening Inaugural Celebration," 170
Pride, of place, 146
Primitivism, 63
Privatization, 123
Profiling, 112, 197n27; global, 122; internationalized, 6; of science, 143; *see also* Stereotypes
Progressive Artists' Group, 39–40, 56
Proportionality, 85
Proust, Marcel, 164
Proximity, transference of, 35

Public participation, 108
Pueblo Indian ruins, 60

Qualified amnesty, 84–85

Race and Reconciliation (Herwitz), 123, 136
Radicalization, 95
Rainbow Nation, 86, 93, 140
Rains, Claude, 183, 184
Ramayana, 46
Raza, Sayed H., 39
Recitation, 17, 157
Recognition, 78–79, 87
Reconciliation, 104
Reconstruction, 4
Redress, 80, 104; demonumentalization as, 108, 124; language of, 104; participatory, 107; poetics of, 108; rightful historical, 99
Rehabilitation, 138
Reichstag, 126
Reifenstal, Leni, 101
Religion: Christianity, 61, 62; fundamentalism, 157; Hinduism, 43, 46, 56; Islamic art, 40; mysticism, 62; secularization of, 14, 17
Renaissance, 28, 61–62, 66; *see also* African Renaissance
Renunciation, 190
Representation, 43
Republican National Convention, 172, 174, 186
Research, priority of, 146
Resistance Art (Williamson), 101
Resources, African, 147
Revaluing, 191
Rewriting, 18
Rhodes, Cecil, 94, 98
Rhodes Memorial Monument, 133
Rich, Peter, 60
Richards, Colin, 63
Rights: customary, 85; dignity and, 116; human, 5, 68, 85
Rightful historical redress, 99
Riskin, Robert, xiii, 182, 185
Rivera, Diego, 45, 67, 69
Robben Island, 7, 86, 132
Robins, Steven, 89

INDEX

Roman Empire, xii
Romanian model, 103
Romanticism, 19, 28, 31
Rossi, Aldo, 118
Rove, Karl, 188
Roy, Jamini, 36
Rugby World Cup, 83, 91
Rugged individualism, 180–81
Rural artists, 77
Rushdie, Salman, 11

Sachs, Albie, 114, 118, 119
Sack, Steven, 59, 112–13
Said, Edward, 26, 194*n*1
Sandstone, 106
Sanskrit, 194*n*13
Saturday Night Live, 189
Schmitz, Bruno, 97
School of Athens (Raphael), 28
Science, profiling of, 143
Scott, Randolph, 2
Sculpture, 47; West African, 63; *see also specific sculptures*
Seattle Times, 186
Second Temple, xii
Second World War, xii, 97
Secularization, 16; of religion, 14, 17
Sekoto, Gerard, 46, 67, 69
Self-becoming, 7, 41
Self-creation, 11
Self-imagination, 10
Self-mirroring, 30
Self-questioning, 78
Self-recognition, 6, 33
Self-respect, 5
Senghor, Léopold, 136, 139, 190
Serlio, Sebastiano, 28
Settler societies, 9–10, 99, 154, 157–59, 161–62
Sexuality, 141
Shepherd, Nick, 5, 103, 108
Sherman, Cindy, 67
Shiva as Lord of the Dance (Nataraja), 51
Siopis, Penny, 101, *102*, 112, *113*
Skotnes, Cecil, 46
Skotnes, Pippa, 109, *110*, 111
Small towns, 22, 185–86; values, 171–72

Smith, Jefferson, 183, 185
Social contract, 180
Solidarity, 94
South Africa, 2, 3, 24, 154; art and, 58; Cape Town, 7, 59, 82, 86, 91–92, 107; Constitution of, 85–86, 88, 104, 116–19, 130–31; currency devaluation, 83; disenfranchising and, 157; FIFA World Cup and, 82, 133; foreign investment and, 92; HIV/AIDS and, 80, 87–89, 140–49; Kwa-Zulu Natal, 87, 140, 200*n*30; media of, 86; modernity, 64; monuments and, 93–100; national narrative of, 82–83; post-apartheid, 105, 114; as postcolonial nation, 81; Rugby World Cup and, 83, 91; transition of, 84, 88; World Cup (2010) and, 90–93, 133
South African Rand, 90
Souza, Francis Newton, 39, 40
Sovereignty, 100, 119; future, 160; settler, 99
Space, 47–48, 105
Spencer, Diana (Lady), 56, 165
Spigel, Lynn, 187
Spilt subjectivity, 34
Spivak, Gayatri, 38
The Star as Icon (Herwitz), 165
"The State of Art in South Africa," 59
Stereotypes, 6, 142, 143
Stewart, Jimmy, 161, 183, 187
Style, 45
Subaltern, 26, 35–38, 45
Subjection, 45
Subjectivity, split, 34
Subliminal construction, 171
Summer Olympic Games (2004), 86
Summer Olympic Games (2008), 87
Surrealism, 43, 67
Sutcliffe, Mike, 200*n*30
Swanson, Gloria, 159

TAC, *see* Treatment Action Campaign
Tamayo, Rufino, 45
Tarantino, Quentin, 175
Tea Party, 162
Television, 176, 187–88; *see also specific programs*

INDEX

Terrorism, 56
Testimony, 107
Theft, 16
Theorization, 197*n*27
Third Reich, 97
Tocqueville, 178–80, 187
Toulmin, Stephen, 197*n*20
Tourism, 3, 4, 7, 90
Township art, 63
Town values, 181
Traditional objects, 2
The Transfiguration of the Commonplace (Danto), 197*n*27
Transformation, 45
Transition, 88, 150; artifacts of, 80; to democracy, 84, 104; dilemma of, 125
Transitional art, 62–63
Transitional justice, 124
Transmission, of knowledge, 18
Treatment Action Campaign (TAC), 88–89
Truth and Reconciliation Commission (TRC), 76, 84–85, 106–7, 120–21, 123, 140
Tshabalala-Msimang, Manto, 148
Turner, Frederick Jackson, 160

Unemployment, 66, 93
UNESCO, 5
United Democratic Front, 114, 123, 149
United Nations, 156, 157
United States, *see* America
Universities, 16–17
University of Fort Hare, 141
University of Natal, Durban, 86
University of Witwatersrand, 61
Use and abuse, 22, 24, 172
"The Use and Disadvantages of History for Life" (Nietzsche), 23
Valance, Liberty, 161
Valentino, Rudolph, xi
Values, 10, 14–15, 21; accumulated, 16; African, 135; of small towns, 171–72; of towns, 181
van Reibeeck, Jan, 99
Varma, Ravi, 33

Verwoerd, Betsy, 86
Verwoerd, Hendrik F., 86
Vha-Venda and Va-Tsonga art, 59, 61–66, 68–70, 73, 75–76
Vietnam Veterans Memorial, 121
View of Part of the City of Benares (Hodges), 29
Visual encomium, 90
Völkerschlachtdenkmal (monument), 97, 98
Voltaire, 24, 31
Voortrekker Monument, 95–96, 96, 100
Vulgarity, aesthetics of, 64

Walker, Kara, 67
Wallerstein, Emmanuel, 74
The Waltons (TV series), 176
Warhol, Andy, 67, 69, 177, 188
Washington, George, 154
Wayne, John, 161
Web (Internet), 105
West African sculpture, 63
West Bank, 159
Western (genre), 160–61
White mining, 3
Whiteside, Alan, 140
Whitman, Walt, 159
Williamson, Sue, 101
Wittgenstein, Ludwig, 69, 70–71
Witz, Leslie, 99
Women, 48, 52
World Bank, 90, 146
World Cup (2010), 90–93, 133
Wright, Frank Lloyd, 128

Xenophobia, 155, 157–58

Young, James E., 106–7
YouTube, 189

Zeal, 161
Zimbabwean ruins, 60
Zionism, 156
Žižek, Slavoj, 168
Zulus, 141; nationalists, 84, 200*n*30
Zuma, Jacob, 104